W9-CRT-047

FRONTO AND ANTONINE ROME

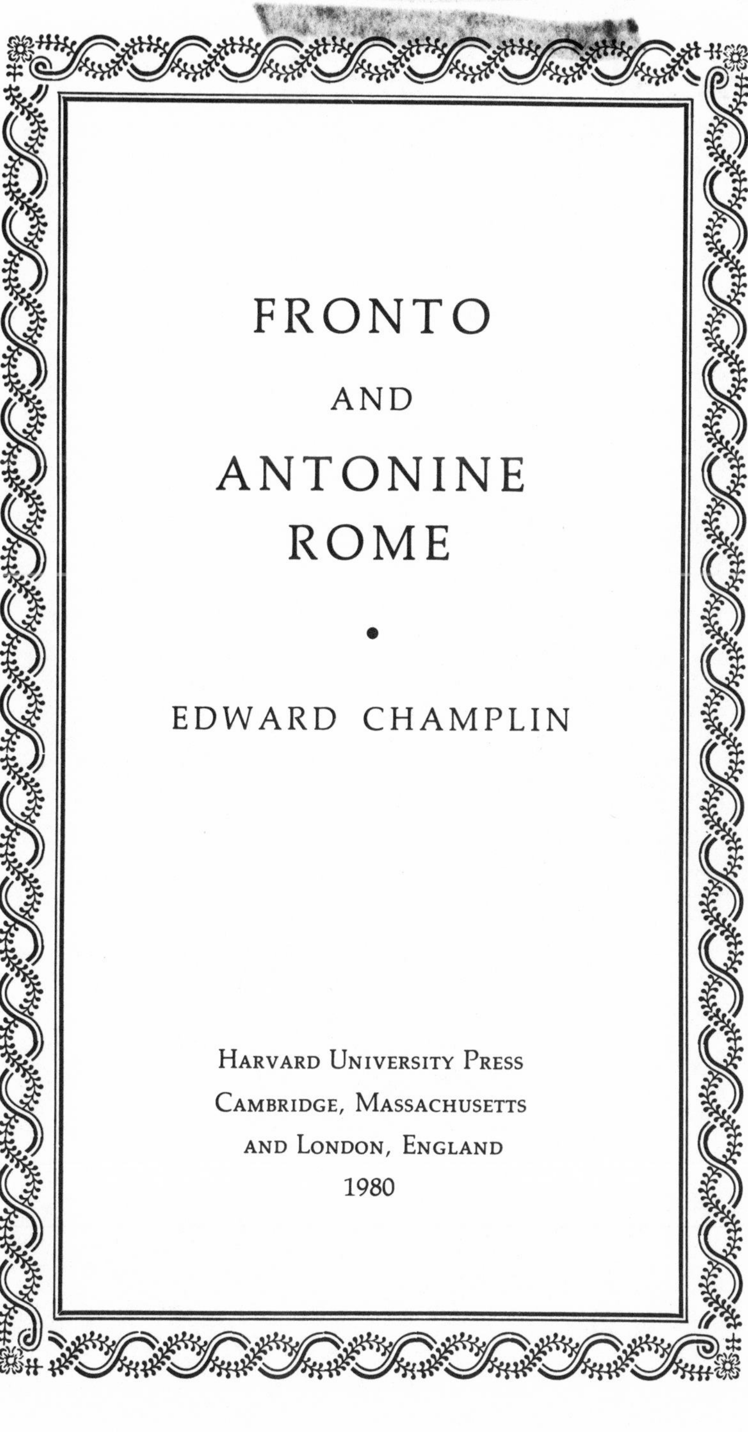

FRONTO AND ANTONINE ROME

•

EDWARD CHAMPLIN

HARVARD UNIVERSITY PRESS
CAMBRIDGE, MASSACHUSETTS
AND LONDON, ENGLAND
1980

Printed in the United States of America

Publication of this book has been aided by a grant from the Andrew W. Mellon Foundation

Library of Congress Cataloging in Publication Data

Champlin, Edward, 1948-
Fronto and Antonine Rome.

Includes bibliographical references and indexes.
1. Fronto, Marcus Cornelius. 2. Rome—Intellectual life. 3. Rome—History—Antonines, 96-192.
4. Orators—Rome—Biography. I. Title.
DG292.7.F47C45 937'.07'0924 [B] 79-28136
ISBN 0-674-32668-7

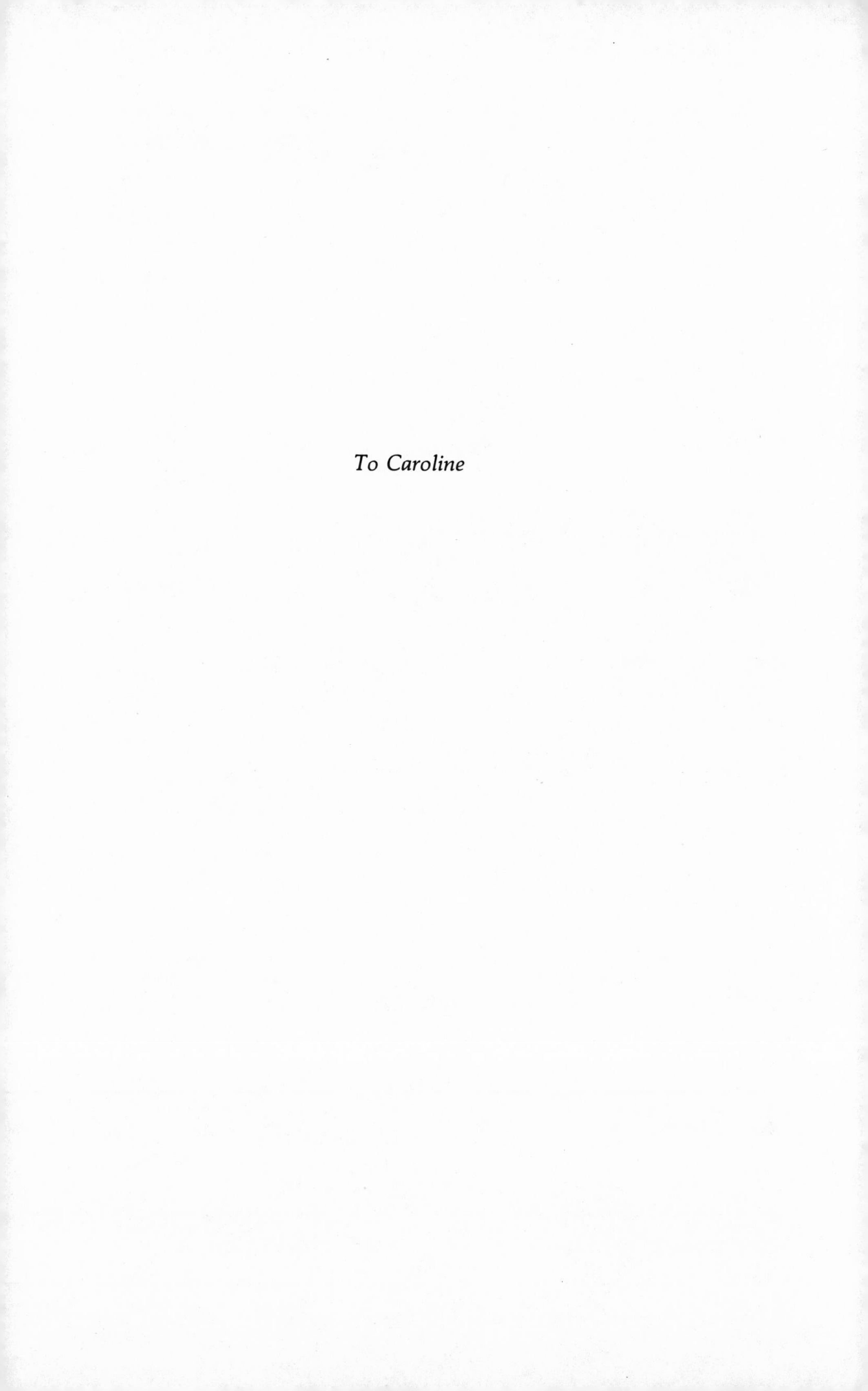

To Caroline

ACKNOWLEDGMENTS

My greatest debt is to four scholars who have done so much to illuminate the history of the principate: Professors T. D. Barnes, G. W. Bowersock, C. P. Jones, and F. G. B. Millar. Whatever is good in this book is due largely to their example and their friendly advice. Its prototype was a D.Phil. thesis supervised by Professor Millar and examined by Dr. J. F. Matthews and Mr. E. L. Bowie, whose kind vigilance detected numerous sins of omission and commission. For advice on certain legal problems in Fronto's letters I was fortunately able to draw upon the expertise of Professor A. M. Honoré. And at a critical stage in its development this book was read with benevolence and greatly improved by Professors A. R. Birley, T. J. Luce, and R. E. A. Palmer. I am grateful not only to all of them for their encouragement, but to all the friends and colleagues who have contributed to the happy years at Oxford and at Princeton of which this book is but one small product. The main contributor to that happiness has been my wife, to whom I dedicate the following pages.

Princeton
March 1980

CONTENTS

FRONTO AND ANTONINE ROME

Note on Texts and Translations

The standard modern edition of Fronto's correspondence remains that of M. P. J. van den Hout (Leiden, 1954). Advances in the study of the text made since then are incorporated with an Italian translation in the version of F. Portalupi (Turin, 1974). Still useful is the two-volume work of C. R. Haines in the Loeb Classical Library, *The Correspondence of Marcus Cornelius Fronto,* published in 1919/1920 by Harvard University Press (Cambridge, Mass.). With the permission of the publisher, I have used Haines's superb translations in my text, tacitly emending archaisms in the English, correcting the very rare errors, and substituting my own versions where the text has since been improved.

INTRODUCTION

THE SECOND CENTURY after Christ, in particular the age of the Antonines, is a period which has exercised a special fascination for subsequent generations. To the later eighteenth century it was without hesitation the happy and prosperous summit of the human condition; under the two Antonine emperors the happiness of a great people was the sole object of government. To the less resolute later twentieth century it is an age of anxiety or of tense equipoise, one scarcely able to contain the new questions and new energies which would erupt in the following century and a half. The major problem has been and remains one of sources. Where once we had the comfortable guidance of a Livy or a Tacitus, a Cicero or a Pliny, we are now abandoned to the uncertain directions of Cassius Dio in epitome and the active treacheries of the collection of imperial biographies known as the *Historia Augusta.* Yet when approached with caution, even these sources can be made to yield more than is at first apparent, particularly when supplemented by coins, inscriptions and papyri, and there is much to be extracted from the voluminous specialized writings of a sophist, a doctor, or a Christian. Gibbon lamented that the historian of Trajan's actions was reduced to working "from the glimmerings of an abridgment, or the doubtful light of a panegyric." If the reigns of Antoninus Pius and Marcus Aurelius are worth understanding, our sources, however problematic and fragmentary, should be valued all the more.

Some fifty years after Gibbon conceived the idea of describing the decline and fall of Rome, Cardinal Mai published the first edition of a part of the correspondence of the orator Marcus Cornelius Fronto, the friend of Antoninus Pius and teacher of Marcus Aurelius and Lucius Verus. Reaction to it formed quickly and has lingered in more or less modified form. Typical were the remarks of the two serious editors who followed Mai: Niebuhr, immensely frustrated, found the orator stupid, frivolous, and the very opposite of eloquent; Naber expressed both dislike and contempt for an author whose works would have been better left buried in the palimpsest whence they had emerged. The problem is one of unfulfilled expectations: the correspondence between Fronto and Marcus Aurelius reveals neither the second Cicero nor the philosopher-prince we want and have been led to expect. To be fair, such disappointment is well justified. The literary value of the letters, both in style and opinion, is low, at least by the standards of the nineteenth and twentieth centuries, while they offer virtually no addition to our understanding of the philosophical life of Marcus Aurelius. But literary and philosophical considerations have combined to obscure the simple fact that Fronto's letters are in two senses a major historical source.

First, Fronto the man was without a doubt one of the great figures of his century. With the weighty exception of Leopardi, whose enthusiastic *Discorso* on Fronto's life and works is still worth reading, a uniformly negative attitude to his personality has grown up since the publication of his letters: the man was fatuous and pedantic, the contents of his letters insipid when their emotions were not downright embarrassing. Nevertheless, Fronto was loved and highly respected by his contemporaries, with the sober Marcus at their head, and by later generations. He was indisputably the guiding genius of Latin letters through three reigns, and was perceived in later times as a second Cicero. He was recognized as the leading advocate of his day. He was an intimate and counselor of the imperial family for over thirty years, and the teacher and mentor of two emperors. Such an accumulation of achievements is rare in any age, and there is much to be gained from applying the simple axiom that whatever this man and the emperor of the Roman world chose to discuss in their letters is, in some sense, important. To read the letters of Fronto without the closest consideration, to dismiss them as fatuous, is to dismiss evidence.

Second, the correspondence itself is above all a document of social history, one of major importance for an understanding of the Antonine monarchy and the Antonine aristocracy. Studies of it have tended to deal exclusively with the literary aspects and much, perhaps too much, has been written on Fronto's fundamentally simple rhetorical doctrines. The importance of these doctrines justifies such research, whatever hesitations one might have about criticism based not on speeches or essays but on private letters, and the curious reader can be directed now to Professor Marache's excellent monograph on the archaizing movement of the second century.[1] History has been correspondingly less well served. Disappointment was again great: here was no excitingly Ciceronian chronicle of daily events, and the letters added virtually nothing to our knowledge of such events between 138 and 167. The tendency has therefore been to mine the correspondence for nuggets of fact while ignoring the whole. This is a major omission. On the lowest level, much is missed by wrenching individual items out of context; numerous and rather serious misconceptions arise. More important, consideration of the correspondence as a whole allows us to reconstruct, however imperfectly, a particular society, that of the governing elite at Rome in the high Antonine Age. Inevitably, that picture is distorted by Fronto's vision, but the very distortion can be turned to good account in the simultaneous reconstruction of Fronto's perceptions of the world in which he moved. Fronto and his society are the twin subjects of this study.

The great obstacle to any study of Fronto is the sorry physical state of the correspondence. To summarize a complicated history, it survives in a single codex from late antiquity, part of which now rests in the Vatican, part in Milan. There is no hint that Fronto himself ever contemplated any collection of his correspondence, and various signs suggest that the present accumulation represents the efforts of different editors at different times working for different purposes. The single codex containing this collection was broken up and its sheets reused with others for the Acts of the first council of Chalcedon, part of which are now lost. Thus, much of the original is lost, the ordering of the leaves which do survive is often insecure, and the palimpsest constantly verges on the illegible, often forcing the reader to consult corrections and marginal annotations of varying reliability. The initial editor (Mai 1815 and 1823) was accused of rendering the manuscript even more illegible; the next two serious editors (Niebuhr 1816, Naber 1867) detested their author; their successor (Hauler) labored for half a century without producing an edition; and the three useful and accessible modern versions (Haines 1919/1920, van den Hout 1954, Portalupi 1974) are based on secondhand knowledge of the original. This state of affairs entails one profoundly serious warning for the historian: where lacunae occur, where readings are dubious, all arguments are provisional at best.

The following study of Fronto is, in essence, an attempt to locate the man in the society which produced him. The first two chapters investigate the background to the life portrayed in the letters. The remainder are concerned with the foreground, isolating in terms of Fronto's roles certain elements of Antonine society which are prominent in his correspondence. This separation into chapters is somewhat artificial: the subjects, like the roles, overlap extensively, and it is hoped that their sequence here is suggestive. From the most public to the most private of these activities, two passions run through and unify Fronto's life as they do his letters: an obsession with rhetorical culture and a love for Marcus Aurelius. They must always be kept in mind, for they are incontestably the prime motives of Fronto's life and they are what, in the end, make him worthwhile.

I

AFRICA

Marcus Cornelius Fronto was born at Cirta in Roman North Africa. The simple fact is nowhere recorded, but must be deduced from stray hints in the correspondence and elsewhere.[1] He emigrated to Rome at an early age, but unlike other emigrants, both successes and failures, he seems never to have returned to his native land, and indeed, but for one or two inevitable official journeys, what is known of his life is closely confined to the environs of Rome and the Bay of Naples. In this he is atypical of his class and his age.[2] There is no sign in his correspondence of any African property or investments, no African affairs appear among his legal briefs, he moved in no recognizably African circles at Rome. As for Cirta and its affairs, they appear briefly in two surviving letters, both embarrassed and apologetic; otherwise there is only a pair of neutral historical references to the Jugurthine war. The impression of indifference is strikingly uniform. Nevertheless, in order fully to understand the pattern of Fronto's life at Rome, it is imperative to look to its prologue, to the province of Africa and the city of Cirta.

Cirta, the second city of Africa, gloried in an exotic past.[3] A magnificent natural fortress, it stood on a plateau flanked by the deep gorge of the Ampsaga River, some fifty miles from the sea. Dominating the whole of Numidia, it first appears in history on the border between two great nomad tribes in the third century B.C. In their struggles it passed in 203 to the renowned Massinissa and remained thereafter the most opulent capital of the new united kingdom.[4] This cosmopolitan position intensified a mixture of cultures. To the Libyan base was added the strong influence of an aggressive Punic civilization to the east: all coins and official inscriptions bore Punic or neo-Punic characters, and Cirta itself was enriched by the libraries of Carthage after the destruction of that city.[5] Further, a community of Greek artists and merchants had flourished within its walls since the third century, if not earlier, and the philospher-king Micipsa subsequently attracted a number of intellectuals to his capital city, "strongly fortified and beautifully built up."[6] Trade with Rome was fostered by the second-century kings of Numidia, and Italian businessmen flocked to the city in numbers sufficient to force its surrender by one monarch to his rival.[7] In the civil wars of the dying Republic their interference was no less strong, for that most unlikely of condottieri, the failed Campanian entrepreneur P. Sittius of Nuceria, made war upon the Pompeian partisan king Juba. For this and other assistance Caesar rewarded him and his Sittiani with the lion's share of Juba's kingdom, thereby introducing a further Italian—and specifically Campanian—element into the local population.[8] Despite his own death in an ambush shortly after his patron's assassination, the followers of Sittius soldiered on, attaching themselves to Caesar's heir, who rewarded their capital with regular colonial status: Colonia Iulia Iuvenalis Honoris et Virtutis Cirta. And in 26 B.C. a formal *deductio* brought yet another infusion of Roman blood.[9] Such was the heterogeneous heritage of Cornelius Fronto and his fellow citizens of Cirta.

From this there developed, not surprisingly, a system unique in the imperial scheme, the "IIII coloniae Cirtenses," first securely attested as such about the time of Fronto's birth. In theory a single republic with magistrates and treasury at Cirta, it nevertheless included three other Roman colonies—Rusicade, an important grain port on the coast; Chullu, also on the coast, west of Rusicade; Milev, twenty-five miles west of Cirta—and numerous smaller *pagi* and *castella*.[10] The Four Colonies, often inaccurately described as a confederation, were in theory bound together by *contributio*, in fact quite dominated by the greatly superior partner, Cirta, which was the only seat of government and jurisdiction.[11] In effect, the individual affairs of the other three colonies were controlled by pro-magistrates, ex-triumvirs of the Four Colonies with the title *praefectus iure dicundo*.[12] Much ingenuity has been invested in the explanation of the origins and growth of this system. It is suspicious that the three smaller colonies bear the name of no imperial founder, but reflect rather their Campanian roots: Veneria Rusicade, Minervia Chullu, Sarnensis Milev.[13] This observation has led naturally to the assumption of a very early and irregular foundation, but an alternative and compelling theory has been advanced.[14] Close relations were maintained with the neighboring colony to the west, Cuicul, which was probably a Trajanic foundation, certain notables holding magistracies in both republics in the second century. It is argued then that Cuicul was originally part of Cirtan territory (as it must have formed part of Sittius' original fief), and that Trajan detached it and its territory in order to implant a veteran colony there, compensating Cirta by granting to its more important subordinates the empty title of colony. In fact, none of the three is referred to as a *colonia* before Trajan, and the system of the Four Colonies makes its first appearance in his reign.[15] On that view, not only were the Four Colonies de facto Cirta and its territory, they always had been. Thus their "confederation" was a solid and historical unit, and its borders will prove decisive in determining the extent of Fronto's African interests.

The area is a large rectangle abutting on the Mediterranean, roughly a square with Cirta somewhat south of its center. Unlike the subordinates of Carthage, Cirta's lesser partners were not spread out into the hinterland, and unlike Carthage Cirta encompassed no potential republics struggling for independence, at least not until the later third century when the Four Colonies appear to have separated.[16] They were all "Cirtensian," their sons and those of less pretentious villages were Cirtensian magistrates and priests, they honored Cirtensian patrons and applauded Cirtensian games.[17] It is possible then that a man might claim Cirta as his patria without being a native of the city. In terms of patrial pride the observation is perhaps negligible, but it does prompt inquiry first as to Fronto's race. The capital sheltered a large cosmopolitan population with an especially strong admixture of foreign blood, but in scores of crossroad settlements or mountain villages there was a much higher proportion of the native population, dominated by a handful with mixed or alien ancestry.[18]

Fronto, in a convoluted Greek epistle to the mother of Marcus Aurelius, excused any linguistic barbarism he might commit by comparing himself to the wise barbarian of legend, Anacharsis, "for he was a Scythian of the nomad Scythians, while I am a Libyan of the Libyan nomads."[19] The wording is ambiguous, for the assertion can be taken simply as "I am an African from Numidia." However, it should be read literally, for in a congratulatory letter to the emperor Lucius Verus on his Parthian success the orator solemnly asserts, "and thus did I made prayer to my ancestral gods: O Jupiter Ammon . . ."[20] The nomen Cornelius should confirm his native descent, a common name unlike some of the rarities betraying Campanian ancestry, and one most probably received with the citizenship by a forebear from a governor who belonged to the Cornelian gens. The paternal ancestry is undoubtedly indigenous, yet nowhere does Fronto betray even a hint that Latin was anything but his native tongue.[21] His family was thoroughly Romanized. General considerations speak for this, particularly his education and the rise of the orator and his brother to the Roman senate and consulship, and there are particular hints that he was at least a third-generation citizen.[22] Such a background will give rise to an important tension, and one not confined to Fronto, between the native and the Roman elements in the provincial gentleman.

Even were there no other evidence, it could be argued with confidence that Fronto was a scion of the educated and Romanized provincial elite. His roots and connections are to be sought in the curial class, the bourgeois aristocracy present in every community, whose wealth was derived from or invested in surrounding estates—Cirta's prosperity, like that of much of Africa, was based on grain and the olive—but whose active lives revolved around the affairs of the central community.[23] The class and its interests are remarkably easy to define by its offices and its wealth, with few local variants. Homogeneity was further promoted by contacts of marriage, friendship, commerce, and investment among peers in various centers. And at the same time there were similar ties and common interests with equestrians and senators in their role as local grandees.[24] It is with this broad upper layer of society that Fronto invariably deals.

The name Cornelius is prominent in the society of Cirta and its near neighbors. Two third-century knights are of special interest for different reasons. One, Q. Cornelius M.f. Quir. Rusticus, was tutor to the son of a senatorial family in the small town of Thibilis, where his grateful pupil dedicated a statue to him in 211/212, and his own epitaph praises his notable eloquence.[25] A second knight shared not his eloquence but his name with the great orator of Cirta: L. Cornelius L.f. Quir. Fronto Probianus was a decurion of the four colonies and resident at Rusicade under the later Severans.[26] At the least these two gentlemen reflect the position attained by some branches of the gens Cornelia at Cirta, and actual relationship with Fronto is a good possibility. Even more relevant is yet another third-century knight, M. Cornelius Fronto Gabinianus, not indeed a resident of the Four Colonies, but a benefactor of nearby Madauros, the birthplace of

Apuleius.[27] Not only did this man bear the names of the orator but, what is more, his father shared the name of the orator's son-in-law, Victorinus: deliberate homage to them is surely indicated, perhaps a client relationship with the family. Finally, a far more important personage can be placed firmly in Fronto's background. Unquestionably the leading figure at Cirta in the age of the Antonines was the knight C. Iulius Crescens Didius Crescentianus, prefect of the Cirtan youth, holder of every civil office in both Cirta and Cuicul, and grandson of a flamen of the province of Africa.[28] A daughter of this august personage was Didia Cornelia, the wife of a senator: her name and rank ought to suggest a connection with the only Cornelian family of equal dignity in Numidia under the Antonines, Fronto's.

The slender evidence indicating that Fronto's origins are to be sought precisely in the equestrian stratum of the Cirtan curial class can be supported by the meager account of his family. Neither father nor mother is mentioned in the correspondence, save perhaps for an obscure allusion to the state of humanity in the time of his parents.[29] However, two relatives do receive attention. A shadowy brother appears in four letters, a man of some importance in his own right who has access to Marcus Caesar and who has been raised by Pius to the highest honors and admitted into the imperial *amicitia*.[30] The orator shows real affection for him, but there is no hint that the two men were particularly close, and other sources must supply him with a name and a career: two water pipes from the Esquiline, where Fronto made his home, bear the names Cornelius Fronto and Cornelius Quadratus; the Ostian fasti produce a Q. Cornelius Quadratus as suffect consul in 147, four years after Fronto; and this man can be identified with " . . . elio Qu . . . " legate of Numidia about the year 142.[31] The brothers Cornelii were both senators and consuls, yet their father remains a cipher. If he had been a senator himself, one might expect some proud echo of his standing in the correspondence, all the more in a generation when African senators had been few and their self-glorification evident. The natural breeding ground for senators was the equestrian class, and the finances required for two senatorial careers should imply an estate many times the amount required for an equestrian census. In fact or in name, Fronto's father was a knight of Cirta.

Useful corroboration may be discovered in a reference to Fronto's only other known kinsman. In a letter of commendation to a certain

Petronius Mamertinus, Fronto asks that he accept a learned youth "among the devotees of our *familia*." There can be no doubt that here, as elsewhere, *familia* means precisely family to Fronto.[32] The exact nature of the relationship is unknown, but its significance is great, for the Petronii Mamertini were one of the rising families of the age, from a Hadrianic procurator, to a prefect of Egypt and the guard, to a suffect consul in 150, to ordinary consuls in 182 and 190. While the pedigree is not quite secure, the rapid ascent of the family is clear, crowned by a marriage to the daughter of Marcus Aurelius.[33] And a good circumstantial case can be made that the family came from Africa and intermarried with yet another curial African family, the Septimii of Lepcis Magna, who entered the senate themselves in the mid second century.[34] Thus Fronto and his brother, Quadratus, should be seen not as isolated phenomena but as products of the process of Romanization which was leading the African aristocracy to its destined role in the Roman senate in the late first and early second centuries, after a proper period of training in the equestrian class.

Fronto was born into the upper class of the four Cirtan colonies, and after his removal to Italy it is with this class that he maintains contact. Their relations divide into two easily defined spheres, Cirta and Rome. Perhaps the most valuable letter in the collection of his correspondence as it survives is that addressed by him to the triumvirs and decurions of Cirta about 158 (*Ad Am.* II.11), valuable not merely in its demonstration of the orator's continued concern for the affairs of his patria, but for its display of most of the important concerns of the correspondence. The subject is, in local terms, the most important possible, the patronage of the Four Colonies, which Fronto gracefully declines, a result signaled to the local worthies by his first three words, "quantae mihi curae." The letter is highly lacunary, as are most of any length in the collection, but a later fragment suggests what the reader might have suspected, that Fronto's cares are not unconnected with advancing age and ill-health.[35] The lost section concluded with the very proper sentiment that the safety of the patria is to be preferred to the augmentation of a single man's *gratia*. Therefore, he suggests, the city leaders should nominate as patrons and solicit the services of those men who are now leaders at the bar, *principes fori* (a pointed reference to his own past supremacy). Proper candidates are duly named, Aufidius Victorinus, Servilius Silanus, Postumius Festus, and their merits are summarized. This leads naturally to a reminiscence of the orator's own past services to the colonies, into which a lacuna intrudes.[36] He then, it appears, proceeded to the mutually agreeable topic of Cirtenses in the Roman senate, distinguished native sons whose influence had materially aided their homeland and in whose company he had played a not undistinguished part. One item in this glorious register survives, a reference to a popular consular who possessed the *ius respondendi*, and the list concludes with the last and greatest honor to have been won by three of Cirta's citizens – and then again the manuscript fails.[37] Whatever that honor was, it afforded the fitting climax to a brisk summary of Cirta's glories which must have gratified both author and recipients. A companion letter (II.10), extant only in its first three words, "meae totius gloriae," surely echoed this theme, whatever its content, interweaving quiet self-praise with compliment to Cirta.

The subject here is an activity fundamental to every society, patronage, but this letter is unique among ancient documents as the reply of a great man to a communal request for his services. Here the main requirement of the local senate is not for benefaction or guidance at home but for the defense of its interests, "negotia nostra," at the seat of empire, specifically in the forum. Two qualities recommend each of the candidates, and in each of the three men they are presented in the same order: uprightness of character and eloquence.[38] The first may be convention, the custom of the good man skilled in speaking, but the second is simple necessity, and no doubt is left as to the real priority: "Wherefore I urge you to choose as your patrons those who now hold first place at the bar." This emphasis is confirmed by the discussion of Cirtan senators, that is, in this context, of service to Rome, the two mentioned being, by no coincidence, a jurisconsult (surely Pactumeius Clemens) and an advocate (Fronto).[39] Further, the *principes fori* suggested have two other relevant attributes which were deemed advantageous to the community and which clearly reflect the two ends of the chain of patronage. First, Cirta: as Fronto himself notes, all have a personal interest in the place, Victorinus as his own intended son-in-law, Silanus and Festus as citizens of nearby *civitates*. Second, though not explicit, Rome: all are senators in the prime of life, preferably consular or senior praetorian, and commanding some influence with emperor and senate.[40]. For the patron the return is simple, *gratia*, that is credit, authority, prestige.[41] It would be remarkable if Fronto had not served as patron of his native city, and here the point of major interest must be not that he refused the honor on this occasion but that he had accepted it frequently in the past. What is more, a sidelight can be cast on his ties with his patria. In this letter he considers it a prime recommendation for two of the proposed patrons that they are citizens of neighboring states. An inscription proclaims Fronto himself to have been patron of the town of Calama; the good fortune of Calama surely sprang from its close proximity to the eastern borders of Cirta.[42]

Fronto's oversight of Cirtan affairs is clearly centered in the city of Rome, not in Cirta. Was there a Cirtan community in the capital? In his letter to the city fathers he recalls one of the greatest glories of his patria, the many Cirtan senators who were its citizens. Few communities in the empire could boast of "very many" senators, and the province of Africa as a whole had been slow in contributing its share. Cirta's achievement, and Fronto's, must be set in a context. Exhaustive investigation has produced only six African knights who held any imperial office before the reign of Hadrian, only two before the last years of Domitian.[43] Advancement to the senate was correspondingly retarded.[44] The first known African knight in imperial service, a man appropriately from the territory of Carthage, received *ornamenta aedilicia*, probably from Gaius Caesar, but after him there is no one before the Flavians and only a handful between Vespasian and Trajan. The Pactumeii of Cirta provide the first consuls under Vespasian and Titus. Thereafter, in the consular fasti up to the time of Hadrian, there are a couple of Carthaginians and perhaps a pair from Thugga in the territory of Carthage.[45] Lepcis Magna produces one or two senators in this period, and a handful of other names may be added, more or less certainly Africans.[46] The Mauretanias, it is not surprising, produce no senator before Pius, except the meteoric chieftain Lusius Quietus (cos. 117).[47]

This harvest of African senators before the Antonine age is meager. Geographical distribution is suggestive. Prosperity is marked out, the big cities—Carthage, Cirta, Lepcis—are represented, with the coasts and the grain-rich plains taking natural precedence. The phenomenon is simply one of Romanization. In Africa, as elsewhere, this was tantamount to urbanization. Therein the ancient cities of the East had a tremendous advantage, and a complementary disadvantage for Africa lay in the vestiges of its strong and alien Punic culture.[48] Outside the great centers, the fertile tracts were exploited by great and relatively few estates; Nero executed six men said to have held half of Africa among them, and a contemporary trickster in Italy could claim a gang of slaves in Numidia large enough to capture Carthage.[49] Native tribes were brought under Roman control only slowly and imperfectly.[50] The great period of urbanization stretched from the Flavians to Hadrian, and in that same span peace was secured by roads and military colonies.[51] It is no accident that Africa first began to make its mark in politics and literature in the late first century. The products of Flavian and Trajanic policy began under Hadrian and the Antonines to enter the equestrian service and the senate along the trail blazed by their fellows from the larger centers, and their numbers become more significant.[52] They were a visible symbol of the Roman prosperity and Roman peace which prevailed in Numidia and Africa Proconsularis throughout the century.

Fronto's entry into the senate, perhaps in the earliest years of Hadrian, was thus not simply the result of chance and personal talent, for Cirta was in the van of Romanization, supplying the first African consuls.[53] Nor was the success of these men fortuitous, for they were introduced into the senate by the emperor Vespasian, doubtless as a reward for services in the revolution of 69. Comprehension of the rise of Cirta's aristocracy, a process in which the brothers Pactumeii are but the first visible peak, is restricted by simple lack of evidence. However, where there are senators we may confidently infer the existence of an equestrian class wherein lay their roots.[54] The relationship between the two is important. The early prominence of Cirtan senators is confirmed in the career of a knight resident at Rusicade, C. Caecilius Gallus, who made his name at Rome itself as praefectus fabrum to various senior magistrates and as judge of the upper three *decuriae*. His eminence is proclaimed by the highest possible honor, the priesthood of the province of Africa.[55] Thus the first known Cirtan knight was the first known flamen of Africa, the choice of Vespasian for his new provincial cult. The temporal coincidence of Caecilius Gallus with the Pactumeii is significant, hinting at an important and representative phenomenon, the presence of a network of Cirtan friendships and patronage at Rome, one for which there is an unusual amount of evidence.

An exceptional number of Cirtan senators are prominent in the records of the reign of Antoninus Pius. Two were already distinguished older contemporaries of Fronto.[56] The eminent soldier Q. Lollius

Urbicus (cos. c. 135) had been decorated in the great Jewish war, governed the provinces of Lower Germany and Britain, and eventually acceded to the highest honor, the urban prefecture. Fronto mentions him once in passing, a neutral reference, in a letter to a fellow Cirtan.[57] His family mausoleum still stands, erected in the *pagus* of Caldis near the patria of the Lollii, the tiny plateau Castellum Tidditanorum, northwest of Cirta: the praefectus urbi was patron of both villages.[58] An epitaph mentions two brothers, the parents and an uncle, but their rank and occupations are omitted. If his family was of modest rank, Urbicus' talents may have required the interest of others. Such patronage could have been derived from the family of the Pactumeii, whose contemporary representative was P. Pactumeius Clemens (cos. 138), patron of the Four Colonies. This nobleman won fame as a jurisconsult, his authority being confirmed by a statue in Cirta itself, by a citation by a contemporary jurist, and by the praise of his compatriot Fronto.[59] These two magistrates, the general and the jurisprudent, could provide powerful incentive and support for Cirtan interests, and such support is attested by strong circumstantial evidence. Thus Lollius Urbicus was not the only man of consequence to be produced by the wholly insignificant Tiddis, for a certain Q. Sittius Faustus, who was created a knight in his old age, had been adlected much earlier *in quinque decuriis* by the emperor Marcus Aurelius; the influence of his great contemporary must be surmised.[60] And the first known procurator from Cirta, M. Claudius Restitutus, began his imperial career in a post in Syria "ad putandas rationes"; he must have served under his compatriot Pactumeius Clemens, who was legate of Hadrian "ad rationes civitatium Syriae putandas."[61]

The existence of a Cirtan community at Rome might be deduced from such evidence; Fronto confirms it, and his general concern for Cirta is best grasped in his patronage of its younger senators. Foremost, of course, was his brother Quadratus (cos. 147), who must have profited by Fronto's eminence to some extent, if not in his senatorial career then at least in his access to the imperial family. But there are others. Aulus Gellius tells of a visit he paid to the orator in the company of his friend Celsinus Iulius, a Numidian, who aided Fronto in discomfiting a grammarian through his intimate knowledge of the works of Ennius. Surely this man was a pupil of the master who so praised Ennius, and the same as P. Iulius Proculus Celsinus, a consul designate and a landowner and native of Cirta.[62] Another friend, it may be presumed, and a native of Cirta as well, was P. Iulius Geminius Marcianus (cos. c. 167), known as a military man but also apparently as an advocate, the same man as "Marcianus noster," who was to act with Fronto in the notorious lawsuit against Herodes Atticus.[63] But closest of all to the orator was the ill-fated C. Arrius Antoninus (cos. c. 170), a man of great civil abilities with an obvious forensic bent.[64] That Fronto promoted his career is most likely, and four letters survive, full of advice, one of them addressed "to my dearest son." The origin of their intimacy is not far to seek: the man's tribe and his patronage of the Four Colonies proclaim a Cirtan origin, and the family had large holdings in the Four Colonies and in Africa.[65]

The list is brief but impressive, and it might be lengthened. A good candidate would be the soldier Q. Antistius Adventus (cos. c. 167) from Thibilis, who was closely connected with Marcus Aurelius and with his fellow Cirtan Arrius Antoninus.[66] Too late, perhaps, for Fronto's friendship were the Cirtans P. Iulius Castus and M. Flavius Postumus, both of praetorian rank under Commodus.[67] However, another junior senator must be included. Fronto believed in selecting patrons from adjacent *civitates*, as he indicates in the letter to the senate of Cirta, and he himself was patron of the bordering town of Calama. A singular contemporary of Fronto was a certain Q. Tullius Maximus "e Libya," consul designate in the later 160s and a budding poet even while in command of a legion; he should be the same as the Libyan Maximus, a lover of rhetoric and an associate of the sophist Aristides at Pergamum in the mid-140s.[68] Tullii are not common in North Africa. Q. Tullii are very rare, and only one of any rank is recorded, Q. Tullius Q.f. Florus, perpetual flamen at Calama.[69] A lover of literature and a neighbor of Cirta would be a natural addition to Fronto's circle.

The role of his patria is clear. Despite continued residence in Rome and despite connections throughout the empire, Fronto retains an interest in his homeland, an interest closely confined to Cirta and its environs.[70] Ties are maintained with family and friends, rights of patronage are accepted or refused, there is perhaps even an unwilling involvement in local politics.[71] More obviously, when Cirtans appear at Rome they stay with Fronto, they are taken on as pupils, their careers are fostered in the senate and at court. The best illustration lies in the man Licinius Montanus, a member of a curial family at Cirta. According to Fronto, Montanus was the dearest of his many *hospites*;

when in Rome he lodged with the orator, he shared intimately in his thoughts and deeds, he was loved by him as few others were.[72] Fifty years and more after Fronto's death, a Cirtan decurion could refer to Fronto simply, with casual pride, as "Cirtensis noster."[73]

The orator's ties with his patria turn out to be close and typical of his age, expressed in solid terms of friendship and patronage. What of Africa, "provincia nostra"? Beyond the confines of Cirta, Fronto's African friends and interests appear to be few and random, in strong contrast even with his contacts in the centers of the Hellenic East.[74] This contrast suggests the key to what was truly "African" in the orator. Above all, Fronto was the learned man of his age, thoroughly familiar with both Greek and Latin culture and the standard-bearer of Latin letters. His only misfortune was that he was born neither Greek nor Roman, but African.

There is an important conflict to be observed between imperial and provincial civilization. Considerable evidence suggests in the educated elite of Roman Africa a conscious suppression of the non-Latin heritage, a practice in marked contrast with that of the Hellenized East. The *lingua punica* was not a source of pride, most particularly in the late first and early second centuries, just when Africans were first beginning to penetrate the courts, the salons, and the senate of Rome. Thus the poet Statius heroically compensated for the origin of a friend from Lepcis Magna with the claim that the man was quite ignorant of Africa: "Your speech is not Punic, neither is your dress, your thought is not foreign, you are Italian, Italian."[75] Knowledge of Punic was mocked as barbarous by one's enemies and caused embarrassment to friends.[76] Important testimony is offered by Fronto's younger contemporary, the renowned Apuleius, who defended his own backwoods birth, "half Numidian, half Gaetulian," with a philosophical appeal to the worth of a man's soul over that of his birthplace. Most significant in one whose background was so similar to Fronto's, he advanced the argument that "among the sluggish Scythians wise Anacharsis was born, among the shrewd Athenians foolish Meletides."[77] The echo of Fronto is striking. He too had used the same image, comparing himself as a Libyan to Anacharsis. A commonplace is suggested, the African man of letters as the Scythian at Athens, wise despite his barbarian patria. Fronto certainly did not forget it, for there exists another letter, also in Greek, to Marcus Caesar "by the hand of this foreigner, in speech little short of a barbarian, but as regards judgment, as I think, not wholly wanting in sagacity."[78] Such a defensive attitude is explained in part by an incident in the career of the African writer Florus, another but older contemporary. He was deprived of the prize for poetry at Domitian's games, so he was told, not because the emperor was prejudiced against his youth, but lest Africa should win the crown of great Jupiter.[79] The problem lies particularly in the tension between two levels of a single civilization, Rome's and the provincial Roman's, at a time when Africans were clamoring for attention. In such a climate it is not to be wondered that Fronto's work should reveal almost nothing of his African heritage. The attitude is in itself an African one, and important in his own development. Provincialism was anathema, the Latin of Africa's educated classes rigidly pure and overinclined to rhetoric.[80]

The concern for Latin and things Roman at the expense of things African was a mark of the educated elite of the province and an index of its Romanization, and Fronto was a true son of the bourgeois aristocracy. The values of this class under the empire are not particularly attractive. The multitude of laudatory inscriptions and the meager literary evidence permit us to form a picture of a truly provincial society, infinitely proud of its achievements, keenly competitive in the public display or expenditure of its wealth, and vociferously patriotic. True to its provincial nature, it tended to be vigorously and faithfully imitative, and nowhere more so than in its energetic pursuit of Greco-Roman culture. Indeed, Africa far outstrips the older Latin-speaking provinces in its enthusiasm. An exuberant intellectual life can be discovered in a raw city of the Numidian backwoods, and the obscurest of towns can celebrate its Cicero.[81] Learning and eloquence were inseparable: otherwise unexceptional worthies were proclaimed "amator studiorum" or "doctissimus et facundissimus"; one knight of Thamugadi was as fluent as he was good.[82] The truly distinguishing accomplishment was the mastery of Greek, signaled by the accolade "utraque lingua eruditus," and a sure sign of the influence of Roman rhetoric.[83] It was displayed flamboyantly.[84] The result of this enthusiasm could be a disturbing lack of discrimination. An epitaph in Cirtan Thibilis renders an exhaustive account of the literary virtues of its young subject, a relative of senators: he was outstanding for his eloquence, industry, and style, a sober declaimer and an easy speaker extempore, the composer of dialogues, epistles, and idylls, and—we are reminded that his talent was remarkable—skilled in the fashioning of eclogues.[85] Bad poetry flourished in Roman Africa.[86]

The second-century province, Fronto's Africa, suffered from a common failing: its cultural resources could not keep pace with its aspirations. In the Greek East under the principate there flourished three centers of the art of sophistry, Athens, Ephesus, and Smyrna; investigation of its practitioners reveals that those unfortunate enough to be born elsewhere migrated to one of these cities, while native sons disdained to leave them.[87] The choice in the West for any intellectual activity was even simpler, for Rome stood unrivaled. Carthage did eventually rise to become the second city, but a clear second: no imperial chairs were endowed there and, most important, there is no hint of the existence in Fronto's day of those schools later familiar to Augustine. The first stray evidence for them appears in Tertullian, in the form of a professor of remarkably poor quality; Apuleius makes no mention of them, and he sought his advanced education elsewhere.[88] Therefore, as it had been for the Gaul and the Spaniard before them, Rome acted as the natural magnet for Africans of exceptional talent, scholars like Annaeus Cornutus of Lepcis, the teacher of Lucan and Persius, or Sulpicius Apollinaris of Carthage, the teacher of Aulus Gellius and the future emperor Pertinax.[89] In due course an African professor would hold the chair of rhetoric at Rome, with the rank of a centenarian procurator: he was a decurion of Sicca Veneria.[90] The best illustration of this migration of the intellectuals is that provided by Apuleius, who clearly sets out Africa's limitations. Carthage had seen the beginnings of his philosophical studies as a boy, but Athens it was which nourished them.[91] Even more damaging, he asserted on another occasion that while most were content to learn from litterator, grammaticus, and rhetor, he (and the contrast is strong) had emigrated to Athens to drain various deeper draughts of erudition, deceptive poetry, limpid geometry, sweet music, austere dialectics, most of all the nectar of philosophy.[92] Apuleius claimed to be a philosopher, and Athens was his natural magnet. For Fronto Rome was the only possible center, and there is good evidence that he went there at an early age to continue his education.

One element of this intellectual migration is an important phenomenon in itself. At the very time when Fronto was working toward his primacy of the Roman bar, the satirist Juvenal briefly captured the strength of his native land: Africa was the veritable wetnurse of advocates.[93] He did not exaggerate, for the profession of advocacy was a favorite preserve of African society, its love of litigation exuberantly recorded in its inscriptions and particularly in the *Apology* of Apuleius.[94] Again, the best went to Rome, where an impressive succession of leading advocates can be traced. The eloquent and wealthy Septimius Severus, the friend of Statius, practiced there under Domitian. In the time of Hadrian and of Juvenal, Cornelius Fronto was the leading advocate, and well into the reign of Pius he was still "causidicus". His successors as *principes fori* were the Africans Servilius Silanus and Postumius Festus. And under the Severi, Minucius Felix was "Romae insignis causidicus."[95] These men represent only the upper stratum, but Juvenal's assertion can be confirmed at a lower level. The less gifted or influential African could advance at Rome by other means, in the service of the emperor, starting his career as advocate for the fisc.[96] That post was instituted by Hadrian, the emperor of Juvenal and of Fronto, and it is worth noting that his reign was the first and only to see a significant increase in the number of Africans in the imperial service.[97] The evidence converges to suggest that from the late first century onward Romanized Africans were attracted to the courts of Rome in significant numbers. Fronto, the best of them, won the consulship. Fifty years after his death a humble African advocate of Moorish ancestry rose to become a brief and unlamented emperor.[98]

Fronto was the African at Rome, the provincial flourishing at the seat of empire. He remembered his patria with affection and he took an abiding interest, however distant, in its welfare and the prosperity of its citizens. But the provincial heritage is ambivalent. The vigorous Roman Africa of the early second century was a new society, Romanization a process of the recent past. The upper classes rejected native culture and energetically adopted the attributes of a civilization to which they were relative newcomers, excelling at some, the art of rhetoric, for instance. This rejection of Africa and identification with Rome was remarkably complete. Thus it was that Fronto, the nomad Libyan and the citizen of Cirta, could write that Mars, "who begat the great Roman race, has no compunction in suffering us to faint at times and be defeated and wounded"; often, he reminds his reader, Rome has won the war after losing the bloodiest of battles, in the Gallic war at Allia, in the Samnite at Caudium, in the Punic at Cannae, in the Spanish at Numantia, in the Jugurthine at Cirta.[99] The conception is startlingly African: "externa non mens; Italus, Italus."[100]

II

ITALY

For the ambitious young gentleman from the provinces all roads led to Rome, and they conspired to bring him there as quickly as possible. The young Pliny from Cisalpine Gaul provides the paradigm in the generation preceding Fronto's. He began attending the lectures in Rome of Quintilian and of Nicetes Sacerdos "when barely adolescent"; he pleaded his first case, probably in the centumviral court, at the age of eighteen; and he undoubtedly filled his attested vigintiviral post, as other young men did, at about the same age.[1] Fronto was similarly marked out for a senatorial career, sitting on the board of tresviri capitales. That vigintiviral office suggests his presence in Rome, barring unusual circumstances, at or soon after the age of eighteen.[2] Likewise, on general principles, his youthful ambitions and his mature success demand an early removal from the provinces to the capital. Most important, for the future leader of Latin letters as for Pliny, Rome was the only possible school.

Fronto was educated at Rome.[3] He names two of his beloved teachers and two only, the philosopher Athenodotus and the rhetor Dionysius.[4] The former, his "master and father," trained him sufficiently in the comprehension and use of *exempla* and *imagines*, or that is what Fronto chose to learn from him. Philosophy, specifically dialectics, lulled him to sleep at lectures with its tedium and its obviousness, and with its disdain for study and preparation. More to his taste was the neat fable of his other master, Dionysius the Slim, composed against the philosopher, "On the Dispute of the Vine and the Oak-Tree."[5] Little is known of these men with Greek names. Athenodotus is recorded as a pupil of that Roman Socrates, the Stoic Musonius Rufus, a master whom he praised unreservedly; so the philosopher Cinna Catulus informed his young pupil, the future Marcus Aurelius.[6] His sphere should have been Rome, then. Likewise, Dionysius points to the capital, but on other grounds. The age at which one would attend the rhetor varied. Most would have transferred from the school of the grammaticus by the age of sixteen, staying with the rhetor sometimes up into their early twenties. Fronto, we know, was probably in Rome at about that age preparing to embark on his senatorial career; he must have gone there to study under Dionysius as well. On the best hypothesis, he may have begun his rhetorical studies in Africa but finished them in Rome. An excellent model is provided by the later career of Septimius Severus, the future emperor, who first declaimed in public at Lepcis Magna at the age of seventeen and soon thereafter set off to Rome to continue his studies, "studiorum causa." There a consular kinsman swiftly obtained for him the broad stripe and he set out on a senatorial career.[7] For an aspiring public man, study at Rome involved more than attendance at lectures.

Fronto was born probably in the last years of the first century and he died in or near the year 167. For five decades or more his life was firmly centered on the city of Rome, its environs, and the Bay of Naples, and his official career was remarkably consistent, if unusual, in that all but one of his known offices were held in the capital, the minor exception offering the closest substitute possible, a quaestorship in Sicily. Thus Fronto's ambit was restricted, but it lay within the only society that really mattered to him. His correspondence as it survives is that of a truly public figure, living and happily working in the salons and the palace, in the senate house and the courts of Rome. These are Fronto's proper environment and here lie his abiding passions, conspiring to form our portrait of him. Of the private man the letters reveal surprisingly little. We can see that he was a kindly and rather simple person and more than a bit of a hypochondriac, but of his religious views or even his domestic routine we learn almost nothing. However, there are two basic elements in Fronto's more private life about which something can be said and which provide essential background to the long years in Italy: his property and his family. The common factor is security.

Fronto was a rich man. In a society where land was by far the greatest source of wealth, he owned at least three substantial estates of which something can be said. First, a mansion in Rome was essential for a Roman senator. Fronto's was on the Esquiline. In a letter from the period of his consulship he mentions "Horatius Flaccus, a famous poet and one with whom I have a connection through Maecenas and my gardens of Maecenas."[8] From the eighth satire of Horace's first book onward, the splendid *horti Maecenatis* with their palace and famous tower have a considerable history, being absorbed after the death of their creator into the imperial property, undergoing considerable alteration, and perhaps being parceled out and sold by Vespasian.[9] Just how much of the original estate came into Fronto's hands is the important question. Most significant, he seems to have acquired the actual *domus*. One substantial room of the building stands today, a self-contained structure just off the via Merulana, known as the *auditorium Maecenatis*: the best modern guess would have it that this was in fact a dining room.[10] Two pieces of evidence converge to link the structure with Fronto and his gardens of Maecenas. First, the two water pipes noted earlier, bearing the names of the orator and of his brother, were discovered near the remains of another large room to the southwest of the auditorium.[11] Second, within the auditorium itself there was found a small fragment of what appears to be an honorific inscription, which has been convincingly restored to read "[Hispania Ci]teriore conv[entu . . .] / Segonti[ni . . .]."[12] In the early 170s, Fronto's excellent son-in-law, Aufidius Victorinus, held an extraordinary governorship of Hispania Citerior and Baetica combined, to deal with Moorish raiders.[13] The fragmentary inscription from the house on the Esquiline should be a relic of the province's gratitude, for as the husband of Fronto's only surviving child, Victorinus in his turn surely came into possession of the gardens of Maecenas.

Fronto's tenure of Maecenas' house on the Esquiline and a part at least of the estate is thus amply assured. Although the size and nature of the property and its buildings in the Antonine period remain quite unclear, the general impression must be that their owner was a man of considerable wealth, more so than might be deduced from his correspondence. The history of the title of the property is impressive, passing by inheritance from Maecenas to Nero, and then from Fronto to his daughter and her illustrious husband. Clearly, the house remained something of a monument, for the location of the orator's residence was still known to late antiquity, and by chance a guidebook from the twelfth century preserves mention of a *domus Frontoniana* on or near the Esquiline.[14]

Next, and almost as necessary for a public man, was a private retreat in the environs of Rome, a place such as Pliny's Laurentine villa which could provide asylum after a full day in the city.[15] In one letter the young Marcus Caesar inquires after his master's whereabouts after they have separated: "Did you go to the Aurelian district or into Campania? Mind you tell me, and whether you have begun the vintage and whether you have brought crowds of books to your country house."[16] The Campanian villa is well attested, but it has gone unremarked that Marcus' words should also imply the existence of a villa with vineyard "in Aurelia," that is, in the area of the via Aurelia running out from Rome and up along the coast of Etruria. The exact situation is unknown, but an approximate location may be deduced from *M. Caes.* III.21, Fronto to Marcus: "I am keeping my bed. If I should be fit for the journey when you go to Centumcellae I shall see you, please God, at Lorium on the seventh day before the Ides." The via Aurelia ran through Lorium and Centumcellae, both of them the sites of imperial residences. It is a fair assumption that if Fronto intended to intercept Marcus at Lorium en route from Rome to Centumcellae, his "Aurelian" villa was somewhere in that neighborhood, but no sign of the estate has yet appeared.[17] Being closer to Rome than the Campanian villa, this place is far more likely to be the subject of certain stray references. Thus news of the victories of Avidius Cassius in the east was brought to Fronto "in my suburban villa," surely the Aurelian, and here were probably the *horti* from which he set out at dawn on 28 March 161 with the intention of reaching Rome that same day.[18]

For a complete holiday the only fashionable area for the Roman aristocrat of the Antonine period was the Bay of Naples, and there too Fronto maintained a villa. Vague hints as to its existence appear in the correspondence, as when Marcus suggests that Fronto's Campanian property included a vineyard, and Fronto himself betrays personal acquaintance with the Campanian coast.[19] Fortunately, something more can be added, for the villa has been discovered and in small part excavated. An inscription to "Cornelia Cratia, daughter of M. Cornelius Fronto," was discovered in the ruins of a mansion on the coast at Surrentum and actually within the walls of the ancient town. This was surely Fronto's Campanian base, set in a plain whose prosperity depended on viticulture and close enough to Baiae for easy visiting with the imperial family.[20] The site of Surrentum is highly impressive, surrounded by sheer cliffs down to the sea and (until recent times) vertiginous ravines on the landward side; the sense of dramatic isolation is reminiscent of Cirta. Given the restricted area of this land island, Fronto's estate must have dominated the town both physically and socially, spread over many acres and commanding several hundred yards of coast with various elaborate maritime constructions, which are the most conspicuous remains today. Of the *domus*, set back from the cliff and surrounded by gardens, the traces are sparse, excavation being severely limited by modern building, but the remains indicate that the word *palace* would not be inappropriate to describe the complex. Indeed, that definition is precise, for it is highly probable that it was to this villa that the disinherited Agrippa Postumus was removed by his grandfather Augustus, shortly before the young man's exile and death.[21] Thus, as was the case with his Roman house, Fronto's Surrentine estate appears to have been part of the imperial patrimony.

The possession and maintenance of three villas, at least two of which were on the grand scale, demonstrate Fronto's comparative wealth.[22] Certainly, he did not flinch at an architect's estimate of one-third of a million sesterces for the construction of a new bath, and it was probably he who undertook the construction of an elaborate nymphaeum at Surrentum and repairs and redecoration both at Surrentum and at the house in Rome.[23] Of casual outlay we catch only occasional glimpses: for instance, his public career and role as patron must have occasioned various expenses—witness the games celebrating his consulship; and, beyond the communal entertainment of numerous friends and students, there are references to financial subventions for some and a gift of two slaves to another.[24] Unfortunately, Fronto's income is even less in evidence. Certainly land and agriculture constituted the major area of investment, and it is appropriate to find him involved to some degree in viticulture at both Lorium and Surrentum, but the size and nature of his estates are beyond conjecture. Of the other common source of steady income, money lending, we hear nothing, but something can be added about windfall income. First and foremost we should expect imperial benefactions. Particularly suggestive here is the common element of his three known residences: all were situated in the neighborhood of imperial palaces (the Esquiline house could hardly avoid it), and two at least had at one time been imperial properties. How Fronto acquired any of them is unknown, but princely gratitude for his unpaid services might be a good guess. Of his wife's dowry, another potentially large sum, we again hear nothing, although it is worth remarking that she may have come from a great family of Ephesus. But we do find in Fronto's letters reference to another and highly lucrative source of profit for the Roman gentleman, inheritance. Cicero and Pliny provide good models, each accumulating millions through the wills of friends and acquaintances.[25] Equally busy as an advocate and a senator, Fronto must have had a similar crowd of friends and grateful clients, and we do learn of one inheritance, five-twelfths of the estate of a certain C. Censorius Niger. Niger, he relates, had performed successfully in a lifetime of war and peace, winning the friendship of leading senators and knights and earning both honor and authority.[26] As procurator of Noricum the man stood at the peak of the procuratorial hierarchy, with a probable annual salary of 200,000 sesterces: even one half of his estate must have been a considerable windfall.

As important as the simple fact of Fronto's wealth is his attitude to it: as a topic of correspondence it holds no interest for him. Thus the Niger inheritance is mentioned only for its embarrassing repercussions, for in his will the knight had indulged in shocking abuse of the powerful praetorian prefect, Gavius Maximus. Moderation was Fronto's guiding principle, avoiding the extremes of avarice and extravagance. Avarice he abhors, he declares in a brief personal apologia prompted by the death of his grandson, never committing a single act of it, and he elsewhere commends his son-in-law for demanding "no reward of anyone for act or speech."[27] Again, "I preferred to be poor rather than indebted to another's help, at the worst to be in want, rather than to beg. In expenditure I have never been extravagant, sometimes only earned enough to live on." The conclusion should be that Fronto was a comfortably wealthy man but not exceptionally rich by the high standards of his class; he himself considered his fortune moderate and left it at that. Essential though it might be to his physical comfort, the property is assigned a clearly subordinate importance: "Studia doctrinae rei familiari meae praetuli."[28]

Even Fronto's warm family relationships are kept to the background of the correspondence, intruding only in certain significant contexts or in the rare outpouring of grief on the death of his grandson. Thus it is especially with his dearly beloved wife, Cratia. The only real fact about her to emerge from the letters is her close friendship with the mother of Marcus Caesar, Domitia Lucilla, whose *clienta* she is called. She stays with the imperial family at Naples, celebrates Lucilla's birthday with her, and transmits messages from her husband.[29] But apart from this particular relationship, it is important to note, the elder

Cratia appears only once in the books of letters to Marcus Caesar, that is, she was of interest in terms of the correspondence solely in her role as the friend of the mother of Fronto's friend and pupil. And the only other mention of her in the correspondence is in connection with the death of her grandson, whom she seems to have predeceased, probably in 164.[30] The marriage was doubtless a happy one – she was "my dearest wife" – and there are hints of mutual affection, but Cratia is a shadow next to Cicero's Terentia or Pliny's Calpurnia.[31] One remark by Fronto in a letter to Marcus is suggestive: "Cratia came home last night, but to me it has been as good as having Cratia that you have turned your maxims so brilliantly."[32] Hyperbole aside, this is a good illustration not of Fronto's affections, but of the interests of his correspondence.

Cratia must remain a cipher, but her name alone is highly significant. Despite modern convention, she was Cratia, not Gratia. The manuscript confusion between semiuncial *C* and *G* should be resolved by reference to the Greek version of her name at *M. Caes.* II.12.1, Krateia, and confirmation is available in the clear epigraphic report of her daughter as Cornelia Cratia.[33] Cratia is, quite simply, a Greek name.[34] Two alternatives offer, gentilicium or cognomen. There exists a Latin family name Cratius/Crattius, which might suggest that Fronto's wife was of Greek ancestry but Italian birth.[35] In that case she might have been a native of Sicily, where Fronto had served as a young man of marriageable age. Or perhaps she was from the highly cultivated area of the Bay of Naples: like the imperial family and much of the aristocracy Fronto holidayed in the area, and he certainly owned an estate at Surrentum.[36] However, any relatives in that area would be very humble folk for the wife of Cornelius Fronto and the intimate of Domitia Lucilla. A better alternative would be Cratia as a cognomen, and as such it does appear once in the upper orders of Rome, in the person of a contemporary lady of senatorial rank from Ephesus, Klaudia Krateia: on various counts she could be a kinswoman of Fronto's wife.[37] Whatever the case, it is amusing that Fronto should portray himself as the barbarian Anacharsis, humbly anxious about the solecisms of his Greek. The image is intentionally misleading, a pose for the leader of Latin archaism, for one of the major surprises to be won from his correspondence is the extent of Fronto's involvement with Greek letters and with the Greek world in general. Ephesus in particular was one of the great centers of the Greek literary world, its leading families connected with an international nexus of highly cultured and politically powerful Greco-Roman aristocrats. A wife from such a background would go a long way toward explaining the remarkably deep implication of a Latin orator in the Greek world.

Cornelia Cratia, the only surviving child of Fronto and Cratia, is an even more elusive figure than her mother in the correspondence, appearing only as a young child or (like her mother with Lucilla) as an adjunct to her husband, the splendid Aufidius Victorinus. In that admirable young man, Fronto's studies and his domestic life intersected happily. He is first discovered in a letter of 143 as "Aufidius noster," bearing news to Marcus of a speech by Fronto, and then in 146 Marcus reports his grandiloquent claim that no man more just than himself had ever come out of Umbria.[38] Victorinus and a certain Seius Fuscianus are reported as the young prince's most intimate fellow pupils, and it requires little imagination to see him as one of Fronto's pupils as well, for their friendship in the correspondence clearly reflects the classroom and Fronto's interests.[39] He became one of the *principes fori* of the day, doubtless with Fronto's assistance, and it is his accomplishment as an orator which is consistently to the fore. Thus in a letter commending a Greek rhetor for a post in Victorinus' province, Fronto praises his son-in-law as a grave and prudent judge in many things, but above all in matters of eloquence, while in an epistle recommending Victorinus himself he lauds his exceptional character and eloquence.[40] Elsewhere he affirms that the young man's oratorial ability was second only to that of Marcus, and he confirmed this opinion by deputing Victorinus to plead in court when he himself was indisposed.[41] And, appropriately, when his son-in-law was absent from Rome, the two corresponded on matters legal and literary.[42] Otherwise, he appears only as the bearer of news or as the recipient of bulletins on the family and Fronto's health.[43] In short, the portrait of Victorinus recalls that of his mother-in-law, for there is scarcely a hint of the brilliant civil and military career well known from other sources: even letters addressed to him in his provinces hold no reflection of his martial deeds. For Fronto, Victorinus' outstanding qualities were his excellent character and his command of eloquence, and he would undoubtedly have argued that his son-in-law's success was the natural outcome of precisely those virtues.[44] Again the correspondence is deceptive: within its limits Victorinus remains as abstract a figure as his wife.

The union of Cratia and Victorinus about the year 159 produced three children. The youngest died at the age of three in his father's province of Upper Germany, and although his grandfather had never set eyes upon the infant, he was overcome with grief.[45] As for the survivors, in a later epistle Fronto the doting grandfather relates in loving detail the childish play of young Fronto (born c. 160) and young Victorinus (born c. 165/166); the pair grew up to hold the ordinary consulship in succession as M. Aufidius Fronto (199) and C. Aufidius Victorinus (200).[46] Fronto lodged high hopes in his descendants. By the selection of Victorinus as his son-in-law, he declared, he could not have better consulted his own interests in the matter of posterity, nor his daughter's in the matter of her whole life.[47] He further stoutly announced that it was in the highest interests of the state that a man like Victorinus have as many children as possible; but he was still delighted to find his grandson Fronto taking after himself, and he attempted to introduce him at an early age to items of great interest to himself, to *chartulae* and *tabellae*.[48] Unfortunately, Fronto's descendants did not fulfill his literary dynastic dreams. The elder, his namesake, who eventually won the proconsulship of Asia, is noteworthy only for his pride, as displayed in the grandiose epitaph of his son and in his own involvement in an extraordinary administrative fiasco during the reign of Macrinus.[49] And his brother Victorinus is remembered merely as the progenitor of a race of senatorial squires at Pisaurum, whose pride in their ancestry seems to have exceeded their own achievements.[50]

Fronto's formal education, his property, and his family: something can be gleaned from the correspondence on each subject, and each provides essential private background to the years in Italy. But this background is all but lost in the public life of the salons, the courts, the senate, and the palace. There the interests of the letters lie, as there Fronto pursued his twin passions, the cultivation of letters and the perfection of his prince.

III

LITERARY SOCIETY AT ROME

THE PURSUIT of learning was Fronto's chief and abiding passion, and learning informs every aspect of his life. Most significant, he asserts in one letter that "the friendship which is grounded on culture [*paideia*] takes the highest place with me," and most if not all of his friendships contain some element of erudition. His *Letters to His Friends* accordingly offer rich material on the literary life of the Antonine era, and since (as it will appear) Fronto existed at the center of the Latin literary world, his correspondence provides a good nucleus for the reconstruction of that world. Because much of the material remains unexploited, a discursive commentary is the first requirement, to present and analyze certain items in the correspondence while working toward some definition of the structure and function of literary society in the second century. It will then be possible to consider a crucial problem: the effect of this society, in which Fronto was the preeminent man of letters, upon cultural developments in his lifetime.

The first of the letters *Ad Amicos*, the introduction to a series of letters of commendation, opens with a solemn statement on the custom of recommendation as hallowed by generations. Then Fronto, the leading advocate of the age, unblushingly introduces to a judge the close friend who is about to plead in the judge's court. Erudition is the dominant theme, the standard catalogue of the litigant's virtues ending with those which specially bound him to Fronto, the study of letters and elegance in the nobler arts.[1] His literary virtues were sufficient to unite this man in all-embracing friendship with Fronto: "We have lived together, studied together, shared the grave and the gay, made trial of our fidelity and of our counsels, and in every way our friendship has brought pleasure and profit." The same man, a certain Sulpicius Cornelianus, is noticed in the subsequent epistle as well, a note of introduction in Greek and addressed to a Greek, which commends Cornelianus for his eloquence and remarks that he is no philosopher. The man himself is otherwise unknown, though it is very tempting from the literary tone of the letter to see in him a man later active in the imperial service, that is, the advocate, rhetor, and ab epistulis Graecis Cornelianus, to whom the grammaticus Phrynichus dedicated his *Ekloge* with recurrent eulogy of both his literary talents and his political power.[2] Appius Apollonides, the recipient of the second letter, cannot be precisely identified, but the Claudius Severus who received the first letter in the series is of exceptional interest.[3]

The family of the Claudii Severi offers a typical combination of political power and active participation in the arts. Its social position was unassailable; the family was connected to various eastern dynasts and had been consular at Rome since the reign of Trajan.[4] Fronto's letter is addressed to a man who placed a high value on culture, but he is not positively identifiable, for culture was a family trait. Thus Cn. Claudius Severus Arabianus (cos. ord. 146) mixed a senatorial career with a mastery of the Peripatetic philosophy which he imparted to Marcus Caesar, and further interests in history and political theory may be deduced from his memorial in Marcus' *Meditations.*[5] Against his identification with Fronto's acquaintance it might be objected that the Cornelianus recommended to him was no philosopher, but the other candidate for the judge in *Ad. Am.* I.1 was also a student of philosophy, Arabianus' son, Cn. Claudius Severus (cos. II ord. 173), a disciple of Aristotle.[6] A life of service in high places is attested for this man as well, a senatorial career and intimate access to the emperor, of whom he was *necessarius, comes,* and son-in-law.[7] And he was a passionate promoter of Greek culture: as a patron he introduced Galen to the emperor Marcus after attending the doctor's anatomical demonstrations, and as a patron he is honored in verse by the sophist Hadrian of Tyre, of whose style he was a lively critic.[8] Moreover, as an equal he was attracted to the friendship of men who, like himself, combined rank and taste. He may be glimpsed discussing Hadrian's talent with Marcus Aurelius, or making a dedication at Athens with the aid of the noble sophist Herodes Atticus (cos. ord. 143), or concerning himself with the health of a boy, Sextus, the son of one of the famed brothers Quintilii (coss. ord. 151) who were also intimates of the emperor and deeply involved in the Second Sophistic as friends of Aristides and foes of Herodes.[9]

The first letter suggests several themes which will recur. The general combination of power and culture is noteworthy, and one concrete result of the combination is here illustrated, the relevance of a man's learning to the judge in a court of law. Further, polymathy is clearly indicated, and a label such as "philosopher" comes under suspicion when the philosopher's friends and interests are noticed; conversely, Fronto's notorious aversion to philosophy will need to be reexamined. Most interesting is the connection with the flourishing world of Greek letters, a contact which will be repeated unobtrusively throughout the correspondence. Fronto, the dominant figure in contemporary Latin letters and one who disclaimed any mastery of Greek, is seen here as the intermediary between two men immersed in Hellenic culture. Close intercourse on a social level is suggested, with a network embracing both cultures: Claudius Severus was noted for his preeminence in both languages, and *fama* had brought to Fronto's ears the praise of Cornelianus' talents.[10] The practical effect on Latin letters remains to be considered.

The same elements recur in the following two letters, but the scene shifts from Rome to Africa and from judge to governor. The first is that recommending the Cirtan Licinius Montanus to the asylum, aid, and advice of the proconsul of Africa, L. Hedius Rufus Lollianus Avitus, and again the man's culture is meant to win official favor. Fronto restates the theme of the previous note, that his closest friendships are founded on culture: "With me eloquence holds the most honoured place."[11] And the praise here closely recalls that accorded to Sulpicius Cornelianus: a list of virtues, the sharing of *contubernium*, general intimacy in every counsel. Montanus was likewise a follower of the noble arts, a man of elegant learning and eloquence, and supremely devoted to Fronto's favorite pursuit, the study of rhetoric. As before, however, attention is attracted more by the recipient of this appeal, and again the interest in learning to be deduced from Fronto's comments can be amply demonstrated from other sources. Indeed, cultivation informs the public actions of Avitus (cos. ord. 144) wherever they are known to us, from the restoration of the theater at Lepcis Magna to the active patronage of the grammaticus Helvius Pertinax.[12] Fronto lodged his trust in the proconsul's love of eloquence, a love exuberantly proclaimed by Apuleius himself, for as proconsul Avitus had graced with his presence one of Apuleius' public orations, and Apuleius (like Fronto) was able to recommend to him a promising young orator. Lollianus Avitus, he claimed, was the personification of the classic ideal, a good man skilled in speaking. His letters exhibited an exceptional charm and learning, and a choice and delightful vocabulary: the terms are especially reminiscent of Frontonian doctrine. As for his eloquence, Apuleius, who had met and courted the most eloquent Romans of his day, insisted that he admired none of them as he did Avitus, in whom were united the particular virtues of each celebrated orator of old.[13] Despite this mastery of Latin oratory, the solidly Italian Lollianus Avitus was no stranger to the Greek literary world: as governor of Pontus-Bithynia, he had advised Lucian of Samosata not to prosecute the dangerously influential charlatan Alexander of Abonuteichus.[14] If that is not enough, there is also a tie with the later asiarch and rhetor Pomponius Cornelius Lollianus Hedianus, kinsman of consulars; and (leading back again to Fronto) there is an intimacy with the Claudii Severi, one of whom accompanied Lollianus to Africa as proconsul's legate.[15]

The eloquent and learned Lollianus Avitus was succeeded as proconsul of Africa by Claudius Maximus, a philosopher and his friend, who presided over the trial of Apuleius at Sabratha in the winter of 158/159.[16] Much of Apuleius' *Apologia* is punctuated by recital of this proconsul's virtues and by appeal to his erudition. The virtues described are standard to the good judge: patience, humanity, shrewdness, caution, justice.[17] But the heaviest flattery is reserved for his learning, for he and Apuleius are comrades in philosophy. Maximus will recognize the allusions to Aristotle, to Plato, indeed to all the ancient philosophers, as Apuleius is careful to point out with each citation.[18] His erudition will serve him as judge and will ease Apuleius' burden as advocate: "Is it not preferable, Claudius Maximus, that I trust in your learning and perfect erudition, and that I disdain to respond to boors and fools?"[19] Maximus is the ideal blend of scholar and man of action, who has heard much in conversation, learned more in reading, and discovered not a little through experience: "virum tam austerae sectae tamque diutinae militiae."[20] Again, there is other evidence to confirm this portrait. Maximus is attested as legate of the province of Upper Pannonia, and an acephalous inscription recently assigned to him records a long and glorious succession of civil and military employments, commencing with service and decoration in Trajan's Parthian campaigns.[21] This man of action's mastery of Stoic philosophy also brought him an appointment as teacher of Marcus Aurelius, and his humanity won an exceptionally affectionate tribute from his pupil.[22] Thus another character of importance in the world of learning can be brought within Fronto's ambit on several counts, even though he does not appear in the extant correspondence. Maximus' friendship with Lollianus Avitus is significant, not a simple bond between two senators alone, but also one between a notable orator and a distinguished philosopher. Apuleius produced and read in court a letter of the former proconsul, introducing it with a eulogy of that *vir bonus dicendi peritus,* to which Maximus would listen with pleasure, just as he would likewise enjoy a lengthy digression on the felicities of Avitus' style.[23] And it is worth reiterating yet again that the philosopher Apuleius delivered and the philosopher Maximus was swayed by what has justly been called a masterpiece of the Second Sophistic.[24] The gulf between rhetoric and philosophy tends to be exaggerated by polemic, not least in the writings of Fronto himself, but even he could on occasion display an interest in philosophy.

Claudius Maximus provides a double link with the subsequent letter in the correspondence, *Ad Amicos* I.4, which is addressed to a fellow philosopher and his own successor as proconsul of Africa, Q. Egrilius Plarianus. In a delightful commendation of his friend Iulius Aquilinus, Fronto presents this Platonist lecturer with singular determination as a practicing sophist. The highest recommendation comes first, that Aquilinus is most learned, and then the second, that he is most eloquent. The discipline of philosophy is mentioned, but it was merely training for the *optimae artes,* just as the study of eloquence improved the man's outstanding *facundia.* The common standards required by the age of all disciplines are duly repeated: Aquilinus is both learned and elegant, and a concrete example is provided by his disputations on Plato. No praise is accorded to his subject or to the brilliance of his interpretation; rather, the twin talents mentioned are the unmistakable marks of Frontonian eloquence, an enviable horde of words and an extensive stock of *sententiae.*[25] Others agree with his opinion, Fronto urges, for great crowds have flocked to Aquilinus' displays, and several senators approve of and admire not his doctrine, but his eloquence. This Iulius Aquilinus is known from epigraphy as a respectable member of that African provincial society marked out by its wealth, its culture, and its public service, the cream of the municipal aristocracy, in this case that of Sicca Veneria.[26] The philosopher had duly filled the role of his station in life, serving on the panel of judges at Rome and seeing military service as prefect of a cohort. In the previous generation a close kinsman, perhaps his father, had served in

Egypt as epistrategus Thebaidos and thereafter as procurator of Dacia Inferior; this man fancied himself a poet, and in the wake of numerous other official tourists had inscribed two samples of his efforts on the much-suffering statue of Memnon at Thebes, one in the Latin language and one (it should be noted) in Greek.[27] To apply the label "philosopher" to Iulius Aquilinus is to admit only part of the evidence.

This mixture of rhetoric and philosophy also tells something about the man to whom it was intended to appeal. Fronto does not apply to him epithets standard to a student of rhetoric, *doctus* and *elegans*, the tributes to an informed taste, but rather those of the philosopher, sober, wise, sagacious, discerning. A brief epitaph from Germany is directly relevant, dedicated by a certain Aelia Timoclea and her children to her husband, "Q. Aelius Egrilius Evaretus the philosopher and friend of Salvius Iulianus."[28] This Evaretus, a Cretan, had migrated from Egypt to Pergamum, where he became acquainted with the sophist Aristides and where he doubtless encountered the jurist Salvius Iulianus among the men of culture incubating at the Asclepium in the 140s.[29] Thus a link between philosophy and Roman jurisprudence was forged in a stronghold of the Second Sophistic and continued on the Rhine frontier. The broad sympathies of Egrilius Evaretus were presumably shared by his patron and (perhaps) his pupil, the proconsul of Africa, Egrilius Plarianus, and Fronto the orator was a happy intermediary between the philosopher Aquilinus and the philosopher Plarianus.

The next letter in this series (*Ad Am.* I.5) reveals yet again Fronto's close contacts with the Greek literary world. Like Claudius Severus, the correspondent Ti. Claudius Iulianus of Smyrna (cos. ?159) combined the inherited power of the eastern magnate—they were both scions of a widespread pan-Hellenic and dynastic connection, and perhaps kinsmen—with the civil and military career of the Roman senator, and both were equally familiar with the leading figures of Greek and Latin letters, Herodes Atticus and Cornelius Fronto.[30] With Aufidius Victorinus and Arrius Antoninus, Iulianus is marked out as a special intimate of Fronto's. Victorinus, with five letters, was the beloved pupil and son-in-law. Antoninus, with four, was a fellow Cirtan who took the place of Fronto's son. Whence then this intimacy with an Asian Greek? In four letters the special regard is made explicit: so solid is their friendship that mundane *officia* may be dispensed with; in a fit of despair Fronto could consider Iulianus to be his only remaining friend.[31] Most suggestive is the opening sentiment of this solemn letter of commendation addressed to Iulianus: "We could assuredly wish, my dearest Naucellius, it had been our happy fortune that, if I had had any children also of the male sex and these were of an age for the discharge of military duties at this particular time, when you are administering a province with an army, my children should serve under you."[32] Such patronage of the young was a common favor between friends, but, more specifically, it was often a mark of kinship. Kinship real or notional is an important element in Fronto's two other intimate friendships, and it might just be that Iulianus was a kinsman of Fronto's wife.

In this, the first of the letters to Iulianus, Fronto appears to be taking customary advantage of such a friendship by recommending to his correspondent's favor a younger man, but the letter is deceptive. The setting is ostensibly military: the young man commended, Calvisius Faustinianus, is to fulfill his military obligations in the provincial army of Iulianus. However, such affairs are soon brushed aside (as were matters of philosophy in the letter to Plarianus), for previous commanders have sufficiently praised the military talents of Faustinianus. His abilities are far more extensive, and a reflection of the unmilitary common interests of Fronto and Iulianus. The reward to be won by Iulianus in showing favor, he is told, is not the youth's loyal industry but the pleasure to be gained from his elegance. Others may praise his martial prowess, Fronto can confirm his erudition; let Iulianus but test his new officer not only in military duties but in judicial deliberations, in literary affairs, in all matters light and serious. Faustinianus is thus presented as a young man of general ability, but the epistle noticeably lacks the extravagant passion found elsewhere in praise of Fronto's *contubernales.* Enlightenment is to be found in the polite embellishments of the concluding sentiments: Fronto could not praise Faustinianus' father sufficiently had not Iulianus already known him; indeed, a quasi-mathematical formula is necessary to express his love for the family.[33] In simpler terms, a cultured senator is commending the son of one learned friend to another. C. Calvisius Statianus, the father, is best known as the prefect of Egypt who espoused the cause of Avidius Cassius in 175, but a previous office bestows upon him official recognition as man of letters, for he was ab epistulis Latinis in the joint reign of Fronto's pupils. In this age the sister office of the ab epistulis Graecis was filled by a remarkable succession of Greek literary figures, several of them practicing sophists.[34] Information on their Latin counterparts is much scarcer but appears to bear out what analogy would suggest, that is, that the office was held by men of considerable rank in the world of letters.[35] It is no surprise that a man like Statianus should turn up in Fronto's circle, and the point of the letter lies not in the qualities of Faustinianus but in the *paideia* of his father.

Both of the other substantial fragments addressed to Claudius Iulianus reflect the erudition of the man. Insofar as it is decipherable, I.19 appears to treat of a literary quarrel with that eternal disciple, Aulus Gellius, but the text is ambiguous and lacks context, and any connection with the *Attic Nights* is hazardous.[36] I.20 will bear more examination. The first section, which concerns itself with Iulianus' zeal in the matter of a certain provincial lawsuit, appeals for an element of levity in the governor's serious deliberations. A dictum of "Valerianus magister" is cited in support; as "Valerianus noster" he turns up again in a few lines; and he reappears once more at the end as the conveyor of news from Fronto to Iulianus. The prominence accorded this man prompts the suspicion that he is in some way interested in the lawsuit and that he has journeyed to Iulianus armed with Fronto's commendation. There are obvious precedents for Fronto's interceding with the judge on behalf of his friends, and the learning of Valerianus is sufficient to account for Fronto's involvement. He is very likely to be the grammaticus Valerianus, a teaching colleague of Pertinax in the 150s and in old age a dinner companion who supplied the literary conversation enjoyed by that emperor.[37] The tight network of literary society may be again observed, for Pertinax was a pupil of Sulpicius Apollinaris and a client of Lollianus Avitus, both friends of the orator Fronto.[38]

A note to the general Avidius Cassius follows the first letter to Claudius Iulianus, but for no discernible reason (unless Calvisius Statianus provides an unstated link). For once there is no obvious literary coloring, simply a straightforward communication of delight in Iunius Maximus, a youthful tribune who has praised his commanding officer. Cassius, however, fits well into Fronto's circle, affording a fine example of the combination of military service with strong literary connections. His father, Heliodorus, had been a Syrian rhetor and philosopher who rose to be Hadrian's ab epistulis Graecis and prefect of Egypt.[39] And not unnaturally there is a connection with the Second

Sophistic, the father being a friend and patron of Aristides, the son a correspondent of Herodes Atticus.[40] Yet the erudition of Avidius Cassius, while providing an obvious basis for acquaintanceship with Fronto, has no evident bearing on this particular letter.[41] There is a more immediate explanation to be discovered in the actions of the tribune. After delivering his laureled despatches and praising his commander in public, Iunius Maximus had journeyed out to visit the ailing Fronto in his suburban villa. There he entertained the old man with tales of the march and of the restoration of ancient discipline, and of Cassius' virtues as displayed en route and in battle. Elsewhere Fronto only once shows an interest in military affairs, and that is in the Parthian campaigns of his pupil Lucius Verus. Here we should have a glimpse of the official chronicler of the war gathering his material. Fronto's preoccupations were few and circumscribed by literary motives.

All of his interests are found combined in his excellent son-in-law Aufidius Victorinus, twice consul (155, 183) and prefect of the city of Rome. As a senator and as an intimate of his fellow pupil Marcus Aurelius, the proud Umbrian was assured of success, and a glorious military career has been well documented.[42] Civil eminence appears to have stemmed, as befits a student of Fronto, from a universally admired combination of eloquence and moral excellence.[43] Naturally, the study of eloquence forms an important part of the correspondence between Fronto and his son-in-law, despite Victorinus' almost constant employment in the service of the empire; the surviving interchange on the subject of Fronto's oration *Pro Bithynis* should be typical.[44] The interplay of life and letters is well illustrated in a rather formal letter of commendation addressed to Victorinus which immediately follows the note to Avidius Cassius (I.7). Its introduction is curt, and familiar by now to the reader of this collection: "Antoninus Aquila vir doctus est et facundus." Again learning and eloquence are the marks of the man's ability and presumably the qualities most likely to engage the favor of the benefactor. However, there are some surprises here. First, Fronto has never heard Aquila declaim; moreover, he has probably never met him. He is reduced to a feeble witticism in support, that the man's name urges confidence: he must be the best of rhetors if he is called the Eagle. Here Fronto is acting merely as the intermediary for other patrons of Aquila, men who are of course learned, honorable, and very dear to himself, and (most important of all) who are apparently Greeks like Aquila himself.[45] These unknowns are the true recipients of Fronto's favor, as he candidly admits: "I want this to be done for Aquila for the sake of those who are pushing him so strongly." He repeats his implicit faith in their sound judgment, but more to the point, he applies the gentle persuasion that these unknown patrons have a proper regard for Victorinus' own wise and sober taste in eloquence. Thus, again, the important element in the letter of commendation is alluded to only obliquely. Victorinus, in turn, is to use his influence with yet another party, the *civitas* within his province, which will select Aquila as "public instructor of its youth." The chain of patronage is striking, stretching back from the unknown state to the provincial governor, to the governor's father-in-law and friend, to that man's learned friends, and ultimately to their client the pedagogue. And it can be observed that one of those links implies close interweaving between the Greek and the Latin literary worlds.

The structure of such social bonds in the service of culture is further illuminated by the next brief note (I.8). Again, the terms are standard: Aemilius Pius is recommended to Passienus Rufus for his excellent character and "the elegance of his studies." No more is said. This time, however, Fronto is not acquainted with his correspondent. Mutual friends are yet again invoked, their report to Fronto ("communium amicorum fama") being sufficient to establish that Passienus Rufus also possesses the two supreme virtues of moral excellence and erudition ("optimum virum bonarumque artium sectatorem"), and Fronto presumes that Rufus has received a similar report of himself. Mere reputation is considered sufficient for entering upon an *amicitia* based on culture, and at the same time for taking advantage of the benefits of friendship by commending a client to the new friend.

Another facet of learned *amicitia* is illustrated in the following letter, the first of the Sardius dossier (*Ad Am.* I.9, 10, 22, 25). Good will extends to the relatives of friends, here the father of two of Fronto's *contubernales*, Sardius Saturninus, who is bound through them to their teacher in the closest intimacy; Fronto's senatorial correspondent is to afford him every assistance should he come his way. This familiarity is confirmed by a letter of consolation addressed to Saturninus on the untimely death of one of his sons (I.22), and the surviving brother is later recommended to Fronto's kinsman Petronius Mamertinus in the third item (I.10). To the standard praise of learning and eloquence Fronto there adds a more personal recommendation: Sardius Lupus was introduced to the forum from the orator's house and *contubernium*, where he had been instructed in all the noble arts, and (again Fronto flatters his correspondent) he was a constant auditor of Mamertinus and the greatest eulogist of his poems. In brief, a young man just starting out on his career is commended to an experienced and influential elder by a shared interest in culture.

The series of commendations to his friends ends with this collection of shorter notes (I.6-10), after firmly establishing Fronto's overriding concern with culture. Indeed, beyond a natural affection for his family, it is difficult to find any activity of the orator which does not betray a literary motif. Certain letters are devoted solely to literary matters, thus lacking the more obvious social implications of *commendatio*, but still offering considerable enlightenment. Most suggestive are the three pieces addressed to Praecilius Pompeianus (I.15, 16, 24). From the only one which survives in substance (I.15) it appears that this man was a participant in those continuous public and private debates (*sermones*) indulged in by the scholarly at Rome and faithfully recorded by Aulus Gellius. In the course of a discussion on the methods of dividing a speech, Fronto had taken an illustration from his own success on behalf of the Bithynians, which he was then revising and of which he had promised much to Pompeianus. This letter is an apology for various delays in publication, one of the few which deals with a subject of much concern to the younger Pliny. If Fronto had such a regard for Pompeianus, it would be worth knowing him better. A homonym of considerable interest turns up on a Gallic inscription, a decurion of Arelate. This Praecilius Pompeianus ranked among the provincial magnates of substance as a judge at Rome, duumvir and munerarius, priest and patron of Arelate, whose citizens voted him a public statue.[46] He was thus a man of wealth, leisure, and considerable rank, comparable to the African Iulius Aquilinus, and identity with the Pompeianus in Fronto is a natural assumption.[47] However, homonymity does not constitute proof, and Praecilii appear in significant numbers at Fronto's patria, Cirta.[48] Nevertheless, the man from Arelate is an attractive candidate and one important clue should allay doubt. Many of Fronto's letters are concerned with the introduction of one literary friend to another, and a widespread network has been discerned in literary society. An eminent sponsor for Pompeianus is available in his compatriot from Arles, the unique and ill-appreciated Favorinus.

There remains a great deal to be said about this exotic Halbsophist. He himself carefully cultivated his image as the leading Hellenizer of his age, assiduously suppressing everything Roman in his thought, his language, and his dress; the corresponding characterization in Philostratus is as tendentious as the rest of his *Brief Lives*.[49] But Favorinus was not so exceptional a Celt as he claimed to be, for Greek culture flourished widely in Gaul, and one enthusiastic "graeculus" of the previous generation, the first flamen of the province of Narbonensis, had been eponymous archon at Athens under Domitian.[50] And Favorinus was more of a Roman than he cared to admit, an equestrian and also flamen of Narbonensis.[51] Aulus Gellius, his disciple, presents a striking picture of a man living at Rome and conversing for the most part in Latin, a scholar passionately interested in Latin grammar and antiquity. Such interests inevitably suggest an acquaintance with the archaizing movement, and a valuable passage in the *Attic Nights* reveals a close familiarity with Fronto – in whose letters he appears as "Favorinus noster" – and an admiration for his prodigious learning and his elegant discourse.[52] There are obvious channels here for intercourse between Greek and Latin culture, but interest should be directed toward the retiring diarist Aulus Gellius. Not an intimate of Fronto, he was introduced into the salon of the ailing orator by his patron Favorinus. In just such a fashion were Praecilius Pompeianus and probably many others brought within Fronto's ambit.

The phenomenon recurs in *Ad Amicos* II.1-3, wherein Fronto appears again in learned discussion by epistle with a man who has been introduced into his salon. The niceties of literary intercourse are well illustrated by the master's striking lack of enthusiasm. A promise is given here that he will gladly read the compositions sent to him by Volumnius Quadratus and correct them. He advises the man to continue his studies in the meanwhile and to exercise his talents whenever he can find the time. For an age of excess in praise or denigration, this lukewarm advice amounts to polite indifference.[53] Here Fronto is merely fulfilling a social obligation, as the opening of the second letter suggests: "Our Castricius gave me your *libellus* yesterday as I was leaving the baths; I asked him to come to me in the morning for the *rescriptum*." The present note is clearly the promised reply. The orator agrees to correct and punctuate certain "Ciceronianos," presumably compositions by Quadratus in Ciceronian style, and his annotations are not to be made public.[54] That Fronto felt such a request necessary—perhaps a nervous reminiscence of the indiscretions of Aulus Gellius in his *Attic Nights*—makes intimacy with Quadratus unlikely, and the use of an intermediary should put him on the fringe of Fronto's acquaintance, somewhere in the vicinity of Gellius. Titus Castricius is the vital link, the distinguished professional scholar who could move easily between the levels of Fronto and Quadratus. Gellius, who of course attended Castricius' lectures, characterizes him well in a handful of anecdotes. He held at Rome the chief position in declaiming and teaching, a man of the highest authority and dignity, admired by the emperor Hadrian for the familiar qualities of learning and character; he was also noted as a man of firm and sober judgment.[55] Eloquence, learning, and moral excellence: a man with such traits could hardly escape that other attribute of the Frontonian age, archaism. Gellius duly records his opinions on the works of Metellus Numidicus, Sallust (the Frontonian hero), and Gaius Gracchus, and his rebuke directed "severely and in the Roman manner" against certain indecorously clad pupils of senatorial rank.[56] It would be particularly surprising to find no mention of such a man in Fronto's correspondence, and the words "Castricius noster" serve to indicate the degree of the friendship upon which Volumnius Quadratus capitalized. Quadratus' own native talents may well have been mediocre, if Fronto's warning in the third letter against poor composition and excessive rhetoric is meant for him.[57]

The quality of this relationship with Quadratus is confirmed by the letter numbered II.6 and addressed to Fronto's beloved compatriot Arrius Antoninus, if Quadratus is properly identified with the Volumnius recommended therein.[58] The terms used here closely resemble those applied to the rhetor Antoninus Aquila in I.7: "He was pointed out to me by learned men and close friends whose wishes are most important to me." Arrius Antoninus will thus be obliging Fronto and Volumnius' unknown friends more than the man himself. Unfortunately, the first part of the letter, which may have recited Volumnius' virtues at greater length, is lost, but these virtues are of little relevance, for the commendation exhibits the same lack of warmth noticeable in the letters to Quadratus himself.[59] Here we are observing not personal friendship but social obligation.

While the letters to Fronto's friends supply most of our material, three other items from the correspondence may be added to the record. One, addressed to Antoninus Pius, is a petition in support of earlier efforts to secure a procuratorship for the historian Appian of Alexandria.[60] Again the Greek world intrudes. Appian, Fronto informs the emperor, is an old acquaintance and a companion in almost daily study, and their intimacy is confirmed by an exchange between the two men of polite but remarkably uninformative letters in Greek which concern a gift of two slaves made to Appian by Fronto.[61] The daily studies to which he refers were undoubtedly undertaken at Rome during Appian's sojourn there as an advocate.[62] His origin and Fronto's use of Greek here might suggest that even Fronto was not above the pursuit of Greek letters as well, but a more characteristic motive for the association may be discovered. We may presume a strong grasp of the Latin language in a man pleading before the emperors at Rome, and Fronto's studies with Appian might well consist of Latin rhetoric. Certainly their friendship reveals a common interest in legal rhetoric—the exchange over the gift of slaves is treated by both as a playful *controversia*—and it would have been sealed by a common distaste for philosophy.[63] Moreover, the two men shared to some degree an interest in Roman antiquity, which is reflected in Fronto's obsession with antique vocabulary and his admiration for pristine virtues, while no one place was better suited than Rome for the research that went into Appian's Roman history. Fronto's request to Antoninus Pius falls into line with other commendations, save that it operates at a higher level, the fruit of this erudite *amicitia* being no less than the grant by the emperor to Appian of procuratorial rank "to enhance his dignity in old age." The extent of such transactions is casually revealed in an earlier passage: previously Fronto had secured for another *contubernalis* the grant of two procuratorships. The emperor himself was not immune to the attractions of erudition, and for advancement in his service its advantages were not confined simply to the great secretariats.

The Greek literary world is inevitably brought into contact with the Roman man of letters through his proposed proconsulship of Asia. One result of Fronto's selection for the office was the summoning of Alexandrian friends to deal with the intended governor's Greek correspondence.[64] The only other trace lies in a brief letter of recommendation of which Fronto is, for a change, the recipient. His pupil Marcus Caesar commends to general favor a certain Themistocles, but again an extensive chain of *amicitia* is exposed. This Themistocles was a friend or pupil of the Stoic philosopher Apollonius of Chalcedon, another tutor of the young prince. Apollonius had sent him to his son in Rome with a command that the son introduce him to Marcus, and Marcus undertook in turn to introduce him to his other master, Fronto, the prospective proconsul of Asia. Apart from this sequence the note reveals little, but some background may be added. In his *Meditations,* Marcus Aurelius reserves special praise for the philosopher Apollonius, but others commented less favorably on the man's avarice and his pride. When he was appointed imperial tutor, a contemporary wit compared his progress to Rome escorted by his disciples with Jason and the Argonauts in search of the golden fleece, and the emperor Pius himself was irritated into alluding to the jest.[65] The Themistocles of Marcus' letter may be one of these latter-day Argonauts. Thus, to explain why Apollonius himself did not approach Fronto directly, we need not invoke Fronto's aversion to philosophy or a supposed disinterest in Greek culture. He may simply have disliked Apollonius of Chalcedon.

One last document, again touching on the Greek world, may be considered not for the evidence it offers but for its cautionary value. It is a brief letter to Marcus Caesar accompanied by an even briefer rescript from the prince, and offering no manifest contact with the literary world.[66] Kindness is requested from Marcus and his father when they come to consider the public accounts of Fronto's client, who is introduced in a single sentence: "Saenius Pompeianus has been defended by me in many actions since he undertook the tax-farming of Africa and he has often assisted me in my affairs." A surviving dedication by the man's wife, Fuficia Clymena, confirms that Q. Saenius Pompeianus was indeed "conductor IIII publicorum Africae."[67] His connection with Fronto may be just what it appears to be here, a simple business affair. However, the involvement in Fronto's *res familiaris* might suggest some degree of intimacy. *Conductores* were by no means beyond the pale of Frontonian society, for the very nature of their profession suggests considerable wealth and equestrian rank.[68] Only two are known for the province of Africa, the other being a certain T. Iulius Perseus, a near contemporary of Saenius Pompeianus and a man of extraordinary accomplishments. This tax-farmer, a magistrate of Carthage, expressed his love for that city by the construction of delightful baths nearby, dedicated to Aesculapius, and he is commemorated as a lion of both Greek and Latin culture in the hymn to Aesculapius written by his friend Apuleius.[69] What is more, he is duly commemorated in the Asclepium at Pergamum by another friend, who was a Roman senator, a Greek dynast, and a notable figure in the Second Sophistic.[70] Perseus' extraordinary connections prompt speculation as to those of his colleague Pompeianus, but there is little evidence. Most interesting is the name of his wife, Clymena, which is Greek, adding a further cosmopolitan touch to the African tax-farmer who died at Rome; and a substantial status might be accorded her, for just at this period the name "Fuficius" penetrates the upper orders of Roman society.[71] The result is slender: rank, Greek ties, and the close acquaintance with Fronto. Nevertheless, the conclusion should be clear. After surveying his correspondence we may confidently be guided by the axiom that unless there is direct evidence to the contrary, all of Fronto's friends—his circle, or his society—shared in his taste for culture.

Fronto's society turns out to be remarkably homogeneous. There are two salient features. First, letters are not cut off from life. Rather than gentlemen abdicating the responsibilities of their station in the pursuit of a life of study, we are faced with learned littérateurs of the highest ranks who are deeply involved in the life and conduct of the empire.[72] Inevitably, *paideia,* and especially the public reputation for *paideia,* has considerable effect directly or indirectly on the larger world, adding an extra dimension to the deliberations of the judge and the governor, the general and the imperial counselor. That suggests the second element to be stressed: there is a network, a sort of freemasonry among men of cultivation, one which sharply and most self-consciously divides them from the *indocti,* the *opici,* and the *rustici.* Within this network lies a complex structure of bonds; witness the recurrence in different contexts of the same names and the same institutions, the same customs and the same opinions, even the same great families. Here the relationship between literature and society is remarkable. On one level the separate classifications of literature break down before the unity of learned society. Polymathy, however superficial, is the order of the day, poetry and rhetoric are confused, the division even between rhetoric and philosophy is bridged, the Greek and Latin literary worlds are intimately interconnected. Thus, viewed simply in its social aspect, culture in the age of the Antonines is both important and unified. Accordingly, cultured society provides an ideal structure for the swift and authoritative dissemination of ideas.

IV

THE MAN OF LETTERS

FROM THE REIGN of Hadrian to that of Marcus Aurelius, Cornelius Fronto was the leader of literary society at Rome. The same period saw the remarkable heyday of the archaizing movement, most closely associated with the name of Fronto, that, however briefly, determined the course of Latin letters. Two questions must be asked, both against the social background: how was it done, and what was the result? If we postpone consideration of Fronto's simple doctrines, the first will be much the easier to answer.

One of the clearest evocations of the mechanics of literary society is to be found in the introduction to the treatise *On Meters*, which was written at Rome sometime in the third century by the grammarian Marius Plotius Sacerdos, being the third book of his work *Artes Grammaticae*.[1] The first volume had been dedicated to the senator Gaianus, a *contubernalis* of his own age and his companion in study. This had come to the attention of Gaianus' father Uranius, likewise a senator, whom it had pleased (says Sacerdos) either by its adequate style or by its dedication to his son. Impelled by this love of literature or of fame, the excellent Uranius had commissioned for himself a second brief volume "de nominum verborum ratione nec non etiam de structuram compositionibus exprimendis." And his activity as patron did not end there, for Uranius commended his scholar to another pair of gentlemen who had also devoted their lives to letters, Maximus "nobilitatis splendore praeditus" and Simplicius "omni laude praedicabilis." These in turn honored Sacerdos with the request for the work on meters, assuredly with ample flattery of his talents. This chain of events can be taken as the model of such transactions. The familiar workings of literary friendship and patronage are clearly traced, but the roots of future success lie firmly in the *contubernium* of youth.

Contubernium is an institution of central importance in the correspondence of Fronto, signifying not merely living together but studying together as master and pupil or as fellow students, always as friends. Its importance extended beyond the classroom, as Quintilian insisted: the *amicitiae* formed by fellow students endured firm into old age, imbued with an almost religious intimacy.[2] Fellow scholars were manifestly an element of extreme importance in Fronto's life, and their numbers over the years must have been considerable. Actual students are attested. The close relationship with the sons of Sardius Saturninus is described everywhere in terms of *contubernium*: these learned youths were instructed in the *bonae artes* at Fronto's house; one of them died there, and the survivor was introduced thence into the forum when his education was complete. One letter recounts the introduction into the forum of a patrician youth from Fronto's house, "filius noster," the news of whose success there was brought back by his other *contubernales*.[3] The closeness with his young pupils is striking, the "almost religious intimacy" perhaps betraying here a paternal element in one without sons of his own. The senator Gavius Clarus, a staunch assistant in his mentor's forensic affairs, was almost an *alumnus*; the learned Calvisius Faustinianus stood in a quasi-filial relationship with Fronto; closest of all was his "dearest son," the senator Arrius Antoninus.[4] And of course his *contubernium* included several older men, the knight Sex. Calpurnius Iulianus; the historian Appian ("studiorum usus prope quotidianus"); Sulpicius Cornelianus ("habitavimus una, studuimus una"); the shadowy Ulpius ("tanta usus studiorum bonarumque artium"); and the eloquent Licinius Monatanus ("quotienscumque Romam venit, in meo contubernio fuit").[5] Conjecture could add many more, notably among his Cirtan compatriots.

Fronto's *contubernium* is of exceptional importance. He has been called a rhetor, mistakenly, for there is nowhere any hint that he delivered lectures or declamations, nor that his *contubernales* were paying pupils; he was a senator and an amateur. His *contubernium* is therefore effectively the core of his learned life, creating an atmosphere of continuous literary ferment in his private life, at Rome. All other modes of dissemination of his doctrines can be seen as mere extensions of a life lived among his student friends.

The first and most important of these modes is the closest to *contubernium*. A report by Aulus Gellius is the principal source: "When I was a young man at Rome, before I migrated to Athens, and had a respite from attending on masters and at lectures, I used to visit Cornelius Fronto for the pleasure of seeing him, and derived great advantage from his conversation [*sermonibus*], which was in the purest language and full of excellent information. And it was inevitably the case that, as often as we saw him and heard his talk, we came away with our taste improved [*cultiores*] and our minds informed [*doctioresque*]."[6] Salient here are the frequency of these visits, whenever there was freedom from teachers and classes, and their value as alternatives to formal teaching, for they never failed to improve the visitor. In effect, Gellius presents Fronto in a series of vignettes as the leader of a flourishing salon.

Fronto's *sermones* appear only five times in the *Attic Nights*, but the record is invaluable, for such discussions are unlikely to have been recorded in the correspondence, and, indeed, only one is mentioned in passing, a conversation on the divisions of a speech.[7] Typical of these encounters is the visit paid by Gellius with the senator Iulius Celsinus, wherein the two friends discover Fronto selecting a plan for his baths while prostrate with the gout. Despite the commonplace setting, he is surrounded by visitors, men remarkable for their learning, their birth, or their fortune. One of these, a learned grammaticus, is humiliated by the orator for affecting to despise the word *praeterpropter*, and Celsinus (doubtless a disciple of Fronto) completes the rout with a sneer that the word in question was more frequently corrupted than explained by grammarians, adding eight lines from Ennius by way of illustration. The grammaticus flees, sweating and blushing profusely, the professional routed by true amateurs; and duly edified, the assembled company disperses.[8] The other four episodes in Gellius are remarkably similar. Each turns on an apparently minor point of vocabulary, thus confirming Fronto's greatest passion, the search for *verba insperata atque inopinata* as the foundation of elegant oratory. And the supremely didactic intent of these conversations is made explicit on one occasion, when Fronto dismisses his audience to their various affairs with the injunction to spend their moments of leisure searching the works of archaic orators and poets for the words under discussion, not (adds Gellius) because he expects them to find any more examples but so that they may be encouraged to read those authors in their quest for *rariora verba*.[9]

Of primary importance is Fronto's audience. Aulus Gellius assures us of the numbers and achievements of his auditors, as for example in the anecdote first mentioned. On that occasion the company had included among the many eminent for learning, birth, or fortune the senator Celsinus and the celebrated grammaticus, with the student Gellius and various architects in the background. In another scene, the annals of Claudius Quadrigarius are read to Fronto "while I and many more were sitting with him," and the orator debates a point with a learned friend, a man of the most elegant taste. In a third the subject is illness, the audience numerous, and the anonymous *familiaris* a well-educated poet of some repute. In a fourth the adversary is the philosopher Favorinus himself, "many learned men being present." The fifth episode is somewhat different; it occurs not in a salon but in the vestibule of the imperial palace, and Fronto is not obviously the protagonist. But the elements are similar, as an audience of Aulus Gellius and a few others overhears a conversation among men of distinction, Fronto, Sulpicius Apollinaris, the senator and orator Postumius Festus, and an unnamed *familiaris* of Fronto, a grammaticus thoroughly steeped in archaic literature.[10] The *sermones* presented by Gellius thus strikingly suggest the propagation of Fronto's opinions to a large and learned audience.

Sermocinatio is a source of erudition second only to actual study and a custom whose importance it would be difficult to overestimate. Some doubt might be felt as to the historicity of the autobiographical episodes in the *Attic Nights*, with their stereotyped conflicts and neat morals. One obvious intention is to relieve with drama the austerity of pure erudition, and the abundance of lively but anonymous interlocutors is suspicious.[11] But much can be accepted at face value, such as Herodes' custom of inviting Latin-speaking students at Athens to his Cephisian villa in the summer and autumn, and Gellius' convalescence there.[12] Moreover, every episode should be authentic insofar as it must mirror commonly accepted practice, and wherever real names are inserted the actions and opinions ought to be consistent with the actual personalities. To the unsympathetic ear these debates may sound highly artificial, but their authenticity as representations of Antonine society is confirmed by abundant parallels. Hadrian himself published at least two books of his own *sermones*, from which chance has preserved a sharp interchange with the famed grammarian Terentius Scaurus.[13] *Sermones convivales* with obvious historical elements still provided vehicles for Plutarch and Athenaeus, and not as a dead literary tradition, for the literary chats of Pertinax' dinner table stand on record.[14] Fronto was not the only one to conduct learned discussions even from his sickbed. Of another erudite senator it was said that "he ranked as one of our leading citizens without exercising influence or incurring ill-will; he was waited upon and sought after, and spent many hours on his couch in a room thronged with callers who had come with no thought of his rank; and so passed his days in most learned conversation [*doctissimis sermonibus*] whenever he could spare time from his writing": not Gellius on Fronto, but Pliny on the consular poet Silius Italicus.[15]

Significant patterns may be distinguished in these encounters, but they conform not to literary themes but to the norms of cultivated society. The scene usually concerns the exposition of a problem by one or more acknowledged masters and the surroundings are informal. Such *sermones* are by no means restricted to students, and Gellius records elsewhere a discussion on the rank and ordering of *officia* by "seniores homines et Romae nobiles atque in morum disciplinarumque veterum doctrina memoriaque praestantes."[16] Debate occurs everywhere, on holiday, on social calls, while waiting for appointments or while simply perambulating, in bookshops and libraries, in the forum and even in the entrance hall of the palace, and of course in private houses, especially in the inveterate form of *quaestiones convivales*.[17] The point to be discussed is raised indiscriminately by a direct question, or in the course of a reading, or even in the discussion of daily business. A recurrent and highly important scene exhibits a recognized *magister* publicly exposing the pedantry, imposture, or ignorance of an upstart, usually after the victim has arrogantly displayed his mistaken erudition in a bid for glory.[18] These academic conflicts are expressed in the fiercest of terms; even Fronto could describe Herodes Atticus himself as a Greekling and unlearned if the occasion served, and he devotes a brief homily to the dangers of ignorance and half-knowledge and to the ease of exposing them.[19] Nothing demonstrates better the closed nature of literary society: rivals vanquished in debate are denied membership in the aristocracy of letters and are treated by their conquerors with the same harsh contempt that the dilettante displays for the masses and the expert for the careless amateur.[20] Not only was literary society in Fronto's day a homogeneous network, but its boundaries were sharply defined, dividing the masters from the masses.

The tendency of such a universe is toward a remarkable uniformity in taste, with an acknowledged master exerting an influence out of the ordinary. Fronto's authority was Olympian. Even Gellius' hero, Favorinus, is mastered in debate: "But for you alone," he admits to Fronto, "the Greek language would have come in first by a long way."[21] (Compare the Caesar Marcus' reminiscent "For as to your elegance what can I say? except that you talk Latin while the rest of us talk neither Latin nor Greek.")[22] And the leading grammaticus of the age, Sulpicius Apollinaris, after informing Fronto that a word he had used was in fact Greek in origin, adds, "But this word would at once have been granted the franchise or been naturalized as a Latin colonist, if you had deigned to use it." That was something not even an emperor could achieve.[23] Fronto was not a professional teacher. Therefore his private *contubernium* and its more public extension, the *sermo*, must be seen as the major modes of dissemination of his doctrines to a clearly defined and receptive literary society. It is especially significant that his tastes and opinions can be observed to be impressed not only on orators but on grammarians, poets, and even philosophers.

The natural counterpart to the *sermo* was the literary epistle, a brief essay on a single topic directed to a particular person. Fronto's letter to Velius Rufus (*Ad Am.* I.11), commencing with the bare theme that figures of speech are what most adorn an oration (a basic tenet of Fronto's), offers a clear example of the genre and is to be distinguished from his personal and didactic letters to his pupil Marcus. Here we have the closest thing to an essay on rhetoric produced by the orator, for while the *epistula* reflects the restricted atmosphere of debate, it can also partake of the character of a published treatise, and such literary epistles were indeed commonly published or circulated widely.[24] Thus the later grammarians preserve extracts from letters addressed to the emperor Hadrian by Annius Florus, by Velius Celer, and perhaps by Terentius Scaurus, and it may be that the *famosissimae litterae* with which the jealous prince attacked the learned Avidius Heliodorus were in fact literary *epistulae*.[25] Similarly, at a later period, Serenus Sammonicus' essay on the sturgeon addressed to Septimius Severus may have been in letter form.[26] To the learned prefect of the city Erucius Clarus, his friend (and Fronto's) Sulpicius Apollinaris wrote in the presence of his followers a brief note on a phrase in Cato; the bare incident was preserved in Gellius' memory, but it appears from another passage in his work that Apollinaris' letters were in the public domain.[27] The extent of Fronto's indulgence in such epistolary essays and of their circulation cannot be estimated.

The obvious vehicle for the dissemination of his doctrines was the actual delivery and publication of orations. A sure gauge of their popularity is offered in a single invaluable passage in which Fronto records for Marcus the effect of a speech on his audience: "What nice ears men have nowadays! What elegance in judging of speeches! You can learn from our Aufidius what shouts of applause were evoked in my speech, and with what a chorus of approval were greeted my words."[28] He proceeds to enunciate for the benefit of his pupil the precept that the glory of pure eloquence must sometimes be moderated to suit the tastes of the audience: the greatest virtue, and the most difficult for the orator to achieve, was to please his audience without sacrificing eloquence, to adorn his subject without sacrificing its dignity.[29] This piece is significant as a mark of Fronto's success, signaling his own obvious talent in adapting his eloquence to his audience. The remarks are overtly self-complimentary. In these days men possess judgment of exceptional elegance, as the fastidiousness of a few on one point demonstrates against the shouts of approval elicited by the whole speech. In this age of meticulous oratorical refinement Fronto is the exemplar. The authority accorded to him elsewhere by Favorinus and Apollinaris in matters of language is echoed here by the prince Marcus, when he imagines Fronto to be the Jovian teacher and judge of every *disertus* and *philologus*, instructing and admonishing them. This particular transport of enthusiasm was ignited not by an especially illuminating lesson, but by the delivery of a speech: Fronto taught by example as well.[30]

To reach an even wider audience publication was necessary. Thus a good number of Pliny's letters reflect the concern of himself and his contemporaries for the publication of every variety of composition.[31] The underlying motive is simple vanity, with an eye to posterity. Fronto's correspondence is concerned once with the publication of speeches, and then with no great anxiety. In letters to his son-in-law and to a literary friend he discusses the preparation of his *Pro Bithynis* for the public in an expanded and enhanced version.[32] The wide popularity of his speeches is twice casually revealed. In what is a standard term for wide circulation, Fronto remarks that he had often praised the divine Hadrian in the senate, "and those speeches are constantly in everyone's hands."[33] And from the East, Lucius Verus requested several speeches of which Marcus had copies; to these Fronto had added the *Pro Demostrato*, despite its attack on a man now standing high in Lucius' regard: "As soon as I was aware of this I was myself anxious to suppress the speech, but it had already circulated too widely [*in manus plurium*] to be called in."[34]

In short, four important channels may be discovered for the diffusion of Fronto's principles, ranging from the most private to the most public audiences—the practice of *contubernium* and cooperative study, the *sermones* of the salon, the *epistula*, and the delivery and publication of *orationes* themselves; among them they cover the spectrum of literary society from the initiate to the neophyte, and literary society by its nature was highly receptive to them. The great question remains: what was the effect of these principles on the content and direction of literature?

Two important trends can be selected as particularly distinctive of Latin letters in the second century, neither of them necessarily new, but each now invested with an exaggerated importance. One was toward the subordination of letters to the doctrines and practices of grammar and rhetoric. The gap between theory and practice was fatally narrowed as erudition and technical skill won the laurels of the poet, the orator, the historian, and even the philosopher, a victory hastened by a superficial polymathy that facilitated the smooth migration of doctrines.[35] Fronto's society provides a good example. The second trend is one specifically toward archaism, a dogma derived from rhetoric but rapidly infecting other disciplines. It is most closely associated with the name of Fronto, and with good reason, for he was not only its leading exponent but virtually its progenitor. In a crucial passage in the correspondence, one concerned with praising Marcus' achievements, Fronto admits that when he was Marcus' age (twenty-two) he had scarcely skimmed archaic literature (*veteres lectiones*), a remark which all but proves that the study of the ancients was not yet a standard part of the curriculum for the generation preceding Marcus.[36] Fronto and the dominion of archaism arose simultaneously.[37]

Of all the literary arts, poetry shows the sharpest decline in the Antonine age and after: there is no poet of the first rank after Juvenal, who was himself the product of a time in which it could be claimed with pride that "this year has raised a fine crop of poets; there was scarcely a day in April when someone was not giving a public reading."[38] The generation before Fronto set a bad example. Pliny dabbled in poetry and praised it in others, particularly commending the the versatility of one man who had a variety of talents, a mastery of oratory, of history, of epistolography, as well as of poetry in the style of Catullus and Calvus and indistinguishable from the originals, for his ability was *varium, flexibile, multiplex.*[39] The boundary between poetry and oratory is especially vulnerable. In an account of his lifelong delight in poetry, Pliny claims that his own hendecasyllables were inspired by reading an epigram of Cicero, for "I began to consider that the greatest orators found pleasure in this kind of effort and regarded it as praiseworthy." And in a long passage of advice to a protégé, he commends the relaxation which those greatest orators discovered in light verse.[40] Inevitably, Pliny was forced to defend the intrusion of poetry into oratory.[41] Yet a generation later, Fronto could propound the axiom that "generally it is verse that gives the best assistance to composing speeches and speeches to writing verse."[42]

Fronto's attitude to poetry is simple. He does not compose it in the period covered by the correspondence and he probably never did. He politely asks to read Marcus' hexameters in one letter, but elsewhere he returns them without the slightest comment.[43] Of what use then was poetry to him? A minor benefit was the sweet *sententiae* to be collected from verse, useful in the composition of *consolationes.*[44] But the paramount value of poetry appears, by no accident, in the passage which spells out Fronto's single guiding principle and the most potent stimulus to archaism, that is, the pursuit of *insperata atque inopinata verba,* "words that are unexpected and unlooked for, such as are not hunted out save with study and care and watchfulness and the treasuring up of old poems in the memory."[45] Poetry was to be ransacked for archaic vocabulary with which to adorn contemporary oratory, hence Fronto's intimate acquaintance with Ennius and with Plautus, whom he idolized, and with all the lesser poets.[46] In the process the soul is removed, poetry submits to oratory, form to content, and appreciation to erudition. Horace is coolly noted as *memorabilis poeta,* but poor Vergil receives from Fronto the ultimate accolade, *verborum diligentissimus.*[47] That the arts of the orator and the poet have reached dangerous proximity is suggested by a passage from his pupil's *Meditations,* wherein Marcus thanks the philosopher Rusticus for teaching him to avoid rhetoric, poetry, and preciosity.[48]

With the exception of poems by Nemesian (and possibly Calpurnius Siculus), the scraps of Latin poetry which survive from the second and third centuries are negligible, but the poets themselves are worthy of remark. The paradigm is the man noticed already in Fronto's company, "his close friend, a very erudite man and at that time a famous poet," who stoutly contested with Fronto a point of grammar and bowed happily to "the authority of the ancients."[49] The erudition of this distinguished poet is the hallmark of contemporary poetry. Comparable to him is Gellius' friend Iulius Paulus, the most learned poet Gellius ever knew, a good man and marvelously versed in the deeds and writings of the ancients; or Clemens, the friend of Apuleius, "the most erudite and sweetest [*suavissimus*] of poets," who sang of the deeds of Alexander in a poem of great beauty.[50] The leading poets of the age are defined as *poetae novelli* by the metrician Terentianus Maurus, not a large school dedicated to "popularism," "realism," and "Romanism," but a small number of individuals who may be characterized firmly and simply as "archaizers in verse": their novelty was part of the new archaism.[51] The three new poets whose names survive are erudite dilettanti. Gellius nicely defines one of them, his friend: "Not only did the poet Annianus have a pleasant personality, he was also exceedingly skilled in ancient literature and criticism, and he talked [*sermocinabatur*] with a wonderful grace and sweetness [*suavitate*]."[52] This poet is portrayed by Gellius as conducting erudite discussions on grammatical matters in the Frontonian manner, and entertaining his friends on his rural estates like Iulius Paulus.[53] The second new poet is Alfius Avitus, otherwise unknown but noteworthy as a member of the senatorial order.[54] Best of the three was the charming, inventive, and very learned Septimius Serenus, whose passion for the archaic should strengthen the identification (which can be suggested on other grounds) both with the poet and avid antiquarian Serenus Sammonicus, the tutor of Geta and Caracalla, and with the Septimius who translated into Latin some fraudulently antique memoirs of the Trojan War. The legacy is Frontonian.[55]

The lower slopes of Parnassus continue to be crowded after Pliny's day. Poets there are none, but gentlemen amateurs abound.[56] More interesting are the professional scholars, and perhaps superior, if Septimius Serenus is included. Fronto's friend Sulpicius Apollinaris, who appears in Gellius as the complete philologue, produced the still extant verse *periochae* for Terence's plays and for the *Aeneid* of Vergil.[57] The dedicated Frontonian Iulius Titianus was known to the subsequent generation as rhetor, epistolographer, chorographer—and poet.[58] The ultimate symbol of the servitude of poetry was offered by the grammarian Terentianus Maurus: his three works, on letters, on syllables, and on meters, are all in verse.[59]

The fate of historiography may be considered more briefly, for it is easily seen as the handmaid of rhetoric. The extreme orator's view of history is fully exposed in Fronto, the end of a long line of orators. History's purpose was didactic, it was the source of splendid *sententiae* and of *exempla* designed to console or to inspire: panegyric was a natural form. But, above all, "historia splendide perscribenda." Style was supreme, content was rigorously subordinated, facts were held to a minimum.[60] Fortune in the form of the Parthian wars provided an opportunity to display this obsession, and the expression of rhetorical ideals was mixed with the less admirable motive of eulogizing an emperor like Lucius Verus. The standard charge against Fronto cannot be denied. His panegyric of Lucius is grossly overdone and the slights upon past emperors are unworthy; objective truth is a minor concern and there is little comprehension. In Fronto's defense it must be urged that we do not actually possess any of his historical work. The *Principia Historiae* is by its nature the most culpable, but it is not history, it is a letter to the subject of a proposed history, quite a different matter. And the opinions contained in other letters were written not with a view to history, but to console Marcus on early reverses in the war or to congratulate Lucius on the brilliantly composed despatches which announced his victory, pieces in which the orator should be at liberty to draw upon or to extol his own discipline. It is especially unfair in the end to condemn the historian for the history he never wrote.[61]

After Tacitus there are no more historians. Two lesser disciplines hold the field vacated by him, both of them redolent of the schoolroom and notable especially for their practical use to the orator in search of examples. The first, Latin biography, immediately evokes the name of Tacitus' junior contemporary Suetonius Tranquillus, author not only of the lives of the Caesars but also of the biographies of illustrious men of letters. The latter collection betrays the true character of the author, for the long list of his lost writings consists almost entirely of grammatical works on a wide range of topics.[62] This prodigious erudition won him two accolades: he was appointed ab epistulis by the archaizing emperor Hadrian, and he is the only contemporary Latin author to be cited by Fronto.[63] Suetonius had two successors in the Severan age, it would appear, the racy consular Marius Maximus and a less flamboyant contemporary whose name has perished with his work.[64]

Far below even biographical essays lies the second subhistorical discipline, the miserable products of history in epitome, hardly more than handbooks of facts and anecdotes of rhetorical interest. There is a startling explosion of the genre in this age of polymathy and Frontonian archaism, even the sophisticated philosopher Apuleius pausing to produce an *epitome historiarum*.[65] Best of the surviving lot, perhaps, is the patriotic effusion of the African poet and professor Annius Florus, which was clearly compiled for a Hadrianic audience.[66] Equally influential was the work of his junior contemporary M. Iunianus Iustinus, the condenser of Pompeius Trogus, who seems to have come under the influence of Fronto and his school.[67] Then there was Granius Licinianus, author of a brief but sometimes useful fragment on republican history which was produced under Hadrian or later. In his way Granius is particularly typical of his age, a gentleman with senatorial kinsmen, an avid antiquarian, an archaizer, and a great admirer of the Frontonian hero Sallust, who he urges should be read as an orator, not as a historian, an operation strongly reminiscent of Florus' essay "Vergilius orator an poeta."[68] Again the influence of Fronto is apparent.[69] Most interesting of all the epitomes is the work dedicated to a young man named Victor by a certain Ianuarius Nepotianus, which epitomizes the previous compilation of Valerius Maximus. The date is uncertain. On one view it is no earlier than the fourth century, to judge by its opinions and an occasionally barbarous vocabulary.[70] But it is more attractive to connect the piece with those inscriptions of Severan date which commemorate two notables of Sicca Veneria, the centurion and knight Victor, and his kinsman Nepotianus e.v., procurator sexagenarius ab actis, procurator centenarius primae cathedrae.[71] Thus a professional rhetor (Nepotianus) compiling an epitome of a previous collection of *exempla* offers a damning portrait of history in the rigid service of rhetoric within fifty years of Fronto's death.

The perennial rival of rhetoric is philosophy. Again, Fronto's opinions are clear and simple.[72] His objections are nothing new, primarily contempt for the pseudo-philosopher and a rejection of the discipline as unconnected with real life; and the latter attitude was defensible in the tutor of a prince, for eloquence seemed to be more useful and less dangerous in the running of the empire.[73] A superficial synthesis is reached: eloquence is practical philosophy and the best philosophers are demonstrably eloquent.[74] The results of such an accommodation are immediately apparent. Fronto's society reveals no fixed battlelines, for students of philosophy were numerous among his friends, and they were often students of rhetoric as well; thus Fronto might have talked just as casually as did his follower Aulus Gellius of "my contemporaries and intimates, followers of rhetoric or philosophy."[75] Gellius tells much of his student days at Athens in attendance on the teachers of philosophy and eloquence, Calvenus Taurus and Herodes Atticus, the same Herodes to whom Marcus Aurelius would award the task of selecting the professors of philosophy at Athens.[76] At the same period we learn of another student who, after completing his studies in rhetoric, applied himself with diligence to all of the schools of philosophy at Athens, yet who was still able to compose a pedantic, pseudo-Vergilian poem, the *Ciris*, which was addressed to a noble and most learned youth and perhaps paid compliment to Herodes Atticus.[77] Apuleius, the self-proclaimed philosopher, is the clearest example of the treachery of labels. His sophistical *Apologia* purports throughout to be a defense of philosophy, while his treatise *On the God of Socrates* is a shallow piece of rhetoric. Apuleius is an anomaly, the only philosopher of the period who has left work in Latin. The general effect of Fronto's teachings is quite unknown, but in his century Latin died as a vehicle of philosophical inquiry. Greek was the language of philosophy, and Athens remained its home.

Perhaps the most important question is the connection between Latin letters under Fronto's leadership and Greek letters, now flourishing in the firm grip of the Second Sophistic. Certainly, the new sophistic movement had a pervasive effect on Latin authors as diverse as Apuleius, Tertullian, and Septimius Serenus.[78] Similar influence on Fronto ought not to be doubted, and through him a general diffusion. His major contribution to oratory was an obsession with pure vocabulary, which reflected the simple credo that the best discourse was the one which pleased its audience and which was highly and appropriately decorated.[79] This striving after *elegantia* led to pedantic erudition, for the finest and least hackneyed words were to be found in the oldest authors, hence archaism and a return to antique purity.[80] Similarly, the keyword of the Second Sophistic was ornament, the pleasure of the audience its chief goal and guide; a history of the movement could consider it in the light of popular entertainment. As to archaism, it is incredible that the same patriotic notion should have come to dominate the two cultures simultaneously without some interaction, particularly when social intercourse is so amply attested among their leaders. That Fronto himself was influenced by Atticism can be taken for granted.[81] Moreover, the subtle and plausible explanation may be advanced that he was the champion of Latin letters against their threatened eclipse by a Greek literature revivified by Atticism.[82] Supporting that view is the praise of Favorinus noted above, that but for Fronto Greek letters would have far surpassed Latin, and the assertion of Marcus that "you have far outstripped those Atticists, so self-satisfied and challenging."[83] Such an interpretation goes a long way toward explaining Fronto's apparent lack of enthusiasm for Greek and his professed lack of mastery.[84] He himself often fails in the struggle to maintain this pose, not only in the employment of common Greek words and phrases, not only in the composition of occasional essays and letters in the language, but also in the devastating admission which slips out once in his *De Eloquentia*, "I can perhaps express my meaning more clearly in Greek words . . ."[85]

Whether inspired to imitate or to repel, Fronto could not have escaped the Greek literary world. In the palace and in the senate of the Antonine period, the refined magnates of the East had taken their rightful place, the fruit of a long struggle upward from the days of Actium.[86] The concomitant invasion of the West by Greek intellectuals is an important and well-documented phenomenon.[87] On the Latin side we have observed even Fronto, the paragon of Latinity, deeply involved in their world. One of the many instances speaks for the rest, the patronage of the historian Appian, with whom Fronto studied daily or corresponded in Greek, and who was but one among several Alexandrian *familiares*; and it will be recalled that the only two teachers of his own whom he mentions are both Greeks. Fronto's reputation as the evangelist of Latin archaism, a picture fostered by himself, has inevitably obscured the important Greek influence, which both attracted and repelled him. His shrinking domain was that inherited by P. Livius Larensis, the genial host in Athenaeus' *Deipnosophistae* at a fictitious banquet set in the years immediately after the death of Commodus.[88] Although Larensis was himself a wealthy Roman procurator and priest, his guests are representatives almost to a man of the Second Sophistic, doctors and grammarians, philosophers and poets. But even in their midst he is no Greekling, despite his huge Greek library and his worship of Homer. He is rather a resolute Latin archaizer, an expert in religious ceremonies and ancient documents of state, and in the best tradition of Frontonian philology he can tell us that it was Lucullus who first named the cherry.[89]

Quintilian had warned against the influence of the *antiquitatis nimium admirator*, and Fronto betrays himself in the exposition of a passage from Claudius Quadrigarius: "For my part, unless my love and reverence for that writer and for all the language of our old authors blinds my judgment, I think that . . ."[90] Indeed, the obsession of a crusade informs his correspondence and the *Attic Nights* of Aulus Gellius, and it goes far in explaining the contempt for ignorance and misunderstanding which marks out the *eruditi* of the age. Obsession is not too strong a word. The most casual survey of Fronto's letters will show how deeply they are colored throughout by a passion for culture. It can be asserted that the sole purpose of his existence was the pursuit of learning, or rather that his few other important interests were firmly subordinated to or connected with the great pursuit. This magisterial obsession with archaism affected the taste of an age.

V

THE LAWYER

A CAREER as an advocate was the natural product of a passion for rhetorical culture and an ambition for advancement in the senate, forensic oratory being both one of the recognized divisions of rhetoric and a traditional path of advancement for the new man at Rome.[1] Advocacy thus offered to Fronto a splendid combination of pleasure and profit, and in the law courts of Rome are to be discovered the roots of his future success in other endeavors. His predictable rise to *princeps fori* goes largely unrecorded, and advocacy is not an immediately evident concern of the correspondence. Nevertheless, sufficient guarantee of its importance in his life lies in the mass of hints and references to the avocation with regard to other matters, in discussions of oratory for instance, or in passages dealing with the *obsequia* between friends, even in modes of expression. "Negotia in foro nostra minima maximaque" intrude everywhere. A note arrives from the emperor: no time to reply, Fronto is just on his way to plead in the forum. Illness prevents him from speaking for a friend: perhaps he will just slip down to the court to hear Victorinus acting in his stead.[2] Because most of the evidence concerns actual pleading for individuals and for communities, the first requirement is an exact record of the circumstances of each appearance in court. From this we can reconstruct to some extent the externals of a forensic career, the types of court, client, and case with which he dealt, the social and political background. And behind that we may deduce a good academic knowledge of the law, an immersion in legal ways of thought, and a real concern for the future of forensic pleading.

Of the cases undertaken for individuals, the first constitutes Fronto's earliest appearance in history, sometime in the 120s, when he was already "first among the Romans in the courts."[3] Returning from a banquet late one night, he was informed by a client that the praetorian prefect Marcius Turbo was already holding court; dressed as he was, he proceeded to the courtroom and greeted the judge not with "salve" but with "vale," the greeting appropriate to the evening. One minor fact is of interest here. If Cassius Dio has transmitted the situation correctly, this is one of the earliest attestations of the praetorian prefect's sitting in judgment.[4] As the exact scope of his jurisdiction is obscure before the Severan period, it would be foolhardy to speculate on the nature of the case. But we may presume that it probably originated in Italy or the provinces, that is, outside the city of Rome, unless the jurisdiction of the urban prefect was being invaded.

Much later, in a letter to Marcus, Fronto requests his good will in auditing the accounts of the tax-farmer Saenius Pompeianus, whom Fronto has defended many times since the man undertook the operations of the *publicum Africae*.[5] It is not difficult to conjecture the general nature of those "plurimae causae," which must have concerned complaints of overtaxation due to rapacity, carelessness, or excessive zeal.[6] The court involved is less easy to fix, but surely located at Rome, for visits by Fronto to Africa are unlikely. In the capital the jurisdiction in cases against *publicani* belonged to the praetor, but the princeps could concern himself at will.[7] It is significant here that Fronto appeals not to the emperor but to the Caesar, requesting his *benignitas* when his father comes to scrutinize the accounts, and Marcus' reference in his reply to his father's *indulgentia* might lead to the suspicion that one at least of Pompeianus' court appearances had been before not the praetor but the emperor himself or his delegate.

A third isolated case is the subject of two letters written some time after 143, the first of which preserves the only substantial fragment of any forensic speech delivered by Fronto, the so-called *De Testamentis Transmarinis*, which is transcribed by Marcus in a letter as his favorite part of the oration.[8] Great caution must be exercised in interpretation. The case concerns a disputed will which has been transmitted by the proconsul of Asia to the emperor, but it has a twist in that the will has apparently not been opened. Fronto makes certain points. First, he protests against the emperor's considering the case at all, thereby setting a dangerous precedent for other governors to refer all testamentary problems to his court. Perhaps the specter of a flood of business for the hard-worked prince is insinuated here, but the true and manifest danger is one of undue delay: first the will had not been opened, then it had been referred to Rome, and the journey had been long. Fronto suggests that a year has slipped by, with two adjournments of the case, such delay permitting those who would have been disinherited by the will to encroach upon another's possessions; the reference should be to *heredes ab intestato* granted *bonorum possessio sine re*. They steal the profits, they lay waste the estates, they consume everything. Another point is then made, that the precious will has been unduly jeopardized on the long journey to Rome. But here two manuscript pages of the correspondence are lost, and the lacuna renders any legal reconstruction hazardous in the extreme. The next flight of rhetoric is an appeal to nature to demonstrate that after death the wool is shorn from the sheep, the elephant loses his ivory, bears their claws, birds their feathers, in other words, a return to the major theme of injurious delay in the matter of inheritance. Whatever the content of the lost part of the speech may be, its tenor is easily inferred from Marcus' enthusiasm for the surviving extravagances.

The legal situation is obscure, and it remains controversial. It appears that those who would be heirs on intestacy have somehow contrived to delay the opening of a will in which they suspect that they have been disinherited, and that Fronto opposes them on behalf of the presumed testamentary heir. On what grounds the proconsul both allowed the will to remain sealed and granted enjoyment of the estate is unknown—perhaps simple collusion with the potentially disinherited, some legal obfuscation designed merely to allow them sufficient time to consume the inheritance, but too many questions remain unanswerable. Had there been a previous trial before the proconsul? At whose request had the matter been referred to the emperor? Had the will been found faulty even before opening, as has been presumed (but there is no evidence to support this), or had it even perhaps been duly opened after some initial delay (Fronto's words do not seem to discount even this possibility)? The letter itself forces such lacunae to the reader's attention, and with these uncertainties it seems unclear even whether the case at issue is one of *querela inofficiosi testamenti* (by his opponents) or of *petitio hereditatis* (by Fronto), that is, whether the orator is acting in prosecution or defense; and his language is suspiciously neutral, not "Where is the *reus* to defend himself?" but "Where is the *adversarius* to plead his case?" Only the court involved is explicitly attested, the emperor's *cognitio*. The fragment clearly was intended for the emperor's ears, but Pius was unable to attend the court on the day proposed for its delivery. In fact, there is nothing in Marcus' comments to suggest that the speech was actually delivered. In the event of a third postponement perhaps the rightful heir came into his inheritance by other means.

An equally obscure and complex case involves the notorious litigation, again before the emperor, between Fronto and the celebrated Athenian sophist Herodes Atticus, which forms the subject of a careful and illuminating dialogue between Marcus Caesar and Fronto (*M. Caes.* III.2-6). Marcus wrote first, urging Fronto to restrain his attack on Herodes in the upcoming trial, "that most hateful affair." Fronto agreed with reluctance not to exceed his brief:

> I quite admit that I ought not to say anything, which does not bear on the case, to damage Herodes, but those facts which do bear on it – and they are undoubtedly of a most shocking nature – how am I to deal with them? that is the very thing I am in doubt about, and I ask your advice. I shall have to tell of freemen cruelly beaten and robbed, of one even slain; I shall have to tell of a son unfilial and deaf to his father's prayers, cruelty and avarice will have to be denounced; a certain Herodes must in this trial be made out a murderer . . . if you think I must do the best for my case, I warn you herewith that I shall not even use in a disproportionate manner the opportunity my case gives me, for shocking charges are made and must be spoken of as shocking.[9]

The affair must have created a sensation, a clash between the leading orators of the age, both ex-consuls and tutors in the imperial house. Its background is tangled and only obscurely hinted at in Philostratus' *Lives of the Sophists*, but the mystery has been carefully unraveled.[10] Despite first impressions, the two men were not principals but advocates, Fronto for the defense and Herodes actually prosecuting: "He is said to be inflamed with a passion for pleading."[11] The "charges" against Herodes of assault, murder, robbery, and impiety were nothing more than standard invective, here echoing tales told by Philostratus of the sophist's bitter relations with his father's freedmen and his miserly conduct toward his fellow citizens of Athens in the matter of his father's will.[12] The real defendant, the man prosecuted by Herodes, was a certain Demostratus, for Fronto's speech is surely to be identified with the *Pro Demostrato* referred to elsewhere in the correspondence, in which he attacked Herodes and a man named Asclepiodotus.[13] Athenian political intrigue then becomes the point of the episode, for years later in the 170s we find the hegemony of Herodes Atticus under attack before the emperor by three political adversaries, Demostratus, Praxagoras, and Mamertinus, who can be identified with three known archons of the mid-second century.[14] Thus a local feud of long standing was twice raised to the imperial level.[15] Why Fronto was called upon to act in the matter remains obscure; that his defense succeeded should be inferred from the publication of the speech.

Another notorious case has caused even more confusion, for a modern misapprehension conceals what was considered by antiquity to be Fronto's greatest forensic triumph. By expanding two brief fragments in an early third-century Christian apology, the *Octavius* of Minucius Felix, there has been constructed in modern times an *Oratio contra Christianos* by Fronto, which has then assumed a disproportionate importance in an ill-documented period of Church history. The evidence is slender. In the first passage of the *Octavius*, the pagan antagonist Caecilius Natalis lists the alleged crimes of the Christians ("I hear," "some say, perhaps wrongly," "tales as detestable as they are notorious"), arriving at the ritual murder of an infant with the drinking of its blood and the consumption of its limbs. Immediately thereafter: "And their banquet is well known, everyone talks of it everywhere; among others, even a speech of our fellow Cirtan bears witness."[16] This is followed by an account of incestuous banqueting. The subsequent rebuttal by the Christian Octavius follows the same sequence. Child murder and cannibalism are the marks of pagan rites: Christians are horrified by the very thought; in fact, they avoid even the blood of animals. As for the vile charge of *incestum convivium*, it is the plot of demons to frighten men away from the truth: "And so on this point even your Fronto did not testify as a witness, he hurled abuse as an orator."[17] Then follows the defense of Octavius, that this custom too is pagan, not Christian.[18]

Where and why was Fronto's oration delivered? Minucius offers no clue. The one fragment contains an aspersion on supposed Christian practices, but it is foolhardy to deduce from that an attack either on the sect or on individual members: the remark need be no more than an insulting illustration or comparison. That is in fact close to what Octavius says, that Fronto was acting as an orator on the attack, not as a witness bearing testimony; and indeed one ought to infer the opposite, that the Christians were not the main target.[19] Further, "oratio" is usually taken to mean "the speech," that is, Fronto's famous alleged speech against the Christians, but it could just as easily be "a speech," that is, one which touches upon the subject only incidentally.[20]

What was the date of the speech? Again, elaborate (and greatly divergent) historical edifices have been constructed on unsupported assumptions.[21] To bring the speech into conjunction with known events as cause or effect is highly dangerous without knowledge of the nature or contents of the speech itself. For unknown reasons, at an unknown date, and in unknown surroundings, Fronto delivered an oration which contained an uncomplimentary reference to Christian practices. Fortunately, there is one major clue.[22] In the final years of Marcus Aurelius persecutions of the Christians erupted. Athenagoras the Athenian makes it clear that the emperor himself was not responsible, while Eusebius' account of the martyrs of Lyon makes the mob the primary villain.[23] Both of these authors mention the same charges leveled against the Christians, indulgence in Oedipean intercourse and Thyestean banquets.[24] These precise references are something definitely and arrestingly novel in anti-Christian propaganda: they are a subtle refinement on the older and more simple standard allegations of cannibalism and sexual orgies. They may well suggest the influence of Fronto's anti-Christian remark, the invention of a practiced orator turning naturally to myth for a striking and appropriate image, and there is some confirmation.[25]

If Fronto was indeed the source of these images from Greek mythology, a suitable context may be found for them in the speech referred to by his fifth-century admirer Sidonius Apollinaris. In a letter to his friend and fellow bishop Ruricius of Limoges, Sidonius develops the theme that a man shows his true talent in time of trial: "So also the great orator, if he tackles a troublesome business [*negotium angustum*], displays his real talent more triumphantly. Marcus Tullius, while in his other pleading he surpassed all other speakers, in his defence of Aulus Cluentius surpassed himself; Marcus Fronto won distinction by his other orations, but excelled himself in his speech against Pelops; Gaius Plinius by his speech for Attia Viriola took away with him from the centumviral tribunal more glory than when he delivered a panegyric that measured up to the matchless emperor Trajan."[26] A forensic speech against a man named Pelops might contain some bitingly elaborate conceits. At the least it could conjure up a familiar series of unpleasant incidents: Tantalus serving up his son Pelops as the main course in a banquet for the gods; Pelops securing the death of Oenomaus, a man who was by one account the lover of his own daughter, and marrying that daughter; Pelops begetting by her Thyestes, who unwittingly devoured his own sons;

Thyestes ravishing his own daughter Pelopeia at the suggestion of an oracle, thereby engendering the avenger Aegisthus.[27] Incestuous intercourse and cannibalistic banquets with a vengeance, motifs easily recalled to anyone familiar with the history of the house of Pelops. The name "Pelops" is sufficient clue: surely we should see in the colorful anti-Christian allegations first apparent in the later 170s a reflection of a learned and rhetorical simile in Fronto's *In Pelopem*, which in turn casually drew upon and embroidered popular contemporary accounts of Christian practices. Appropriately, the *In Pelopem* offers further attractions as the oration referred to in the context of the *Octavius*. Clearly, the speech of "our fellow Cirtan" was familiar to educated third-century audiences; according to Sidonius the oration against Pelops was Fronto's finest effort.[28] And a forensic speech would hold a special appeal for Minucius Felix, himself not unknown among advocates of the day.[29] Chance, preserving one fragment torn out of context, has unduly obscured Fronto's triumph.

Nothing is known of the speech beyond Sidonius' general characterization as "negotium angustum," recalling perhaps the difficulties of the case or (more probably) its restricted and unimportant nature, or perhaps both. Neither charge nor court nor opponent is known.[30] As late as the fourth or fifth century a Peloponnesian magnate could claim descent from Pelops; the orator's victim might have been both Greek and well-born.[31] At the least the name is patently Greek, yet further evidence of Fronto's wide dealings with the East.

In addition to speeches on behalf of individuals, there are instances of Fronto's acting for communities, the evidence confined in each case to a single item. One is tantalizingly suggestive. In preparing for his Asian proconsulship he called upon the aid of *splendidi viri* from Cilicia, because he enjoyed a large host of friends in the province "owing to my always having advocated the public and private interests of the Cilicians before" Antoninus Pius.[32] Likewise there is an oration *Pro Ptolemensibus*, cited by the grammarian Charisius for its use of the genitive plural "parentum tuorum," that might be forensic.[33] Certainly a speech on behalf of a community and delivered before a single person with reference to his parents should suggest an address to the emperor, perhaps before his *cognitio*.[34] But the Ptolemais involved cannot be identified with any certainty from the several available, and therefore the circumstances are beyond recall. Perhaps the most attractive city of that name is the one in Cyrenaica, which might hold some interest for a native African; the reference could then be to an event in the previous generation in some way connected (for example) with the devastation caused by the Jewish revolt in the last years of Trajan and the first of Hadrian, Pius' "parentes."[35]

More solid is a third item, referred to by the late author Fulgentius in his *Expositio Sermonum Antiquorum:* "*Iustitium* is said to be a public mourning, whence Fronto also says in his speech *Pro Nucerinis,* 'Finally a *iustitium* was announced to the people.' "[36] Fulgentius' pamphlet is a curious mixture of genuine citation and cool forgery, none of it trustworthy without external confirmation.[37] The *Pro Nucerinis* has accordingly been branded as highly dubious. However, Fronto enjoyed a double connection with the town of Nuceria that must not be overlooked and that makes him a natural patron: with his Campanian villa at Surrentum he was a near neighbor of the place, and two centuries earlier his patria, Cirta, had been colonized by Campanians, some of them men of Nuceria. Patronage of the Nucerians is thus rendered highly plausible.

Finally, Fronto alludes with pride to a speech *Pro Bithynis,* which was assuredly a forensic success. In two letters he treats of the revision of the oration:

> [To Praecilius Pompeianus] And, indeed, if I remember rightly, when we were discussing the rhetorical heads of a speech, I claimed, and with some pride, that I had in that speech very thoroughly analyzed in argument and confuted the assumption [*coniecturam*] which turned on the charge of murder by mandate.[38]

> [To Aufidius Victorinus, on additions to the speech] . . . particularly a passage on my past life, which I think will please you, if you read that excellent speech on a similar subject in defence of P. Sulla left us by M. Tullius; not that you should compare us as equals, but that you should recognize how far my mediocre talent falls short of that man of unapproachable eloquence.[39]

The parallel with Cicero's *Pro Sulla* should not be pressed beyond the observation that Fronto's own past ought to be bound up in some way with the events under dispute, and that like Cicero he probably considered his own honor (and perhaps more) to be at stake. Such connection need involve no more than an earlier patronage of the provincials or of a Roman official in the province.[40] The presence of Fronto presupposes a suitably elevated court, and the case is serious, for there is an allegation of *crimen mandatae caedis*. "Iterum Bithyni": the litigious provincial council should be Fronto's client here, with its exceptional record for the prosecution of senior Roman officers.[41] The turbulent city factions, the class conflict, and the rivalry among cities, so familiar from Pliny and Dio of Prusa, will then provide a suitably violent background for the trial in Fronto.[42] At first glance it might appear that the Bithyni stood accused of murder and that Fronto refuted the charge. He gives none of the circumstances of the speech, for his correspondent was familiar with them, and his concern here is explicitly rhetorical, not legal or historical: "coniecturam . . . divisisse argumentis ac refutasse," that is, he refuted the *coniectura* of his opponent that turned on the charge. The obvious culprit for the charge of murder by mandate (a rhetorical, not a legal, concept) should be the proconsul of Pontus-Bithynia, not its assembly, and Fronto's speech on behalf of the Bithynians was presumably delivered in prosecution of an ex-governor on various counts in the senate.[43] The obvious charge would be *repetundae* committed with *saevitia,* and parallels can be adduced of death resulting from a governor's greed.[44] Such an interpretation explains Fronto's apparently ambivalent attitude to his success. Aufidius would be pleased, he suggests, by the addition of the section "de acta vita" to the published version, and the orator is especially proud of his confutation of the defense; yet later he adds, "I took a dislike to that speech, and will not be ashamed to confess hatred and aversion," and something to the effect of "so the speech came back home to me after I had publicly disowned it, and it would have taken up its abode with me again."[45] *Odium* and *simultas* are strong words and repudiation a strong action, while the addition of an apologia to the original speech must be significant. Behind these should lie not a dislike for rhetorical imperfection, which Fronto obviously did not feel, but perhaps repugnance at the successful prosecution of a senator by a member of the same order.[46]

The register of Fronto's cases takes us some way toward an estimate of the externals of his forensic career, but there is more to be considered in his success as an advocate, not actual speeches but the next best thing, letters which perform the function of *orationes*.[47] The convention employed is made explicit in the first of his *Letters to His Friends,* in which he carefully recalled the judicial connections of *litterae commendaticae*. Recommendations, he asserts, were originally expressions of good will whereby every gentleman sought to introduce one friend to another, and thus to create new friendships. The custom developed in one sphere into the offering of testimony as to character in courts of law, as long as justice was not impeded, that is. This role Fronto's present letter of commendation is intended to fill.[48]

Addressing his epistle to the judge concerned in the case, he proceeds to act as if he were in court, speaking to the character of his intimate friend Sulpicius Cornelianus: "following a long-established precedent, I venture to speak in praise of my friend before you." A catalogue of the man's virtues follows, and (after a long lacuna) an appeal to the judge's favor. However, it appears (despite the mutilation of the text) that Fronto goes beyond a mere testimonial and enters into the circumstances of the trial.[49] This has been interpreted as "the broad wink of *gratia*" passing between judge and advocate, but this "prohoemium" of the orator on the custom of recommendation was surely intended to be not a plausible excuse for undue influence but rather the reverse, a careful repudiation of anything dishonest. As he himself explains, it was meant to prevent the judge, Claudius Severus, from taking the letter as a slight to his *gravitas* and his *auctoritas*. Both Fronto and Severus were highly honorable men, the latter an ardent student of philosophy, and there is no hint of a crafty quid pro quo here.[50] Fronto's argument is not to be scorned. Defense of a man by his friend and testimonials to his character were elements familiar to Roman courts. Here Fronto merely transfers his plea from the court to an epistle, carefully rebutting in advance any suspicion of undue influence; illness would be a plausible reason for this novel but quite reputable procedure. If this letter can then be regarded as a form of written plea substituted for spoken advocacy, others should be considered in the same light.

The best example of a written plea is the epistle addressed to Fronto's beloved friend Arrius Antoninus.[51] The nature of this piece, implicit in style and vocabulary throughout, is made explicit at the outset: "Volumnius Serenus of Concordia, if in what they have told me he has subtracted nothing from the truth, nor added anything to it, has every right and claim to my services as his advocate and intercessor [*vel patrono vel precatore*] before you. But if I seem to overstep the limits of a letter, the reason will be, that the facts of the case require some legal advocacy to be mixed with the letter [*ut cum epistula coniuncta sit quaedam causidicatio*]." First, by a series of questions, it is established beyond a doubt that Serenus had been a decurion of Concordia, and that he had properly participated in the duties and the privileges of his order. A precedent is cited. Then the charge against Volumnius Serenus is noted: opposition to his reinstatement to his former rank after a period of exile, "as if he illegally forced his way into the senate." A previous trial proved inconclusive. The orator appeals to Antoninus' compassion for the excessive disgrace suffered by the man, by his family, and by society at large; an earlier judge had sympathetically reduced the length of his exile. Fronto requests immediate restoration of rank to the old man.[52] It may be asked how a rather obscure Italian decurion was able to approach Fronto, and why the orator agreed to help him at such length. The answer is clearly indicated, for the son of Volumnius Serenus was apparently a Roman knight and his grandson was a member of Fronto's own order. Influence had certainly been exercised, for it was others who related to Fronto the details of Volumnius' plight.[53]

Confirmation of the importance of intermediaries is to be found in the letter on behalf of a certain Baburiana, likewise addressed to Arrius Antoninus, and concerning the modification of a legal decision which had gone against her. Because of the well-known intimacy between Fronto and Antoninus, many had sought the elder man's *suffragium* with the younger. Fronto had listened with care to all petitioners, but had supported only those "probe petentes." Baburiana should be a local worthy similar in rank to Volumnius Serenus, for she has in some way defaulted on a construction project within the province and jurisdiction of Antoninus. The same query as to the connection with Fronto may be made of her. An answer appears in a mutilated remark made in the course of the letter: " . . . men dear to me, and I would most gladly oblige them, only so far however as is compatible above and before all with a regard for your justice."[54] The use of intercession by other parties to win the *suffragium* or patronage of a great man is a common enough phenomenon. Here it appears that in the first instance Baburiana, and possibly Volumnius, had recourse to friends of Fronto to gain his powerful advocacy. Their interest thus becomes of concern in his *obsequia* to his friends, and their problems become *amicorum causae*. And noteworthy here is the echo of Fronto's previous insistence on justice, for again he distinguishes between proper *causidicatio* and the suspicion of improper *gratia*.

His most vehement epistolary plea is discovered in a partly preserved letter to the emperor Marcus, whose reply opens with what may be a jest—"so my master will now be my advocate also!"—and closes with the promise that "the speech in which you have advocated our cause, I will show at once to Faustina." The affair is a complicated one, concerning a dispute over the will of Marcus' wealthy kinswoman the younger Matidia, great-niece of the emperor Trajan and sister-in-law of Hadrian. Contention arose over certain codicils which Matidia had long ago annulled by opening, but which some unscrupulous persons had sealed up again while she lay unconscious and dying. Should the codicils stand? The matter is complex, and further complicated by the fragmentary state of the two letters, one to Marcus, one to Victorinus, which discuss it.[55] Under the will proper, the empress Faustina was heir, her daughters were legatees, and certain dependents of Matidia, both men and women to an unspecified number, each received an annuity of fifty thousand sesterces, to be paid to them by Faustina. If the disputed codicils were upheld, Matidia's *alumni* expected to receive instead a lump sum of one million sesterces each; the money thus dealt out in legacies would exceed three-quarters of the value of the inheritance, and the lex Falcidia would have to be invoked to insure that the heiress, Faustina, received at least one-quarter of the value of the estate. Marcus was in a real quandary as emperor, as judge, and as husband of the heir and father of legatees. Three choices were open to him, to disallow the codicils, to accept them as a valid part of the will, or to persuade Faustina not to enter upon the inheritance at all. Fronto was truly appalled that any but the first choice could even be considered, and deeply worried that philosophy might pervert the emperor's judgment. The result was an advocate's *oratio*, not a legal opinion, and it must be treated as such.

The surviving portion of the plea begins with a scathing attack on the sneaks (*cellae filios*), particularly some engorged female parasite or other, who will walk off with a good portion of what would belong to the imperial treasury if the codicils were upheld.[56] If they are upheld, the Falcidian law will require a *distractio bonorum*. Among the goods to be sold thus are numerous valuables, including a celebrated string of pearls. Such a sale will inevitably cause scandal: if Faustina purchases them she will be accused of collusion with herself as heir to snap them up cheaply while reducing the amount eventually to be paid to the legatees from the estate; if any other person buys them, Marcus' daughters will lose their legacy and he will be the man who despoiled his own children to enhance the already swollen gorge of one of the parasites.[57] The legal situation is obscure, but clarity was not Fronto's object here: for that Marcus had numerous learned advisers.[58] The rhetoric, however, is brilliant, particularly the cumulative picture of the unworthy beneficiaries of the codicils. They are children not of the earth, Fronto asserts, but of hidden places, the cellar or perhaps the inner chamber (*cella*). These people are defined to Victorinus as Matidia's "Variani alumni," but here the innocent term is twisted into deadly literalism: "nescio quae ista altilis alumna," suggesting a fattened parasite. Inevitably, then, these *alumni* will devour the lady's inheritance as well, and the pearl necklace is picked out for its juxtaposition to their already swollen gullets.

Fronto then briefly considers the third choice available. Should Faustina refuse the inheritance altogether, intestacy would ensue, both will and codicils would fail, and the intestate heir would succeed, if there was one. Here Fronto appeals to Marcus' family piety: a most noble and nobly born lady, one highly deserving of Marcus' favor, should not die intestate. And he ends with a flourish, pointing dramatically to the gross incongruity of a personage who was honored with a public funeral yet whose testament was disallowed. Then, still in the character of the advocate, he concludes with a brief appeal to Marcus as a judge who has up until now shown himself to be just, grave, and righteous in all cases.

The emperor's reply to all of this contains no hint of irony or of resentment at the written plea. His praise of Fronto's letter and his assertion that his master's *sententiae* lie closest to his heart should make his opening remark suggest not mockery but surprise and gratitude for his teacher's intervention in the affair: "after a consultation with my *amici* up to this moment, I have carefully collected all the points which weighed with us, so as to write fully to my lord [Lucius Verus] and make him assessor in this business also."[59] Fronto's forceful letter might thus be seen as the equivalent of an appearance before the emperor and *consilium* in court. The deliberations were weighty indeed, for among the extant *responsa* of Q. Cervidius Scaevola, a jurisconsult well-known as Marcus' friend and counselor, appears one dealing with the disposal of a necklace of thirty-five pearls according to the lex Falcidia.[60]

Of all the possible motives for engaging in advocacy, Fronto's correspondence clearly betrays the two which had been succinctly defined by an advocate of the previous generation as "amicorum causae" and "coloniarum et municipiorum clientelae."[61] Other standard stimuli are noticeably absent: the pursuit of money or influence or glory or oratorical skill.[62] This is only to be expected, for the Fronto of the letters is the established lawyer, the leader of the forum who no longer has a career to make for himself. The ancient duties of friend and patron are sufficient. That he was indeed *princeps fori* is amply demonstrated by the two salient elements of his career, the extent of his *clientela* and the courts in which he appeared.

At the heart of Fronto's pleading lie his *amicitiae*; ranging from Marcus Aurelius down to Saenius Pompeianus, such friendships almost inevitably reveal some literary element. But beyond these is the *clientela* from a remarkably broad area. By way of contrast, in the previous generation Pliny had represented the provinces of Baetica and Africa, but those briefs had been thrust upon him by the senate; otherwise his interests were confined to certain minor Italian towns, Comum, Tifernum Tiberinum, Firmum.[63] But Fronto's contacts, as revealed in a mutilated correspondence of no greater extent than Pliny's, spread throughout the empire. With regard to Africa, he had vigorously defended the interests of Cirta in his youth and he was a patron of neighboring Calama; and what is more, a man from Mauretania owed him *fides* and he was to render thanks in the senate on behalf of the Carthaginians. Italy is not so visible, but there is the speech for Nuceria and of course individual contacts elsewhere, for instance with a man of Concordia. But the real surprise lies in the East: Fronto prosecuted the governor of Bithynia for the provincials; he more than once defended Cilician friends before the emperor; he acted in the matter of an Asian will; he defended Demostratus against the Athenian Herodes Atticus; he acted in court with the Pamphylian senator Gavius Clarus; his greatest triumph was won against a Pelops; he spoke on behalf of the citizens of Ptolemais.[64] The explanation for much of this lies initially in Fronto's widespread literary friendships, cases undertaken as *obsequia* to friends cultivated for their *doctrina*.

As for the courts, again there is a telling comparison to be drawn with Pliny. Pliny's activities divide unequally between the great trials in the senate, where it is evident despite his self-glorification that he was usually one speaker among many, and those in the court of the *centumviri*, "my arena," in which he fought the great majority of his battles. Only once does he appear before a *iudex* (though other cases are hinted at), never before the emperor.[65] The contrast with Fronto is illuminating: at least eight appearances before the emperor's *cognitio* are attested, one before the praetorian prefect, perhaps one in the senate. There should be no doubt as to Fronto's relative power as a patron and desirability as an advocate.

Fronto's cases shed dramatic light on his legal practice, but his attitude to the law itself remains elusive. One major question concerns the extent of his legal knowledge. A sharp distinction must be drawn between the jurisprudent and the advocate with his rhetor's ability to entertain *disputatio in utramque partem*.[66] Yet it would be wrong to assume, simply because the lawyer has different interests at heart, that his knowledge of the law is therefore meager. In general, it is difficult to imagine a leading advocate who enjoys only a nodding acquaintance with the law; at the least we should envisage in him a sound knowledge of the law pertaining to particular briefs, similar to that acquired by the modern lawyer. The professional *causidicus* might hire a jurisconsult and his opinions, but the gentleman orator was always expected to have included a firm grounding in the law among his studies.[67] Moreover, as magistrate, promagistrate, or imperial legate, he might expect sooner or later to appear in court as a judge himself. And, most significant, the lawyer might take his place as a legal adviser next to the jurisconsult. Thus, when acting as judge, Aulus Gellius turned for advice to his friends, "men experienced and celebrated in advocacy and the affairs of the forum."[68] At a higher level, on at least three occasions, Pliny served on Trajan's *consilium* at imperial investigations into various minor cases arising from the provinces, and once he is discovered sitting with the prefect of the city.[69] Similarly, the historian Cassius Dio, who also made some early reputation as an advocate, turns up more than once as adviser at imperial *cognitiones*.[70] We may conclude that the opinions of educated men with practical courtroom experience were of considerable weight in the interpretation and application of the law.

It is true that Fronto does not dwell upon matters of law, but then he made no pretense to expertise. Nevertheless, he has been accused with some contempt of considerable ignorance.[71] The case against him rests primarily on three pieces of evidence, each of which entails the same serious caution, that the manuscript is incomplete: the passage on the overseas will is merely one mutilated extract from a much longer speech; the surviving argument of the acephalous letter on Matidia's will appears likewise to form part of a longer *causidicatio*;

and the discussion of the curial status of Volumnius Serenus is highly lacunose. Thus, without all of the evidence, it is difficult to claim conviction for any attack on the orator's handling of a brief. Each case has additional perils. In the first, no one has satisfactorily explained how or why the proconsul delayed the opening of the will, nor indeed is it even clear whether Fronto is acting in defense or prosecution.[72] In the second, the phrase "bonis lege Falcidia distractis" has caused trouble. Fronto is mistaken, we are told, for there is nothing in the lex Falcidia concerning *bonorum distractio*.[73] However, co-owners (in this case the legatees whom Fronto found so abominable) could always require the sale of property owned in common (here, with the empress), with a view to the division of the proceeds. Fronto's position here is that of the advocate, not the jurisconsult; he can be accused of disregard of the law but not of ignorance. The lex Falcidia would have to be invoked, certain imperial treasures would have to be sold, and the intervening steps are immaterial. Whether the sale of the treasures would actually be required in this case or not—it is hazardous for us, who do not have the details, to judge Fronto, who did—the orator, who is here in full flight, is perfectly free to offer and expand upon a rhetorically effective hypothesis. As for the third case, there is no fault in the letter as it stands, merely ambiguities, and it must be remembered that the plea is one for the exercise of leniency by an officer in his jurisdiction, not the defense of a litigant at a trial, despite its own professions. This letter was addressed to a *iuridicus*, the other two are pleas to emperors, one of them in a matter where consultation with a *consilium* is explicitly attested. Is it likely that Fronto could have presented a case before the leading jurists of the empire without a sure grasp of the legal situation? Whatever the extent of his legal knowledge, the case for incompetence will not stand.

That Fronto did not choose to ponder legal theory argues only a lack of interest, not of acquaintance. His friend the philosopher Favorinus was discovered by the delighted jurisconsult Caecilius Africanus to be expert in Roman law and familiar with the commentators upon it.[74] But for this chance anecdote recorded by Aulus Gellius, Favorinus' knowledge of the law would have gone unsuspected. Fronto, to whom even Favorinus bowed in matters of the Latin tongue, must also through his studies have had a thorough knowledge, if not deep understanding, of Roman legal writings, the product of his consuming quest for words. On a natural assumption, *studia doctrinae* would again have contributed to success in other endeavors.

The importance of law in Fronto's life is strikingly suggested by the legal jargon and metaphor which permeate his daily correspondence. Thus, in one complicated protestation of love for Marcus: "See that you do not turn informer [*delator*] or appear as witness before your daughter, to make her think that I love you more than her."[75] Or, a *defensio* is submitted in excuse for delaying a visit to Lucius Verus; on another occasion, no defense is needed, "res ipsa testa est."[76] In an attempt to demonstrate the contrast between state and private customs, the florid epistle to Appian naturally includes a lengthy section on litigation, and the exchange of letters itself is little more than a *controversia*.[77] The best instance of this legal mode of expression is a letter from Fronto to the emperor Marcus which begins with an excuse for the delay in writing, demanding the customary indulgence of *dilationes*, "ne fraudi sit." To Marcus' fear that Fronto's love for him has lessened, Fronto replies, "Look, I beseech you, that you do not rob yourself [*ne temet ipse defrudes*] and of your own accord demand a diminution [*detrimentum*] of love." And with regard to his hopes for Marcus' promise as a youth he continues: "I indeed, being granted all that I wished and prayed for, have been cast and fined in my very wishes and prayers; to meet that fine I put in my doubled love for you, not, as was the custom in the old time for fines to be inflicted, at the rate of half less a thousand [asses]."[78]

Two letters in the correspondence go so far as to make their points through fictitious lawsuits. The first is addressed to his master by the pupil Marcus Caesar, *Contra Somnum pro Insomnia*.[79] Immediately, the plaintiff Marcus accuses himself of *praevaricatio*, for sleep is with him both day and night, but he thinks his "friend" will withdraw in offense at this *accusatio*. His *epichiremata* are presented by the calling of witnesses, first Homer of the *Odyssey* and the *Iliad*, then Ennius *noster*, then the shepherd Hesiod. At last Marcus tires of this sport, in which he has indulged more for Fronto's pleasure than his own, and he retires to sleep, praying that it will not attack him in its turn. It is interesting that this light-hearted exercise is a reply to a warning from Fronto against excessive nocturnal labor, for another letter survives from a much later period on the same theme. It takes the form of a fable intended to persuade Marcus Augustus to sleep at least, even if he cannot relax amid the carės of state.[80] Vesper and Lucifer are at law over the boundary between their domains, and Somnus also demands a hearing at their *cognitio*, appearing as a relative of Vesper who suffers from *iniuria*. Somnus then takes over, as the tale of his origin unfolds. When Jupiter had observed men to be settling *iurgia* and *vadimonia* at night or postponing them to another night (*comperendinari*), he created Sleep to rule them after dark, all the other gods having refused the task. And to make the new ruler acceptable to his subjects, Jupiter gave to him the power of bestowing sweet and hopeful dreams. The application to Marcus is apt, for he is to be upbraided for judging cases at night: "Now what if no one had stolen fire from heaven, would not the sun suffice you for your judicial duties? Do realize in your conscience that you are tied to a daily falsehood, for, when you say that you "appoint the day" for trial of cases and yet try by night, then you are bound to be untruthful, whether you condemn or acquit. If you condemn anyone, you say, 'There appears to have been gross negligence' [*parum cavisse videtur*]; where indeed but for the light nothing could appear at all."[81]

Marcus as judge appears elsewhere in the correspondence. Even as Caesar he was detained for whole days listening to *causidici* while he longed for his studies or the company of Fronto, and his conscientiousness as judge is elsewhere well attested.[82] What appears only in the correspondence is his impatience with the duty of judgment, and that impatience is directed particularly against the hateful and wearisome clamor of the advocates—he hastens to exclude his master, who is no mere advocate, but an orator.[83] The boy who could trifle with a *controversia* on sleep soon abandoned such a sterile pastime. At an early age he is discovered requesting from Fronto better material for practice composition, for in the last suggested *hypothesis*, a case before the *centumviri*, he had found nothing but *epiphonemata*, exclamations.[84] When his friend Aufidius Victorinus ridiculed the orator while praising judges, Marcus felt the attack keenly, and the writings of the learned jurist Titius Aristo confirmed him in his dislike for the meaner tricks of advocacy.[85] It can be suggested that Marcus' youthful crisis of conscience, when set against his distaste for *causidici* and his concern for justice, is less a rejection of rhetoric in favor of philosophy (as it is commonly taken to be) than a specific rejection of the impurities of advocacy for the purity of jurisprudence. Fronto's disappointment at this conversion is visible to a degree in the parable on Sleep.

The early apostasy of Marcus struck at the part of the law closest to Fronto's heart, the teaching of forensic rhetoric. Here the passion of the scholar and the duty of the gentleman meet again, in the ancient custom of *tirocinium fori,* whereby young men were attached to the leading *patroni* of the day, escorting them everywhere and assisting them in their speeches to court or assembly.[86] This was the best and most practical method of learning how to plead in court, and in Fronto's case it appears as an element in his basic practice of *contubernium.* The best illustration lies in his relations with the junior senator L. Gavius Clarus. The two lived together in great amity, the younger attending to the elder and being promoted by him, and all of Fronto's business in the forum, both great and small, was cared for by him.[87] Fronto's son-in-law and pupil is likewise revealed acting with him in court and duly succeeds him as one of the leaders of the forum in the next generation.[88] In one letter we see the master waiting at home in trepidation while one of his noble *contubernales* undertakes his first appearance in court. When other pupils bring news of the young man's success, Fronto writes to his father a sentiment worthy of Pliny: "He went down to the forum noble by birth, he came back from it more noble by eloquence than by lineage."[89] The relationship is encapsulated in a letter of introduction for another protégé: "Sardius Saturninus has a son, Sardius Lupus, a learned and eloquent man, introduced to the forum from my home and my *contubernium,* and instructed by myself in the noble arts."[90]

The key word, again, is *contubernium,* here the all-embracing relationship between a senior and a junior gentleman. While serving the older man everywhere, the younger received not only practical training but a grounding in etiquette and introduction to the right people. The elder received practical assistance and satisfaction at the success of a friend. But what is more, he insured the future leadership of the law courts.[91] It was one way in which the successful orator and senator, often a *novus homo,* could repay his debt to advocacy.

VI

THE SENATOR

THE AUGUST SENATE of Rome was an institution of central importance in Fronto's life, an element in all of his activities from adolescence to death. His career as a senator and his appearances in the senate can be chronicled in some detail, and beneath this surface may be discerned a deep regard for the well-being of his order. Two features predominate throughout his career. One is, inevitably, the orator's passion for eloquence, which will produce a somewhat atypical picture of senatorial life. But the other is a central fact of imperial history, and one rendered with exceptional clarity in the correspondence: the shadow of the emperor falling over every aspect of senatorial life. To Fronto, good relations between emperor and senate were a matter of vital concern; rhetoric would be, of course, his only mode of expression.

Fronto's active senatorial career was of a remarkable consistency, and it offers a valuable lesson. With the possible exception of his vigintiviral post, it was pursued under two emperors, Hadrian and Antoninus Pius. An inscription survives, dedicated by the citizens of Calama in Africa Proconsularis to their patron M. Cornelius T.f. Quir. Fronto, and recounting the earlier stages of his *cursus honorum*: triumvir capitalis, quaestor of the province of Sicily, aedile of the plebs, and praetor.[1] Little can be gleaned from this. The Sicilian quaestorship (c. 120?) arouses interest as the one post assuredly held away from Rome, and that at no great distance.[2] Fronto seems to have remained in the capital both before and after his Sicilian employment and to have undertaken no military service of any sort. The praetorship, if held at the minimum age of thirty, would have fallen to him about 125. Certainly if the anecdote of Cassius Dio is correctly assigned to the 120s, Fronto's supremacy at the bar, like Pliny's earlier prominence, was established around the period of his praetorship, and the two achievements would not have been unconnected. His tenure of the magistracy can be assigned (to be safe) to the period c. 125/130.[3]

The subsequent consulship was not won until 143, after an interval of at least thirteen years, a long period of silence between the end of the inscription and the beginning of the correspondence. This was the crucial part of a man's career, the stages between praetorship and hoped-for consulship. Most opportunely, there is a neglected passage of autobiography, submerged in a conventional inquiry into the sources of Marcus' love for him: "What benefit has your Fronto bestowed upon you so great that you should show him such affection? Has he given up his life for you and your parents? Has he braved perils vicariously in your stead? Has he been the faithful governor of some province? Has he commanded an army? Nothing of the kind."[4] The letter itself cannot be dated more precisely than to the period of Marcus' Caesarship, though the pressure of work that Fronto complains about in the previous letter would best fit the period after Marcus' reception of the *tribunicia potestas* (147).[5] At any rate, the year should be considerably after 139 to account for the intimate tone of the letter and to allow time for Fronto to have avoided some of these services to Marcus. At a stroke, then, he confirms what we might well have surmised, that after his praetorship he held neither legionary legateship nor proconsulship nor provincial legateship. The conclusion is inevitable, barring exceptional conditions, which are both unattested and unlikely: in order to accede to the consulship Fronto must have held at least one of the prefectures of the treasury in Rome.

Further precision may be attained through comparison with the known prefects of either treasury who reached the consulship and the relevant portions of whose careers have been transmitted intact. First, the junior post of the *aerarium militare*.[6] If we subtract as irrelevant those senators who held provinces or led armies at any time between praetorship and consulship, and if we disregard two men whose careers display clear and explicable anomalies, the list of senators comparable to Fronto becomes extremely short: we are left only with the advocate Pliny and the jurist Salvius Iulianus, both of whom ascended directly from praetorship to *militare* to *Saturni* to consulship.[7] Similarly, for the more senior post of the *aerarium Saturni*, by eliminating the ineligible and by again discounting four clear anomalies, we are again left with the same two men, Pliny and Julian, praetors, prefects, and consuls.[8] There is no reason to assume any special dispensation in Fronto's selection for the consulship, and it can therefore be argued with confidence that he held both treasury prefectures.

The parallel with the careers of Pliny and Julian is not fortuitous. Pliny was a noted barrister, Julian a great jurisconsult; Fronto, the pre-eminent advocate of his day, joins their company with ease. The advantage of legal training in dealing with the affairs of these prefectures, particularly the senior office, is amply demonstrated by the variety of legal problems arising from the financial business they handled, and indeed we may discern a marked preference in the senior prefecture for men with legal backgrounds.[9] It would be difficult to imagine Fronto not holding such an office, with the ever-present example of Pliny before him, and such a sequence of offices is in harmony with the tenor of his own career, early and late, the career passed never far from Rome of a senator whose interests lay neither in military glory nor in government service. His two triennial tenures may be assigned roughly to the late 120s and early 130s, before the dark last years of Hadrian.

Service as prefect of the treasury of Saturn should have led to a swift nomination to the consulship: if not immediately, then within two years.[10] There may, however, be a hiatus in Fronto's career, the result of some discord with the emperor Hadrian. He is properly circumspect under Hadrian's heirs, but his dislike of the emperor is clear and there are veiled references to damaged *dignitas* and even to personal danger. Even with the accession of Pius there is some delay before the consulship of 143. This is perhaps neither unusual nor excessive, nor was forty-eight (to take an approximate age) abnormally old: many new men had to wait twenty-five years and more after their quaestorships.[11] Reason for delay may be sought above all in the more important and time-consuming occupation of educating a Caesar. And after the recent years of insecurity, a new emperor facing hostile factions and a restive senate would feel obliged to reward his political friends and placate his opponents.

When the honor of the consulship was bestowed, it was keenly appreciated, but the conspicuous feature of Fronto's tenure is his desire to be quit of it.[12] This is not mere accident. The correspondence of the following two decades and more is resolutely domestic, seldom raising its view in any but the most disinterested manner beyond the confines of Rome and Italy, until a major disaster threatened in the East, requiring the presence of one of his imperial correspondents. Not surprisingly, there is no suggestion of any desire for a consular province, and considering the ever-precarious state of his health, the silence of Fronto's letters as to any sort of *cura* nearer home may be taken to imply the absence of such posts. The exception is, of course, the proconsulship of Asia or of Africa, for this crowning glory of a senatorial career was an honor hardly to be refused. Fronto's turn came about the year 157/158, and the lot assigned to him the province of Asia. Unfortunately, the honor coincided with a bout of ill-health; it is unclear whether he recovered sufficiently to take up the office.[13]

Fronto's career offers the clearest possible indication that a man's importance in the state is not necessarily measured by his official *cursus honorum*. His was the barest minimum, with no military experience and virtually no provincial service.[14] Extensive activity at the bar and in the salons of Rome is to be expected from the start, and later an intimacy with the imperial family. Above all, the most serious consideration must be given to the ill-health which plagued his later years and jeopardized his proconsulship. Circumstances and inclination thus conspired to keep him in the neighborhood of Rome, and of the senate house.

The normal activities of the curia call for little report in the correspondence, a silence encouraged by the fact that the principal correspondent was supremely well-informed on the affairs of the senate. But it must not be assumed from this silence that Fronto was not assiduous in his attendance. As late as 161 a busy session could delay for a day his reply to a letter from the emperor himself. The date is of interest, late 161, for on any reckoning Fronto was then of an age when attendance at the senate was no longer required.[15] The labor concerned here was presumably a particular project of his own, for the routine of the house gave him no pleasure, if we may judge it by his chafing at the golden chains of his consulship.[16] But where there was occasion for grand rhetoric, Fronto's interest was sure to be aroused.

The obvious attraction for the leading advocate of the age was the senatorial court, in which there was still sufficient opportunity for the display of Fronto's talents. The slim records of the reign of Pius yield three sensational trials in the senate, one for murder, two for treason, and all of eminent senators.[17] Of Marcus Aurelius, his biographer states curtly that "he assigned the senate as judge to many investigations, especially to those which most concerned him," one of these commissions being the trial of the supporters of Avidius Cassius, with the restriction that heavy punishment was forbidden.[18] It would be surprising if Fronto never appeared before the house in his capacity of advocate, and there are a few casual references. In the 140s an interest at least is betrayed: he loves and honors Pius "since the excellent decision in the senate, which, while safeguarding the interests of the provinces, at the same time gently rebuked the offenders."[19] The notorious skirmish with Herodes Atticus may have taken place before the senate, though again the emperor's presence overshadows the affair. The speech *Pro Bithynis*, reminiscent of the *repetundae* trials involving Pliny, was probably delivered before the senate. And a heavily mutilated text from a letter to Fronto's close friend Claudius Iulianus seems to have reported a trial in the same court.[20]

However, Fronto's finest hours in the senate were passed in the delivery of *actiones gratiarum* to the emperor, and it is these which hold the interest of the correspondence. He had considerable practice in the genre. Hadrian he had often praised in the senate, he told Marcus, and those speeches remained in circulation, and Pius himself he had eulogized when designated to the consulship.[21] These were undoubtedly splendid occasions, Rome's best orator reciting the praises of the emperor before the senate, and Fronto's investment of so much effort in them suggests that they were to be taken seriously. He hoped that they would survive as literature, and as instruments of propaganda they would surely have been invaluable. "Him [Pius] I must now so praise that my praise be not hidden away in the Journals of the Senate, but come into the hands and under the eyes of men."[22] Such productions must therefore be carefully examined for their semiofficial picture of the age.[23] Fronto is particularly remembered for two, one in thanks for his consulship, and one on behalf of the Carthaginians.

Fronto's *gratiarum actio* for his consulship was delivered to the emperor Antoninus Pius in the senate on 13 August 143. It does not survive, but there are references to it in the letters and elsewhere, and similar speeches from analogous occasions supply parallels and occasionally direct borrowing. Moreover, an exactly contemporary panegyric of the emperor in Greek does survive, from the hand of the young sophist Aelius Aristides.[24] And the framework for the eulogy of a prince is provided by the so-called Menander Rhetor: the prooemium, devoted to the specific circumstances of the oration, was to be followed by a laudatory biography of the future monarch from youth to accession, followed then by an account of his civil and military achievements as the visible sign of the four virtues (*andreia, dikaiosune, sophrosune, phronesis*), with reference to his family and friends, and then by a general summary of the new golden age, rays of which have shone through everywhere in the preceding speech.[25] Of these, Fronto would have pointedly emphasized the quietly civil virtues of the future emperor throughout. Pliny had provided the paradigm for comparison of the present mild age with the difficulties of the recent past, and Claudius Mamertinus would stress the same theme later. Aristides especially was to contrast the dangerous later years of Hadrian with Pius' mild temper and unstained clemency. Fronto, as a senator and a familiar friend of Hadrian, would have added more personal remarks. He had feared Hadrian and perhaps suffered in his career, for he was to claim that Pius' *dies imperii* (10 July 138) saw the rebirth of his own health, his dignity, and his security.[26] He was bound to make some such comment in this speech, for it was no ordinary occasion: Fronto's consulship coincided with the glorious completion of the emperor's first quinquennium.

The orator promised to praise the virtues of Pius, both physical and mental, in his speech: *prosopon, morphe, tropoi, aretai.*[27] The emperor's lack of martial accomplishments suggested a single grand image, one of striking aptness. Pius' biographer concludes his list of the emperor's qualities with the remark that he was rightly likened by good men to Numa Pompilius, and the sentiment is repeated in its proper place in the final chapter of the biography: Pius was rightly compared to Numa, "whose felicity and piety, whose peace and sacred rites, he always preserved." The context here is primarily religious, but there is a secondary note of pacifism, which is brought out by the comment of the *Epitome de Caesaribus* that Pius was a Numa in a reign untroubled by wars.[28] Whence did the image derive? Marius Maximus knew it in the early third century, for he turned it into an erudite joke: the family of Marcus Aurelius (who was of course Pius' son by adoption) was said "[going back to the beginning] to derive its blood from Numa." Yet there is no sign in inscriptions or coins that Pius considered himself or was considered by his successor to be the new Numa, despite an avowed interest in the figures of the earliest history of Rome.[29] The single contemporary reference to Pius as

Numa appears, appropriately, in the work of an accomplished orator, M. Cornelius Fronto: "The same devotion to peace is said to have withheld him from action absolutely justified, so that in his freedom from empty ambition he is clearly comparable in all the line of Roman emperors to Numa alone."[30]

Pius as Numa should be the masterly creation of a panegyrist, a theme to be repeated and developed throughout his speech by a man who delighted in the multiple image apt in every point.[31] We can use it in the recovery of two *capita* at least, from the encomium of Pius' first five years. The two obviously Numan elements are religion and peace. In a list of his father's virtues submitted to Marcus in the 160s, Fronto emphasizes the late emperor's piety: "Your father, that godlike man, who in his *providentia, pudicitia, frugalitas, innocentia, pietas, sanctimonia* excelled the virtues of all rulers."[32] This should recall to some extent sentiments pronounced in the panegyric two decades before, for Pius early established his special claim to the virtue of piety, bearing the name from the beginning of his reign; Aristides certainly returns to the theme several times in his speech of 144, and an inscription erected in 143 by the senate and people of Rome honors the emperor "ob insignem erga caerimonias publicas curam ac religionem."[33] The time was also ripe for praise of the bringer of peace; for literature, inscriptions, and coins combine to suggest a period when relative calm prevailed after troubles in the East, in Germany, and in Britain.[34] The British campaign, which was successfully concluded by Fronto's compatriot, the governor Lollius Urbicus, won for the emperor in 142 or 143 the designation "Imp. II."[35] Chance has preserved one of Fronto's comments. As the biographer points out, Pius conducted several wars through his legates, and the theme was happily appropriated for its neat contrast by the panegyrist of the warlike Constantius Caesar, who reconquered the province in person: "Fronto, not the second but the other glory of Roman eloquence, when he was giving the emperor Antoninus praise for the successful completion of the war in Britain, declared that although he had committed the conduct of the campaign to others, while sitting at home himself in the palace at Rome, yet like the helmsman at the tiller of a ship of war, the glory of the whole navigation and voyage belonged to him."[36] The pilot image was apt and popular: the very next year Aristides developed it at some length in his praise of the emperor.[37]

A little more of the speech can be recovered. Fronto tells us once that he praised the emperor's *virtus* and his *facta*, elsewhere his *facta* and his *dicta*.[38] What details he chose to enlarge upon may be guessed.[39] One element is sure, however, the standard praise of the emperor's family, which should appear in the account of his domestic virtues. Pliny had elected to depict the wife and sister of Trajan as models of the Roman matron; Ausonius would prefer to illustrate the character of Gratian through the familial piety shown toward father and uncle and the honor bestowed on his brother.[40] Fronto was able to employ both devices. First, attention would be directed to the deified Faustina, to the felicity of the emperor's married life and his pious regard for her memory. The opportunities for a warm-hearted friend and first-class orator were irresistible. On the occasion of another laudation of Pius, perhaps that delivered when Fronto was designated to the consulship,[41] the emperor had been satisfied with most of the usual praise but truly moved by the orator's remarks on Faustina, which were as true as they were eloquent: "For this is the plain fact: by heaven I would rather live with her on Gyara than in the palace without her."[42] Such a success must have appeared in the principal panegyric as well. The emperor's lost children would be mourned, and then, moving from his piety and his grief to his happy generosity, the orator would celebrate the surviving daughter and two adopted sons. Here again the orator's personal involvement would be woven into the theme, perhaps with the graceful apology made by another consul in a later age that in praising his pupil's talents he might seem to be praising his own.[43] Marcus Caesar, the pledge for the future, was a suitable theme to lead up to the peroration, and Fronto indulged himself in a miniature panegyric with an account of his family—Lucilla was mentioned—and his physical features, his habits and his virtues, treated perhaps in marked parallel with those of his adoptive father.[44]

Fronto's *gratiarum actio* of August 143 was a triumph. Marcus was beside himself with delight, and later generations vindicated Fronto's hopes that his speech might live on as literature. It seems to have had a powerful effect in forming posterity's view of the happy age of the Antonines.

Tantalizing fragments survive of another speech delivered to the emperor before the senate, on behalf of the citizens of Carthage.[45] The occasion of this *actio* is not difficult to discover. In it Fronto refers to restoration work carried out by the emperor: " <si> cut Rhodum <cond> idisti," "atque urbes <it> a ut incolumes <si> nt iu . . .

imum . . . restituas." Context is supplied in the *Historia Augusta*'s list of the *adversa* of Pius' reign – an earthquake laid waste the cities of Rhodes and Asia, the forum of Carthage was burnt – and Pius' exceptional generosity in the relief of disaster is well attested.[46] Foremost among his benefactions to the African capital was the construction of vast new baths unequaled in the West outside of Rome for their size and magnificence.[47] The date of construction is fixed only loosely by a highly fragmentary inscription of dedication recording Pius' fourth consulship (other indications are lost), Marcus Caesar, and "the other children."[48] However, the period indicated, 145/161, can be further reduced by reference to a medallion of Aurelius Caesar Aug. Pii fil., with the date of 153 and a representation of Dea Caelestis near a round temple; it is a most plausible conjecture that the goddess' shrine at Carthage was damaged or destroyed by the fire in the nearby forum.[49] Fronto's speech (as it will be reconstructed below) seems to bear some confirmation. The job of restoring a single temple would be an easy one compared with that of restoring the baths, which were left to be completed by Marcus and Lucius. The Carthaginian fire should then be assigned to the period of the late 140s or early 150s, some short while after the earthquake at Rhodes in 142 or 143 and Pius' reconstruction work there, to which Fronto referred in his oration.[50]

Recent inspection of the palimpsest of the Carthaginian oration has added a few words and phrases, and numerous corrections.[51] Two leaves of the folio survive. The first appears to contain an account of Carthaginian (or perhaps African) history. The recto, while almost completely illegible, lends most support to this theory with a fragment in which a reference must surely be seen to Antony and Cleopatra.[52] The subject might then be some connection of Antony with the province of Africa, perhaps during his period with Cleopatra, and the section preceding this (verso) fits in well with a description of civil war.[53] Such a historical digression or prologue would be essential in a speech of this nature, to recall the former glories of the now stricken city and to rehearse the benefactions of past Romans. This would form a natural prelude to the introduction of Pius Augustus as the new founder of the city, and that image can be discovered on the dedicatory inscription from the Antonine baths: "[. . . ? ut a primis imperatori]bus colonia co[ndita?, ita] . . . beneficiis eius au[cta]."

The second leaf has arrived at the praise of Pius himself. Here the orator appears to be indulging in a rhetorical contrast between the generosity of Pius and the rapacity of a previous emperor (or perhaps of a governor); that is, "bad" elements and "good" seem to alternate in the fragments.[54] The speech is nearing its end, and on the last page appears an easily reconstructed passage praying for the emperor's safety, which is held to be synonymous with the security of the empire. The religious note had been sounded immediately before, for the word *delubris* stands out at the end of the previous page, and the tenor may be plausibly recovered. The account of the emperor's benefactions would end, suitable to his renowned piety, with the *delubra* he has erected, one of them presumably the temple of Caelestis. Thus the pious monarch has rebuilt or is rebuilding Carthage, "just as you built Rhodes." Fronto prays to the rest of the gods of all peoples and of all cities for Pius' long-lasting good health, on which depends the safety of the whole world. The cities are to be maintained unscathed by the gods while Pius restores them, and to conserve their famed virtues with the help of the emperor, "nostrarum variarum fortunarum subsidium."

What emerges from the consideration of these exiguous fragments is precisely what was to be expected. The *Gratiarum Actio in Senatu pro Carthaginiensibus* was a simple encomium to the senate of the great city's great benefactor, and beyond the natural stress on the emperor's material beneficence would have contained the conventional tributes to his piety and his mildness. A delightfully tart letter from Pius to Fronto survives, to give a unique glimpse of the recipient's point of view. Praise is showered on a particular panegyric delivered by the orator, but exceptional distaste for the custom itself is manifest.[55] Nevertheless, the opinions of individuals were irrelevant, the ceremony was essential, and senators like Fronto continued to praise the emperor to his senate.

Scraps are preserved of a speech delivered *in senatu* that for once has no apparent connection with Fronto's major concerns, but it turns on a theme worthy of close attention, the dignity of the senator and the senate. The fragments are remarkably obscure:

> What nice ears men have nowadays! What taste in judging of speeches! You can learn from our Aufidius what shouts of applause were evoked in my speech, and with what a chorus of approval were greeted the words "in those days every bust was decorated with patrician insignia"; but when, comparing a noble with a plebeian race, I said, "As if one were to think the flame kindled on a pyre and on an altar to be the same because both alike give light," at this a few murmurs were heard . . .

> Instead of Polemo the rhetorician, whom you lately presented to me in your letters as a Ciceronian, I have given back to you in my speech, which I delivered in the senate, a philosopher, if I am not mistaken, of the hoariest antiquity. Come, what do you say, Marcus, how does my version of the story of Polemo strike you? Of course, Horatius Flaccus supplied me with plenty of smart things to say on that subject.[56]

The story of Polemo was a commonplace, the conversion of a sybarite into a philosopher, but more generally an example of a sudden and dramatic change for the better.[57] How Fronto deployed this matter is unclear. The speech was certainly delivered during his consulship; therefore it may have played directly or indirectly on sentiments contained in the satire to which he refers: thus, Fronto the consul who so longed to leave office and flee to Marcus at Baiae, may have found amusing Horace's words "ponas insignia morbi, fasciolas."[58]

The fragments quoted from the speech are especially puzzling. Several of the audience had murmured when they heard the second sentiment. "Admurmuro" could imply either approval or disapproval, and it is not clear here whether the senators are murmuring at the orator's opinions or at his manner of expressing them, though the latter might be more attractive in the context. Worse, the relationship of the noble and the ignoble race with the funeral pyre and the altar is strange, and that a practiced orator should compare either with a funeral pyre is surprising, especially an orator such as Fronto, who insisted on the aptness of his similes. Fortunately, the first fragment offers illumination. There is surely a contrast implied here between the past, when every bust portrayed a patrician, and the present, when the Roman nobility is but a shadow of its former self; hence the rather effective image of the light cast by the flame of a funeral pyre. The first remark brought forth shouts of praise, the second a few murmurs of, surely, disapprobation. Fronto's tale has a didactic intent. Why, Marcus may ask, has he told him this? In order that the Caesar may learn to adapt his speech to the tastes of his audience, just as he honors successful gladiators, even if they are criminals, at the request of the people.[59] Fronto had forgotten or ignored this cardinal rule, and he had come perilously close to offending a part of his audience.

It thus appears that a Roman consul could inform the senate that the *nobilitas* was dead or dying, a somewhat outrageous remark. Not unnaturally, this particular consul ranked eloquence in others higher than noble birth.[60] The relevance to himself, a new man and one who rose by eloquence, is obvious, and the speech to the senate may betray some antipathy to pedigree. Such dislike can in fact be glimpsed in the otherwise obscure fragment which survives from a letter addressed to the solidly equestrian Cornelius Repentinus, commending his protection of Fronto's friend Fabianus. The villains of the affair are obvious: ". . . nor will you find [such among] the nobles: hold rather that they were full of sufficiently undisguised hatred."[61] Another fragment, from the speech for the Carthaginians, may betray a similar bitterness.[62] But the most interesting manifestation may be found in Fronto's concept of *philostorgia*.

Fronto's prejudices in this matter are most clearly displayed in his commendation of a senator from Asia Minor: "Simplicity, continence, truthfulness, an honour plainly Roman, a warmth of affection [*philostorgia*], however, possibly not Roman, for there is nothing of which my whole life through I have seen less at Rome than a man unfeignedly *philostorgos*. The reason why there is not even a word for this virtue in our language must, I imagine, be that in reality no one at Rome has any warm affection."[63] Precisely the same sentiment is discovered in the recommendation of an African of the curial class: "Worthy, upright, *philostorgus*, a quality for which the Romans have no word."[64] Several emotions may be combined here, not least Fronto's own warmness of heart,[65] but it is significant that in his *Meditations* Marcus Aurelius particularly thanks Fronto for teaching him that on the whole those whom we call patricians are especially *astorgoteroi*, that is, lacking in warm affection.[66] Thus, Fronto's concept of *philostorgia* may particularly reflect the eternally ambivalent attitude to Rome displayed by the provincial, who can both admire and imitate the virtues and deplore the deficiencies. Fronto's speech to the senate in 143 can then be seen as a footnote to an old problem, the place of the *novus homo* at Rome.[67] And the circumstances of the speech then cast light on its contents, for it was delivered in the course of his consulship: the new man had arrived, and he could regard himself as the truest representative of the Roman senate in the modern age.

Fronto was a provincial gentleman, but a simple statistic reveals his preferred environment: of thirty-eight letters addressed to his friends, twenty-six are to fifteen men of senatorial rank, ten to five men of nonsenatorial rank, and two to the senate of Cirta.[68] The new man's pleasure in his well-merited success is evident. Pride in his achievements cannot fail to shine through Fronto's letter to his native city, declining active patronage of it. He suggests three notable orators in his stead, all of them senators. And the opportunity is seized for a review of past patrons and successful native sons, occasion for satisfied praise of both self and patria: ". . . we should have a well-known man and a consular with the *ius respondendi*. I too, as I hope, while young and strong, played no obscure part in civil affairs. There are many other natives of Cirta also in the senate, *viri clarissimi*. The last honour is the greatest, three of your citizens . . ."[69]

"Ordo noster" is the key, evoking not the dubious power of the senate but the social rank and moral authority of its members. Exclusiveness is the salient trait, and full value must be accorded to the word *noster*. Thus, in commending a philosopher to a proconsular friend, Fronto can add a common seal of approval to his virtues, for not only have crowds flocked to hear the man lecture, but (and a clear contrast is intended here) many men "of our order" have both approved and admired his eloquence.[70] In praise of Censorius Niger it is urged that the man was an intimate of Marcius Turbo and Erucius Clarus, "those two excellent men," Fronto glosses quite unnecessarily, "who were the one leader of the equestrian, the other of the senatorial order."[71] And an appeal to a senatorial friend includes a clever argument against loss of dignity, for the convicted man to whom he is to show mercy is the grandfather of a senator: because of the man's disgrace "a troop of Roman knights, a part of the senate is dishonoured in the person of one man."[72] The pride and the unquestioning elitism implicit throughout the letters are stated explicitly in a commendation of a young senator to the emperor: there are simply special *iura* between two members of *ordo noster*.[73]

This concern of Fronto for the special dignity of the senate and its members had one important effect on imperial relations with the senate. Of Marcus Aurelius in general it can be observed, with his ancient biographer, that "no emperor paid greater deference to the senate."[74] Part of the explanation for this may lie in his own character or training by others: certainly when Fronto proposed as a theme for composition the appearance of a Roman consul in the arena, the young Marcus indignantly refused to discuss the matter.[75] Nevertheless, part of Marcus' exceptional deference to the senate may be attributed directly to the teachings of Fronto. Marcus as emperor was sedulous in his attendance of the senate, if he was in Rome, whether or not there was a motion before the house; and when he wished to propose anything himself, he would appear in person, even if that involved a journey from Campania.[76] Fronto loved the emperor Marcus and he was concerned for the dignity of the senate; inevitably, his influence on their relations was exerted through his major passion, oratory.

The orator clearly instilled in his imperial pupil a deep respect for addressing the senate. When he offered explicit advice on the use of *eloquentiae studium* in the duties of a prince, the long list of illustrations began with: "for it falls to a Caesar to carry by persuasion necessary measures in the senate."[77] Marcus is urged to cultivate a talent which will be of use in many important matters, or does he think that his choice of words is unimportant in affairs which are conducted verbally? "You are mistaken if you think that an opinion blurted out in the senate in the language of Thersites would carry equal weight with a speech of Menalaus or Ulysses, whose look in the act of speaking and their mien and attitude and melodious voices and the difference of cadence in their oratory Homer . . ." The following two pages of the manuscript are indecipherable, but it is evident from marginal glosses that Fronto developed the theme of loss of *auctoritas*, which was introduced in the Thersites passage: "There is no one, however authoritative, who, when his skill is at fault, is not looked down upon by him who has greater skill."[78] These opinions are to be found in a late item in the correspondence, but similar sentiments can be discovered at an earlier period. In a very early plea for the careful choice of words, Fronto asks rhetorically who will force Marcus—the free son of free parents and possessed of more than the equestrian census, a man asked for his *sententia* in the senate—who will force such a personage to say "vestimenta lavere" rather than "lavare"? No one, of course, but we who have dedicated our lives to pleasing the ears of learned men, we must pursue such trifles with the greatest of care. Surely the implication is here, again, that the civilized audience will despise an unskilled orator, however eminent he may be.[79] But Fronto had nothing to fear, for Marcus was a willing pupil. In a later epistle his teacher remarks with satisfaction that whenever Marcus has spoken in the senate or the assembly he has never used a far-fetched word or an obscure or jarring image, for he has learned that the eloquence of a Caesar should be like a trumpet, not like the flute, in which there is less noise and more difficulty.[80]

The important point is that Marcus Caesar *was* a willing pupil. As a boy he had been embarrassed by flattering "lies" told about him by Fronto "especially in the senate,"[81] and this genuine solicitude appears in an early letter to Fronto: "But as to my despondency, nevertheless, I am still nervous in mind and a little depressed, lest I shall have said something in the senate today such that I should not deserve to have you as my master."[82] This particular anxiety is recalled by Fronto to Marcus years later, in the autumn of 161.[83] Did he remember the speech he had delivered in the senate when little more than a boy, in which he had used the image of a little leather bottle (*utriculus*)? "You were much concerned lest you had employed an image little suited to the dignity of the place and of a senator." Now that he is emperor, Marcus' anxiety is renewed, and Fronto's letter is intended to soothe his more general fears that he is losing his command of eloquence. He points out to the emperor the pleasure and good will with which the senate and the people hear him speak. What other prince ever used figures of speech? Here Fronto slips back into his old role of master with a lively critique of a recent imperial *oratio* to the senate on the plight of Cyzicus after an earthquake, praising in one place the emperor's audacity in introducing the speech with a *paraleipsis*, questioning in another the precision of his use of the word *obsecro*.[84] For Fronto, the exercise was sufficient proof of Marcus' concern. There was much to praise in the speech, but for Fronto its great virtue lay in the simple but forceful combination of brevity and force, one reminiscent of the earthquake itself in its effect on its senatorial audience. Marcus had learned his lessons well.

In his *Meditations*, Marcus touches only once upon the senate, but there he is concerned precisely with speaking in the house, and the expression strikingly recalls Fronto: "Speak both in the senate and to every man with propriety and without affectation. Use words that ring true."[85] His numerous surviving verbal and written communications are of a piece, conscientious, painstakingly thorough, obsessed with clarity, intensely earnest.[86] When Avidius Cassius rebelled, it was reported that Marcus would have preferred a peaceful solution to civil war; one of the means he is alleged to have proposed was a debate for the empire in the senate.[87] Marcus Aurelius, oratory, and the senate: his old master would have been delighted by a story which combined his loves so well.

VII

THE FRIEND OF CAESAR

THE WORD *aula* appears nowhere in Fronto's correspondence, and he protests more than once that he was exceptionally remiss in the *officia* between himself and his prince, yet Fronto was unmistakably a courtier.[1] Most of his letters are addressed to the emperors, or to members of their family, or to senators and knights high in their service, but *amicitia* is subordinated to *amor* throughout, affectionate intimacy tending to obscure the formal connections between a subject and his emperor. Nevertheless, even the enlightened rule of the Antonines could not escape the trappings of a monarchy. Definition of the court is by proximity to the ruler, including his relatives, his personal friends, his advisers, and the officers high and low of his household; and ceremony dominates its conduct. More exciting, beneath the placid surface lie the standard operations of influence and intrigue.[2] And all of these forms and functions are reflected to a remarkable extent in Fronto's deceptively sedate correspondence.

Fronto's career as a courtier began, appropriately, at the court of the learned Hadrian; indeed, the emperor's notorious literary preferences may have stimulated the archaic interests of an educated and ambitious young man eager for his quaestorship.[3] The relations between the two men are best captured in a letter to Marcus Caesar concerning Fronto's oration of thanks for his consulship, delivered almost exactly five years after Hadrian's death. He claims that this speech was composed with an exceptional care born of his great personal love for Pius, and in it a natural comparison with his earlier contacts with Hadrian arises: "I often praised your grandfather, the deified Hadrian, in the senate, with a steady and a ready zeal . . . Yet if your filial feeling towards him will allow me to say so, I wished to appease and propitiate Hadrian, as I might Mars Gradivus or Father Dis, rather than loved him. Why? Because love requires some confidence [*fiducia*] and intimacy [*familiaritate*]. Since, in my case, confidence was lacking, therefore I dared not love one whom I so greatly revered."[4] This is a remarkable confession. Despite a previous avowal of frankness, Fronto is not being perfectly open here, and for good reasons: the events of 136/138 were still in men's minds; he owed his consulship to the grace of Hadrian's pious son; and Hadrian's grandson Marcus was still his pupil. Yet even with these restraints the portrayal of the deified Hadrian as a god of war and the underworld is ominous. The structure of the final sentence should be observed with care. To love, one needs *fiducia* and *familiaritas*; because there was no *fiducia* in their relationship, Fronto did not dare to love. It should follow from this that there was indeed *familiaritas* between Hadrian and Fronto, that he was in fact already *amicus Caesaris*. He fits well, then, into that picture drawn by Hadrian's biographer of *familiares* able to place no trust in an emperor who would eventually turn upon them.[5] Hadrian was especially notorious for humiliating his learned friends by deriding their erudition while showering them with honors.[6] Thus the friend honored above all by the emperor was Favorinus, the Gallic sophist and also a friend of Fronto, yet Favorinus was bullied, persecuted, and perhaps hounded into exile.[7] And several other learned *familiares* felt sooner or later the wrath of the *doctus princeps*.[8] Fronto was a rising star in Latin letters, and his own words betray familiarity with the emperor, but no love. Did he too fall from favor?

An astonishing note of bitterness pervades Fronto's attitude to Hadrian, indeed, nowhere does the orator refer to the prince without disparagement. At their best, his remarks are confined to an ambiguous reference to Hadrian's enthrallment by music and rich banquets, or a strong sneer at his pretensions to antique eloquence.[9] At their worst, they border on the vicious. Under Hadrian's rule countless soldiers had been slain by Jews and Britons, and Trajan's great conquests had been abandoned to the empire's enemies while the emperor toured his realm building monuments and exercising the army. It was Hadrian's poor leadership that was to blame for the decline after Trajan: energy better directed toward maintaining discipline was dissipated in the oppression of his friends and addresses to the troops.[10] Hadrian's biographer duly notes that the emperor turned in time against all of his friends, often with violence.[11] And this grim reminiscence surfaces again in Fronto, in an otherwise unmotivated allusion to the many monuments of Hadrian's travels which are scattered about Europe and Asia, "as well tombs built of stone as many others."[12] Behind these dark memories and the startlingly open contempt—never afterward did the army see such a general—there should lie a real hatred shared with the senatorial order, the hatred expressed in the senate's unanimous attempt to annul the acts of Hadrian and to deny him deification in the first days of the subsequent reign.[13]

Two passages in Fronto's correspondence require particular attention. One occurs in a note to Pius congratulating the emperor on the anniversary of his *dies imperii*, "a day which I count as the birthday of my own health, reputation, and safety."[14] The implication is unstated, but surely to be considered, that before Pius' accession Fronto felt that he had neither health, nor *dignitas*, nor safety. The inclusion of safety is a surprise, yet the idea of danger recurs in a solemn declaration made at the end of his days: "my whole life through there has not been on my side a single act of avarice or of treachery, but on the contrary many of generosity, many of friendship, many of good faith, many of loyalty, undertaken, too, often at the risk of my life."[15] This is a dramatic note in the placid age of the Antonines. Mortal danger can have been encountered by a peaceful scholar and advocate only in the sordid and dangerous last years of Hadrian, years of complicated and bloody dynastic maneuverings and of alienation and death among the intimates of a suspicious prince.[16] There is no reason to doubt Fronto's veracity here, for in letters to the son and grandson of Hadrian memories of the danger would tend rather to be muted than played upon and embroidered, and the outpouring of grief in which one of these memories is discovered ("On the Death of His Grandson") rings with sincerity.[17] The *periculum capitis* incurred more than once was evidently the result of loyalty to friends, implying thus an indirect rather than a direct involvement.[18] The obvious employment for a loyal friend who was also the pre-eminent advocate is defense in a court of law, and there was at least one great capital case in this period, the trial of the heir presumptive on a charge of treason.[19]

It is clear that Fronto considered himself to be in personal danger at some stage in his life, and bitterness toward Hadrian is marked in a man who was a prominent figure in the literary world during the reign of a jealous scholar prince, and the leading advocate under a tyrant. Some discord seems to be indicated, perhaps a chill in relations rather than outright enmity. It was Fronto's claim that his *dignitas* had suffered before the accession of Antoninus Pius; there may indeed be a hiatus in his senatorial career.

The turning point in his life at court was his appointment as tutor to Marcus Aurelius, which probably came soon after the accession of Pius.[20] He affected to regard 10 July 138 as the birthday of his new life, and the new emperor was one who genuinely respected all true scholars and artists, and one who could be generous in his praise of Fronto's particular genius.[21] Accordingly, in explicit contrast to Hadrian, "Antoninus I love, I cherish like the light, like day, like breath, and feel that I am loved by him."[22]

However cordial the personal relationship between ruler and subject, the court demanded a certain degree of ceremony between them. Indicative is the important daily ritual of the *salutatio*.[23] In a revealing passage Fronto protests that he is no courtier; he had commanded no armies and ruled no provinces, nor had he risked his life for Marcus or his father: "Not even those everyday duties about your person does he discharge more than others; nay, he is an infrequent visitor enough. For neither does he haunt your house at daybreak, nor pay his respects daily, nor attend you everywhere, nor keep you always in sight.[24] The passage is misleading, for whatever his attitude may have been, his correspondence reveals Fronto's close and continuing involvement in the affairs of the court. Thus he is to be discovered among the *turba salutantium* seeing Pius and Marcus off into the country, or in literary conversation with senators and grammarians while waiting in the antechambers of the palace.[25] And that his attendance upon the monarchs was assiduous, perhaps even daily, is betrayed by the briefest of notes to Marcus Caesar: "I am laid up with pain in the sole of my foot. That is why I have not paid you my respects [*non salutavi*] these past days. Farewell best of lords. Greet my lady."[26]

Moreover, a formal group of apologies, which are individually of little significance, together reveal a social duty. One of these prays to the gods for a happy and prosperous New Year for all of the imperial family, Fronto's fears for his health in the crush of well-wishers preventing a personal appearance. Marcus returns his greetings and rejoices in his caution, for the *salutatio* will be repeated more quietly in two days, and Cratia has already adequately fulfilled her husband's *officium*.[27] In a second note, Marcus' daughters are wished a happy birthday and his family a long life; Fronto's crippled feet prevent him from being among the first to embrace the prince. In a third, the gods are called upon to grant Marcus himself a happy birthday; this time stomach problems forbid Fronto's attendance, and Marcus reassures him that he had immediately surmised some such illness to account for his teacher's absence.[28] And in a fourth exchange Fronto excuses himself from embracing Pius on his *dies imperii* because of severe back pain, but he assures the emperor that the proper vows have been discharged and renewed before his household gods. Pius' reply has an audible ring of formality, if not of the secretariat.[29] The essentially formal nature of these occasions is clear from the bloodless brevity of all of these missives, from the ritual undertaking of vows, and from the numbers of people involved. It is no accident that the correspondence between Pliny and Trajan should provide precise parallels for each occasion, for in the briefest of notes the legate in Pontus and Bithynia informs his emperor of prayers undertaken for his safety and prosperity at the New Year, on his *dies imperii*, and on his birthday, all of which Trajan acknowledges with equal concision.[30] These were great public occasions celebrated throughout the empire; at Rome the emperor would naturally hold a grand reception, which all of his friends were sure to attend.

Behind the protocol, the reality may be difficult to estimate. Caesar's friends were a large and amorphous crew, and obscure cronies could wield excessive influence, while the title of *amicus Caesaris* could be the merest formality accorded to rank or office.[31] Fortunately, Antoninus Pius' high regard for Fronto and the orator's influence with his emperor are confirmed in a single letter of great interest.[32] The first section of it is lost, but it apparently included a recapitulation of previous favors won by Fronto for others from the emperor. One sentiment survives, that the *modestia* of Fronto's friends had insured that he could make no unworthy request.[33] The remainder of the letter recalls that on two different occasions Fronto has requested and been granted procuratorships for his *contubernalis*, the knight Sex. Calpurnius Iulianus. These two *beneficia* he chooses to regard as four, for Pius has also twice been pleased to accept Iulianus' *excusatio* from his duties. Fronto has now been petitioning the emperor for two years on behalf of his old friend and fellow student Appian of Alexandria, who will (he feels sure) exhibit the same *modestia* as Iulianus had done. Appian's motive is neither sordid *ambitio* nor *procuratoris stipendii cupiditas*, but an honorable desire to embellish his *dignitas* in his old age. At the first time of asking, Pius had seemed to listen benignly; at the second, his reply had been favorable, but with the affable remark appended that if he granted

Appian's desire a crowd of advocates (and a certain Greek rival was named) would demand similar treatment. Appian, however, had a claim to special consideration, on Fronto's submission: "there is age, there is childlessness, which calls for consolation to relieve it." And Appian is simply more honest than his potential rival. Then, in the last surviving section, Fronto makes a show of magnanimity: his own simplicity, veracity, and (here the courtier) "the assurance of my love toward you" suggest to him that the fairest solution is to favor both Appian and his rival for Fronto's sake, but the condition is added that the rival should also petition for two years, following Fronto's example, and then, if he wishes, he may likewise obtain his *excusatio*. The rest of this perplexing letter has perished.

Despite its obscurities, this epistle is of primary importance for clarifying the workings of the imperial service. The acceptable, perhaps inevitable, operation of *suffragium* within the system is striking, and Fronto's *gratia* with Pius is shown to be extremely high.[34] Comparison with Pliny is yet again instructive, for his correspondence records numerous requests pressed upon the emperor, several of them patently unsuccessful and none so ambitious as to seek a procuratorship; but Pliny was not an intimate of the imperial family.[35]

However, it must be emphasized that this letter deals not with offices but with honors, insofar as Appian is concerned, an important distinction. The key word is *excusatio*: one might win the honor of an office without assuming its burdens. Thus *excusationes* from various offices are proudly displayed on several cursus inscriptions, and in terms of advancement dispensation from an office could be considered equivalent to having performed its duties.[36] Fronto attributes Iulianus' *excusationes* to his natural modesty, not to any calamity or change of heart, and he clearly considers their granting as equal in honor to the granting of office itself. Because Appian will show the same moderation, the implication is surely that he too will excuse himself from the honor; and, indeed, old age and childlessness are not potent recommendations for active procuratorial service, nor is a reminder that Fronto's clients have previously declined Pius' offers. If that is so, Appian's remarks in the preface to his history require closer examination: "I am Appian of Alexandria, one of the leading men of my homeland. I pleaded cases in Rome before the emperors until they judged me worthy to be their procurator."[37] The thought has been carefully phrased. Fronto's insistence on dignity in old age suggests that it was his friend's retirement from the courts which prompted the honor, and his repetition of *modestia* and *excusatio* suggests that Appian would decline the position: on both points the deceptive text of Appian offers no denial, for, whatever he might seem to imply, he says neither that it was his service in court which brought the honor nor that he actually held the office. It can be concluded without prejudice to the efficacy of Fronto's influence that Appian did not serve as procurator; indeed, the honor without the office may have been a sign of special favor.[38]

One other episode in the relations of Fronto with the emperor Pius is preserved that both sharply defines the relationship and further illustrates the operations of influence on the prince and intrigue around him. Fronto's friend Censorius Niger has died, leaving Fronto heir to five-twelfths of his estate in a will which violently and inexcusably vilifies the praetorian prefect M. Gavius Maximus. Fronto's embarrassingly delicate position is discussed in letters addressed to three interested parties. The note to Maximus himself has been in part destroyed, but enough survives to show how Fronto tackled his problem.[39] First he appeals to the past: Censorius Niger had been Maximus' friend before enmity had arisen between them, and Fronto swears that he had often seen Niger weeping over the discord. The discord itself had so clouded the man's mind with grief and anger that he was not responsible for his intemperate words. A second and unrelated consideration is also introduced: that Fronto's own *amicitia* with Gavius Maximus, having begun without any reference to Censorius Niger, should continue independent of any dissension between the two knights. The apologia as we have it is thus twofold, one part excusing Niger's excesses, the other justifying Fronto's acceptance of the inheritance. Such elaboration was necessary, for the affair had wider implications. Grave offense had been taken by Gavius Maximus, "clarissimus et nobis observandus vir," who as praetorian prefect is characterized by Pius' biographer as *vir severissimus*. Worse, for Fronto, the emperor placed extraordinary confidence in this man, retaining him at his side for almost twenty years.[40] The quarrel takes on even darker shades: a letter of explanation to the emperor himself is necessary, and (surprisingly) Fronto must pledge his continuing loyalty to the prefect lest Maximus give ear to malign men and enemies of Fronto.[41]

The letter to Pius offers further information on the affair. Although he can neither condone nor take responsibility for Niger's transgressions, Fronto feels that he must intercede for his late friend. Against this single misdeed should be set the man's character, *frugi, fortis,* and *innocens,* his notable achievements in war and peace, his friendship with the leaders of the senatorial and equestrian orders, and the marks of honor and authority which he had won from Pius himself. Fronto then digresses to defend his own position: "Possibly some might say that I ought to have given up my friendship with him when I realized that he was not held by you in the same favour as before."[42] It thus emerges that some *frigus* between the emperor and his procurator had clouded Niger's final years. It is difficult not to see the potent influence of Gavius Maximus behind the rupture, and this influence is probably the target of Niger's testamentary outburst.[43] If that is the case, some parts of the abusive will may have verged upon *maiestas,* and by accepting the inheritance Fronto might have put his own *amicitia* with the prince into jeopardy, to the joy of the elusive "maligni homines." At the least, the passage illuminates a convention: when the prince abandons a friendship, the loyal courtier should do likewise, and it appears that Fronto is anticipating criticism when he stoutly maintains that one who has lost Caesar's regard is to be pitied rather than hated. After these remarks, lacunae in the manuscript defeat any logical reconstruction, but it is noteworthy that the final sentiments twice connect the gods with the solemnity of friendship.[44]

The innocuous third item of the group is the most important, and it constitutes an adroit piece of maneuvering. The situation is briefly explained. Then, innocently, Fronto tells the Caesar Marcus, "I was anxious that you should know of this, as of all that concerns me."[45] Clearly this note was intended to arouse his interest in Fronto's plight and his intercession with the emperor. By the time of this affair Marcus was a power in his own right, consul twice and invested with tribunician power and proconsular imperium, immersed in the business of state, trying cases at law, and holding his own *salutatio*. His *obsequia* toward his father were legendary, and, in return, "such sway did he have over Pius that never did he easily promote anyone without consulting his son."[46] Marcus' role as intercessor with his father on Fronto's behalf is neatly revealed in the orator's brief note for his friend Saenius Pompeianus, the African tax-farmer: "I commend him to you that, when his accounts are scrutinized by our lord your father, you may be induced both by my recommendation and your own constant practice to extend to him that characteristic kindness, which you habitually show to all."[47] The conclusion is obvious, that much of Fronto's influence at court derived from his friendship with the powerful heir apparent, rather than from any real intimacy with Pius, and indeed it is to Marcus Caesar that he addresses his excuses from *salutatio* and his protestations that he is no courtier, and it is through Marcus that the emperor receives information, best wishes, and excuses.[48] The book of letters to Antoninus Pius contains only two brief items from Pius and five from Fronto, not figures indicative of intimate familiarity. The conclusion of the Censorius Niger affair is lost, but that relations among the living were somehow patched up cannot be doubted, and that Marcus was the mediator seems most probable. The episodes elicit a pair of conclusions which should be pursued further, that the crown prince played an important role in his father's court, and that Fronto had enemies willing to draw him into intrigues.

The clearest illustration of Marcus' position lies in another brief letter of recommendation addressed to him, a letter similar to that concerning Appian's procuratorship in revealing the workings of the imperial service. It differs in dealing not with *amicitia* but with patronage in minor bureaucratic appointments: "This Aridelus, who is taking my letter to you, has attended to all of my wants since he was a boy, from a passion for partridges to important duties.[49] He is a freedman of yours; he has watched over your affairs with diligence,[50] for he is honest, temperate, brisk and industrious. He is now a candidate for a procuratorship *ex forma suo loco ac iusto tempore*. Assist him, my lord, with your interest, as far as may be. If you do not recognize his person, when you come to the name Aridelus, remember that Aridelus has been recommended to you by me."[51] The key words here are "ex forma suo loco ac iusto tempore." They have been taken to mean "according to the text of the regulation, in conformity with his rank and seniority," thus providing the only explicit ancient testimony to the rules of appointment and promotion which are deemed to be at work behind the procuratorial hierarchy.[52] Unfortunately, the text is much too unsound to bear such a weight.[53] And the words themselves can be understood simply to say that Aridelus is now petitioning for a procuratorship "in the proper manner, on his own behalf, and at the proper time." On that reading, the letter collapses as a demonstration of unattested "rules" of promotion, and more important, it takes its proper place as a clear illustration of the simple etiquette of seeking patronage.

Marcus Caesar had both influence with his father and patronage of his own to dispense, and as a philosopher in training he well realized the perils of his position. As early as 138, when his household asked him why he seemed so distressed at his adoption by the emperor, he had replied by recounting the evils inherent in empire.[54] One of these evils appears in a letter to Fronto of the year 143. The first surviving paragraph makes the point that in all his efforts at composition his only model is Fronto: "I do right in thinking of one man only when I take my pen in hand."[55] The problem is that as a prince Marcus is surrounded by false flatterers who might lead him astray, and to express this fear the best of Fronto's archaic authors are called to witness. Ennius, says Marcus, talks of counselors whose foolish advice is meant only to please, while Plautus warns against treacherous courtiers who surround the king saying one thing but thinking another. And even more aptly, Marcus writes: "These drawbacks used formerly to be confined to kings, but now, indeed, even the sons of kings have more than enough of men who, as Naevius says, flatter with their tongues and nod assent and carry out their every wish."[56] The context is literary, but experience is obvious.

The perils surrounding the *regis filius* naturally concern his tutor. In one extraordinary discourse addressed to Marcus, Fronto cleverly expounds the allegory of the Orpheus myth in terms of a prince and his *amici*, the prince's talent to charm lying not in music but in his eloquence.[57] In the lost portions of the letter other matters have been considered, leading to a retelling of the myth, which concluded (it would appear) with the sheep and the dove united in the company of Orpheus with the eagle and the wolf. To those who interpret the fable aright, Orpheus was a man of outstanding *ingenium* and *eloquentia*, virtues which Fronto had often before noticed in Marcus.[58] Of course, the combination attracted many admirers. These friends and followers, although representing many nations and different customs, he brought to live together in peace, the mild and the fierce, the gentle and the violent, the meek and the proud, the timid and the cruel; and he taught them to learn his own virtues and to lose their faults of *inpudentia*, *contumelia*, and *malivolentia*. Marcus, the modern Orpheus, was better fitted than any man to bring together his *amici* and *sectatores* in mutual love, for Nature had provided him with all of the virtues, leaving education little to add—even before assuming the toga of manhood he had been the good man skilled in speaking—and the greatest of these virtues was that of joining his friends together in concord, a task more difficult even than soothing the savage beast. Here the allegory is quite abandoned. The deadly enemy is envy among Marcus' friends, the envy caused by favor shown to one of their number. If Marcus can keep it from his *cohors* of friends, they will remain harmonious and well disposed, but if it spreads, the trouble in suppressing it will be enormous.

Fronto's remarks, it may be presumed, reflect personal observation of court intrigue, but the general sentiment arises from a particular incident: "I love Iulianus—for this discussion originated with him—I love all who are fond of you." Marcus' reply to this survives to cast some light.[59] Fronto had visited this Iulianus at his sickbed for Marcus' sake, sending to the prince afterward a long account of their conversation, together with the "verba suavissima, consilia saluberrima" of the Orpheus tale. In Marcus' usual protestation of affection and gratitude for this gesture may be detected a hint of crisis averted. Fronto's letter had reassured him "how great is the confidence you have in my friendship." Subsequently, however, Marcus writes, "And that is why I am often full of wrath and indignation against you when away and guiltless, because you make it impossible for me to love you as I wish, that is, for my soul to follow your love up to its supreme height."[60] Despite the polite verbiage, Marcus' words imply that for once his friendship with Fronto has been strained, and the context naturally suggests that dissension among his friends was the cause. Fronto is advised to press on with his present plan concerning Herodes, for Herodes loves him and Marcus is working "in that quarter" (*istic*). Evidently, advances are being made on both sides toward a rapprochement between the two orators with the Caesar Marcus as mediator, the Orpheus for his friends.

The discord alluded to must arise from the notorious trial which displayed the two famed orators as opposing advocates. Marcus had written to Fronto before that clash, urging him to exercise moderation in his attack on his rival, for the passions aroused by the trial could not fail to damage the prince's circle of friends. Again nameless men of ill-will toward Fronto appear, men who will observe his indignation *maligne* and rejoice to see him acting "unlike himself," but the Caesar's real concern was the embarrassment of a conflict between two worthy friends, "for I love both of you, each one for his merits, and I do not forget that he was brought up in the house of my grandfather, P. Calvisius, and I educated under you."[61] Fronto in his turn was perplexed that Marcus should extend his *tutela* to such flagrant misdeeds as Herodes stood accused of, and he asks his counsel as to how he should proceed, promising to let Herodes off lightly if that is indeed what Marcus wishes. Despite the seriousness of the charges (which he cannot help reiterating), he reassures the prince that the courtroom battle need not produce lasting discord.[62] His letter concludes on a delicate note: "Farewell, Caesar, and love me, as you do, to the utmost. I, indeed, dote on the very characters of your writing: wherefore, whenever you write to me, I would have you write with your own hand."[63] That Marcus had not written in his own hand is taken as a sign of regal displeasure, and Fronto's fears on that score are confirmed by a hastily penned postscript insisting that the prince realize that others will be acting against Herodes as well, and perhaps with greater violence.[64] Marcus' reply to this reassures Fronto of his love, courteously thanking him for the opportunity to advise his master: the orator is to adhere to the facts of the case he defends, but to refrain from any attack on Herodes.[65] Fronto capitulates completely. He will act in this and in every case as Marcus wishes, and should he ever err in the future the prince must not hesitate to correct him. Thus subdued, he outlines his proposed conduct of the case, to the point even of advising Herodes how to react.[66] The Orpheus fable is only too aptly applied to an episode which displayed warring friends forced together in the yoke of the prince's *amicitia*.

The moral is not unexpected, that the courtier and his concern for the *gratia* of his prince must take precedence over the advocate and his concern, if not for justice, at least for presenting the strongest possible case for his client. Years later Fronto can calmly claim Herodes as his close friend despite the continued circulation of his speech against him.[67] The code of conduct is neatly illuminated in another letter of uncertain date. In a postscript Marcus requests that Fronto write a few appropriate words of condolence to Herodes Atticus, just bereaved of his newborn son.[68] The *consolatio* duly appeared, a standard production with one variant. Solace is to be found by Herodes in the continued preservation of Marcus Caesar, in whom all reliance is placed, who can cure all ills—and Fronto will not deny that he is Herodes' rival for Marcus' love.

Tension among the prince and his friends is a topic of concern even under the rule of a philosopher. The *Meditations* of Marcus Aurelius dwell upon the ephemeral passions of court life past and present, the first book especially revealing an extraordinary concern for his conduct toward those around him.[69] The greatest influence upon Marcus was undoubtedly the noble Q. Iunius Rusticus (cos. 133), *stoicae disciplinae peritissimus* and grandson of a Stoic philosopher and consul who had been executed by Domitian.[70] In his private thoughts the emperor thanks the gods for allowing him to know this man, and Marcus' biographer calls him the disciple of Rusticus, following his teachings before all others.[71] As a philosopher and as a man skilled in the arts of peace and war, Rusticus was held to be the prince's mentor in every matter, private and public. Consequently, the honor accorded him was unusual, for he received Marcus' embrace even before the praetorian prefects, he was honored with a second consulship and the prefecture of the city, and he was glorified posthumously with several statues.[72] This man provides a sharp contrast to Fronto. The greater marks of honor were accorded to him, not to Fronto, and it is clear that the orator was not an intimate of the emperor's counsels. The difference is not one of mere personalities. Marcus loved Fronto as a kind and honest man, while his relationship with the austere Rusticus was punctuated by bouts of anger.[73] The difference was rather a function of the prince's marked preference for philosophy over rhetoric. Therefore, friction between the philosopher and the orator might seem inevitable on more than one count. Marcus makes it clear that Rusticus' teaching included an overt attack upon Fronto's domain, for the philosopher forbade him several pleasures, "not to run off into zeal for sophistic, or to write on speculative themes, or to discourse on edifying texts, or to exhibit in fanciful colours the ascetic or the philanthropist. To avoid rhetoric, poetry and urbanity, . . . to write letters in a simple style."[74] In reply, Fronto confined himself to an attack on the discipline of philosophy. Only once is Rusticus mentioned in the letters, but the sketch verges on caricature. When Marcus was Caesar, Fronto had often asserted that even Victorinus could not aspire to the beauty of Marcus' talent as an orator: "Then that friend of mine, Roman Rusticus, who would gladly surrender and sacrifice his life for your little finger, yet on the question of your natural ability gave way against his will and with a frown."[75]

In effect, the reign of a scholar emperor promotes a confusion between the court and the world of learning, as men of letters are found in positions of highest influence, and the overlapping of professional rivalry and court intrigue is inevitable.[76] Dramatic feuds such as that between the consular brothers Quintilii and the ubiquitous Herodes Atticus break out indifferently in the theater, the law court, or the presence of the emperor.[77] Such clashes are absent from the pages of Fronto, but there are hints of coldness, if not of open dissensions. The notorious legal conflict with Herodes arose from quite unrelated matters, but Fronto could not resist calling his learned rival *graeculus* and *indoctus*. The philosopher Iunius Rusticus is mentioned only once, despite his intimacy with the Caesar, and then in no flattering light. The same treatment is accorded to Apollonius of Chalcedon, who was able to seek a favor from Fronto only at several removes and through their common pupil, Marcus; some contemporaries, including Pius himself, considered Apollonius to be arrogant and mercenary. Clearly, this Apollonius was coupled with Rusticus and Claudius Maximus (who is absent from the extant correspondence) as one of the three men for whose friendship Marcus thanked the gods. All three were noted Stoic philosophers. Their combined influence suggests one further source of tension at court, that between Fronto and his own pupil.

From an early age Marcus Aurelius was fascinated by philosophy, assuming the dress and conduct of a philosopher at the age of twelve; he was *frugi, verecundus, gravis, serius*. His personal principles could not avoid affecting his conduct as a prince. The *Historia Augusta* records public indignation at a general harshness in his relations with others, one which stemmed from philosophy, and an indifference to popular pleasures—at the circus he would read a book or listen to conversation or subscribe documents.[78] Popular resentment was shared at court, by Fronto himself: "I have occasionally inveighed against you behind your back in somewhat strong terms before a very few of my most intimate friends. Time was I did this, when you went about in public gatherings with too serious a face, as when you used to read books either in the theatre or at a banquet . . . on such occasions then, I would call you an austere and unreasonable, even at times, stung by anger, a disagreeable sort of person."[79] The vehemence of this past emotion is startling, heightened by its sudden and anomalous appearance in a correspondence overflowing with assertions of mutual love. Even the letter in which it appears is an elaborate demonstration of that love, for in this instance Fronto maintains that while he himself might complain about his pupil he would not suffer others to do so in his hearing, just as he would prefer to strike his own child than to see another strike her. Elsewhere Fronto the orator campaigns fiercely against the snares of philosophy set for an emperor, but here alone he attacks the daily conduct of the philosopher prince himself, conduct over which he apparently has no control.

The incidents of anger betrayed here tend to confirm the conclusion to be drawn from the sum of other stray items, from Fronto's ignorance of Marcus' high regard for Herodes Atticus, from Marcus' displeasure over the Herodes affair, from Fronto's protest that he was not an assiduous courtier, from his apparent omission from any imperial *consilium*, and most of all from the complete ineffectiveness of such adjurations to Marcus as the *De Feriis Alsiensibus*.[80] When the manuscript of the correspondence was discovered, some readers were repelled by the apparent trivia of its contents, and indeed no secrets of empire are revealed; the accidental brush with Gavius Maximus affords the only unsettling glimpse of naked power, while the patronage of such men as Saenius Pompeianus and of Aridelus is more indicative of the normal workings of a system than of any unbridled influence. Fronto's position at court must be strictly defined, the result of a warm mutual affection which guaranteed him access to the emperor and a benign interest in his affairs. Had his pupil been a devoted student of rhetoric rather than of philosophy, he might have been a power in the state.

The correspondence casts some needed light upon a shadowy but important figure at the court of Antoninus Pius, Domitia Lucilla, the mother of Marcus Caesar. Marcus was to remember her briefly but affectionately in his *Meditations*, primarily for her piety and her generosity, and for her abstention from evil thoughts, exotic food, and extravagance.[81] This philosopher's image of a somewhat puritanical lady may be contrasted with the equally conventional account of her character which Fronto addressed to Lucilla herself, in one of the two letters written to her in Greek. He suggests, after the event, that she should have invited to her birthday feast several kinds of women, those who love their husbands and children and are chaste, those who are truthful and sincere, and those who are kind-hearted, accessible, affable, and modest, for all of these virtues are to be found united in her.[82] The other epistle to her is equally charming, an apology for the delay in producing his speech of thanks for the consulship, wherein he playfully introduces a horde of incongruous similes. Carefully he lets drop one useful item, that the encomium of Pius would mention her, and he concludes with an implied compliment by asking her indulgence for any words he has used which are obsolete, barbarous, or otherwise non-Attic.

Fronto's familiarity with Lucilla is a constant element in the correspondence, the phrase "domina mea te salutat" being a common conclusion to Marcus' letters, matched by Fronto's "dominam saluta"; and his Cratia was much in Lucilla's thoughts.[83] The relationship with Fronto's wife is noted elsewhere, when she visits Lucilla and celebrates her birthday with her. Then she is Lucilla's *clienta* who needs no food but will live contentedly on her mistress' kisses.[84] The word *clienta* is arresting. With Fronto's flattery in other letters, it suggests that Lucilla's affection for Fronto and his wife ought not to be ignored, despite the elaborate expression conventional to the age. There are signs that Lucilla was a personage of some importance. She certainly had some influence at court, either her own or through her son; for her protégé, the future emperor Didius Iulianus, won the vigintivirate through her suffrage. And she attracted the envy of other friends of Caesar, for it is recorded that when Pius and his caustic friend M. Valerius Homullus (cos. 152) chanced upon her worshiping at a shrine of Apollo, Homullus whispered, "That woman is now praying that you may die and her son may rule."[85] Fronto's birthday letter to her reveals something of her situation. As consul he is unable to attend the celebration, but he imagines himself as the *eisagogeus* at her door, allowing in only those worthy to attend the festival. Foremost among those whom he would exclude are false flatterers who arrive with good will on their lips and insincerity in their hearts; deceit is their goddess, and when they smile they hide their mouths to conceal their malice and their treachery.[86] The rest of his observations are lost, but these should be sufficient to suggest that Lucilla was worth courting and deceiving. *Amicitiae muliebres* were as much a problem at the court of the Antonines as at any other, and a long record can be compiled of the influence wielded by the wives, mothers, and mistresses of the Caesars; Valerius Homullus, for one, could not fail to recall the analogous situation which had obtained exactly a century before.[87]

At the court of Antoninus Pius it is even easier to overlook the emperor's other son, Lucius Ceionius Commodus, the visible monument to Hadrian's thwarted dynastic schemes.[88] Adopted and reared by Pius, he received no mark of favor before his successive quaestorship (153) and consulship (154), and no title beyond that of *Augusti filius*; indeed, his inferiority to Marcus was emphasized by the imperial progresses, wherein Marcus rode with Pius, Lucius with the attendant praetorian prefect.[89] His education was not neglected, and it is no surprise that he shared several teachers with Marcus, the philosophers Sextus and Apollonius, the orators Caninius Celer, Herodes Atticus, and M. Cornelius Fronto.[90] No letters between Fronto and his pupil survive from this early period, but such items must have existed, just how many is uncertain; perhaps as much as one or two books have perished.[91] Some estimate of the relationship may be formed from the five books to Marcus Caesar covering the period from 139 to 161, for his brother is mentioned only once and then as an afterthought. On an occasion which may concern Lucius' consulship, Fronto praises a speech of Pius which matched in nobility his most noble deed; "but your brother's speech also delighted me, for it was polished and politic at the same time."[92] Thus the correspndence of the good courtier faithfully reflects Lucius' historical position, and the prince is kept offstage until Pius' action brings him suddenly into the limelight.[93]

The correspondence between Fronto and the emperor Lucius Verus is not long, nine items from Fronto and six from Lucius, but the mercurial relations between the two men invest it with a drama absent from the ultimately bland affection of the exchanges with Marcus. Here protestations of love invariably accompany recriminations or explanations, and the tone is set very early, in the first exchange of letters in 161, after the death of Pius.[94] After an absence of four months Fronto had returned to Rome. He appeared at the palace to pay his respects to the new emperors just moments after Lucius had left. Why, complained Lucius, had Fronto not sent word in advance, and why had not Fronto or Marcus summoned him to return? If Fronto sent for him today he would come running; it was the hardest duty of his new station that he could not come every day.[95] Fronto's reply to this complaint is exemplary. Of course he was not at fault in the events of yesterday, as he would presently explain, but if he had been he would not reproach himself even now. A reception with honor could not afford him joy equal to that derived from Lucius' concern over his absence, for while every senator was received by the emperor with honor, few were inquired after so diligently. Anger and regret are the signs of a prince's love, for if he did not love Fronto he would neither miss him nor be angry with him. From this clever misconstruction the accomplished courtier launches into a (now fragmentary) discussion of one of his cherished themes, the apportionment of the emperors' love among the crowds of retainers who surround them.

In the second half of the epistle comes the defense. On his return to the city, Fronto had thought it best not to rush immediately to the grieving emperors, but to inquire of their freedman Charilas if it were convenient for him to visit the palace at that time; and he goes so far as to quote from his letter in Greek to that official, who appears to have been an imperial *cubicularius*.[96] The rest of the explanation is lost, but an excess of tact is the obvious excuse, a plea that he did not wish to disturb the emperors—a plea which could be attested by the letter to Charilas. Most interesting is the emperor's friend having recourse to an intermediary at court, and the senator's appeal for the advice of a freedman "as a man of prudence and a friend." The power of such imperial freedmen is not a phenomenon confined to the reigns of "bad" emperors.[97] Thus a bald statement in the biography of Marcus has it that "great power indeed was held under Marcus and Verus by [the freedmen] Geminas and Agaclytus." The life of Verus adds, truthfully or not, that this Agaclytus was married by Lucius himself to the widow of Marcus' cousin, against Marcus' wishes, and includes the names of others who influenced Lucius, all but one of whom Marcus dismissed after his brother's death.[98] Fronto's letter is a useful reminder of the importance of these unobtrusive figures, and his respectful address to one of them is remarkable, again nicely defining the degree of his intimacy with the palace.

The tension between Lucius and his *magister carissimus* reappears in a subsequent letter dispatched by Lucius from the East.[99] The pressure of his military duties and the daily change of events have delayed his sending an account of them, but faith in Fronto's love has prevented any worries on that score. Others would have been angered by Lucius' neglect; Fronto (he is sure) will pardon it. And, in a clever borrowing from Fronto's own teachings, he points out that others demand the exchange of *officium* for *officium*, Fronto only love for love.[100] While the outcome of events was so uncertain, Lucius did not wish to try Fronto's love for him with his worries, nor could he dissemble them to his Fronto, the master of truth and simplicity.[101] He was sure that the ancient pact between them was sufficient to excuse his negligence. Then, to the reader's astonishment, the polite flow is sharply interrupted: "At all events, when in spite of repeated appeals from me you never wrote, I was sorry, by heaven, but remembering our compact, not angry."[102] And the apology continues even more humbly: "Peccavi, fateor." Fronto's humanity is appealed to at some length until the letter as we have it breaks off. That this unexplained lapse in relations between the two was resolved is evident from the subsequent correspondence. To attribute the meanest of motives to Lucius, we might surmise that the first victories in the East, which are the occasion of this letter, stimulated his reconciliation with the man best suited to be their chronicler, and indeed that the lost portion of this letter first suggested the project which occupied Fronto's declining years.

The reason for the breach is not beyond conjecture. The Historia Augusta paints a lurid picture of Lucius' riotous conduct in the East and on his way there. Some of the details are pure invention, but others have a plausible ring, tales of reckless gluttony, of dallying with musicians and actors while others led his armies; and some confirmation is available in the unusual pamphlets dedicated by Lucian of Samosata to the flattery of the emperor's concubine, the learned and beautiful Panthea of Smyrna. Lucian was particularly impressed by her glittering entourage, which included not merely maids and eunuchs but a number of soldiers as well.[103] Neither Marcus Aurelius nor Lucius' generals can have cared for such a court, and it seems that Marcus dispatched a high-ranking agent of his own to keep an eye on his brother.[104] The standard view of Lucius as a careless and luxurious prince can be discovered even in the discreet pages of Fronto's correspondence, and the source of the tension between them may lie in these deficiencies of the prince's character, a tension compounded by rumor when they were apart. In the so-called *Principia Historiae* Fronto notes one of the common charges against Lucius, that he summoned actors from Rome into Syria even under the cloud of war, and Lucius' biographer adds the corollary that, when the war was over, the emperor brought home from Syria such a troop of entertainers "that he seemed to have ended not the Parthian but the Thespian War."[105] Fronto, the emperor's apologist, makes an imperial virtue of his pupil's taste for actors, with Trajan as the example: "His actions seem to be based on the loftiest principles of political wisdom, that the emperor did not neglect even actors and the other performers of the stage, the circus, or the amphitheatre, knowing as he did that the Roman people are held fast by two things above all, the corn-dole and the shows."[106] Even in the brief correspondence Lucius' actors turn up, as he relates to Fronto a dispute with another courtier in which Lucius maintained that Pylades' very similarity to his instructor Apolaustus (a favorite mentioned by the biographer) is proof of his superiority over Apolaustus in acting.[107] This he will prove "in the presence of all, and with you too, if you are present, as a witness," but this is said in jest, *cum ioco*: perhaps his panegyrist would not wish to witness the emperor's trifling recreations in person. Another vice worked up by the biographer was Lucius' gourmandising, the most scandalous incident being the serious illness induced by gluttony that delayed his departure for the Syrian front.[108] The episode might be dismissed as fiction were there not preserved a letter from Fronto expressing his joy at Lucius' recovery after a three-day fast and some bloodletting, and pleading for temperance and moderation and for the continuation of the present enforced abstinence.[109]

For his part, the prince of pleasure can have had little time for the advice of an elderly valetudinarian. Freedmen and actors were his chief friends. Dissension among his courtiers, Fronto's favored theme, is almost forced upon him. The most curious example concerns, appropriately enough, a banquet. The episode is preserved in a letter so lacunose that neither writer nor recipient is named, but Fronto and Lucius are highly probable, and a reasonable reconstruction can be offered to reveal Fronto struggling to show deference to his prince while stoutly protesting against the conduct of one of the prince's friends.[110] How much has perished is unclear. The first fragment indicates that someone had inquired of Fronto by letter or by intermediary if he could see him. Fronto assented. The unknown then used Fronto's friend Tranquillus as his go-between, just as he had used him at the banquet. This relation of the circumstances is then interrupted by an astonishingly blunt comment directed to Lucius: "It makes little difference to me, who of the friends you hold dear has an affection for me, except that I take prior account of him who is less disdainful of my friends."[111] A line is lost after this. Then comes the remark that "he also saw him at once," referring probably to the unknown offender and Tranquillus, respectively. "Tranquillus found me, when he was coldly received, still forbidding but less . . ."[112] Then, after another gap, the letter concludes with praise of Tranquillus' diligence; he would never have offered his services in this affair "did he not know how much you love me." Despite the apparent confusion a clear sequence can be evoked from these fragments. At a banquet one of Lucius' friends had somehow insulted an unknown friend of Fronto in his hearing, and at the same dinner the offender had asked Tranquillus to appease the indignant orator. Subsequently, after the banquet, the man had asked to see Fronto and had sent the same emissary, Tranquillus, who was again met with cold disapproval but perhaps with a greater willingness to accept an apology. The important element in this untoward incident is the involvement of the emperor, to whom (as in the Censorius Niger affair) Fronto felt obliged to send an account, perhaps because Lucius had already heard another version; indeed, the remark that he cares little which of the prince's friends loves him may suggest an estrangement between the old man and the court. The motive for Tranquillus' role should be emphasized; he interceded not as a mediator in a private quarrel but as a reconciler of two friends of Caesar. It appears that Lucius demanded the same harmony within his circle that Fronto had preached to his brother. The identical sentiment is discovered yet again in a letter accompanying a parcel of speeches sent by the orator to his pupil in the East. In one of those speeches, the *Pro Demostrato*, a certain Asclepiodotus had been attacked. When Fronto learned that this man was now a favorite of Lucius, he attempted to suppress the offending oration, but it had already circulated too widely. What more could Lucius desire? "Asclepiodotus, since he has earned your approbation, should also become to me a very dear friend, just as by heaven Herodes and I are now on the best of terms, in spite of the speech being published."[113] Whatever the personal strains involved, the friends of Caesar were bound to submerge their differences in their love for him.

Frigus and reconciliation are likewise the subjects of another letter, which also exposes some of the maneuvering involved. The beginning is lost, but even the first partly preserved line offers an opinion familiar to the courtier, that when one has been granted an honor that honor is coveted by all others.[114] Fronto is now out of favor at court, but he and Lucius are covertly scheming to reinstate him without giving offense to his rivals. Lucius had approved of Fronto's counsel in the matter, openly persevering in his refusal even to greet the orator for three or four days, but privately admitting him to his chamber, "so that you were able to give me a kiss without exciting anyone's jealousy." Fronto's gratitude is fulsomely expressed, concluding with the sentiment that the kiss is the greatest honor that he has received from Lucius. This leads him to recall what he chooses to regard as marks of the prince's special favor, his support of the elderly orator in rising and walking, his cheerful and gentle greeting, and his conversation gladly started and prolonged, concluded only with reluctance; for in these insignificant signs of the emperor's solicitude and good will one could discern that which men seek most, love and honor. These last remarks might be discounted as mere hyperbole had it not emerged from the previous section that such a small gesture as a kiss must be hidden, lest it arouse the envy of other courtiers; and, indeed, such marks of favor or disapproval may prove a sure guide to the realities of power. Fronto appears in a new guise, the intriguer outmaneuvering his rivals at court, and as unctuous a flatterer as any.

Despite their unstable relationship, or during its periods of stability, Fronto could command considerable influence with the prince. One of Lucius' notes to him ends with the offhand remark that Fronto's friend Valerius Antonius should submit his petition so that in his rescript the emperor may demonstrate his *gratia*.[115] And the warmest of Fronto's many letters of recommendation is addressed to Lucius on behalf of the penurious ex-praetor Gavius Clarus, that is, the L. Gavius Clarus known from inscriptions as the scion of a distinguished family of Attaleia, in Pamphilia.[116] Antoninus Pius had gladly paid the expenses of the man's praetorship, and Lucius Verus knew him well, Fronto is sure, for the orator has often spoken of him with the emperor. After rehearsing Clarus' qualities at length, Fronto recommends him to Lucius' trust and protection, but the precise nature of the aid required is lost with the rest of the letter. However, Clarus' mission suggests a general answer, for he is off to Syria to secure certain legacies left to him in the will of a dear friend; Lucius Verus the emperor and friend of Fronto had his headquarters in Antioch.

The Parthian War cemented Fronto's *amicitia* with Lucius, for the emperor's victories required the encomium which the orator was only too willing to provide. One brisk letter reveals Lucius gathering materials for the great work, the dispatches of his generals, his own orders, commentaries from the chief commanders, his speeches to the senate, transcripts even of his negotiations with the barbarians.[117] Advice is submitted: Fronto should dwell on the initial reverses of Rome and the overwhelming might of the Parthians; as Lucius candidly admits, this will set off the magnitude of his own deeds. His debt to Fronto is expressed without equivocation: "In short, my achievements, whatsoever their character, are no greater, of course, than they actually are, but they can be made to seem as great as you would have them seem."[118]

The historian is submerged in the panegyrist. Two items give a foretaste of the projected history, the prolix letter to Lucius professing unbounded admiration for the eloquence of his dispatch to the Senate that confirmed the victories in Armenia, and the so-called *Principia Historiae.* The first employed Lucius' evident mastery of rhetoric to demonstrate in great detail how his years of study led directly to his victories over the barbarians.[119] The second is not the intended prologue to the history but a letter to Lucius written before his war commentaries have arrived, setting out with a wealth of illustration the fashion in which the historian will treat Lucius' deeds, Fronto acting as Homer to his Achilles.[120] It is clear that the emperor's original advice was to be closely followed, for the power of the Parthians is dwelt upon in a long historical prologue; then the main body of the work will proceed in the form of parallel accounts of the two great Parthian Wars "within our memory," with the martial achievements of Trajan everywhere outshone by those of his great-grandson. Thus Fronto will compare the armies, Trajan's confident soldiers with Lucius' motley legions of untried recruits and slothful veterans, demoralized by the soft life encouraged by Trajan's successor. Lucius the noble commander is then to be introduced, sharing his men's hardships in the best of traditions and correcting their faults, just and clement in his dealings with ally and foe alike. So extravagantly is he to be praised that even his notorious fondness for actors is to be raised to an act of statesmanship. It follows from this that the last exchanges between master and pupil are uniformly cordial, Lucius requesting copies of Fronto's speeches, Fronto sending these speeches although depressed by ill-health and the loss of his wife and his grandson, Lucius briefly consoling; and in the last datable items of the correspondence the two men are left contemplating their meeting with pleasure, after the emperor's long and glorious sojourn in the East.[121]

Fronto maintained that he was no courtier, but the assertion is belied throughout the correspondence. Neither a high officer in the imperial service nor an influential adviser nor an assiduous attendant of the court and its ceremonials, he was simply a warm friend of the imperial family and thus able to win its favor in a variety of interests.[122] Any influence on the emperors, however moderate, seems inevitably to have aroused envy, for Fronto is repeatedly to be found in conflict with other courtiers, to the displeasure of his prince, or (equally significant) preaching upon the virtues of harmony. The uncomfortable coexistence of these two activities is neatly reflected by an unflagging concern for the proper etiquette which informed all dealings with the emperor and his *amici*. And at all points it is difficult to distinguish absolutely between the unfeigned love of the friend and the fervent flattery of the subject. Thus a remarkable picture of the Antonine court emerges from Fronto's domestic correspondence, revealing a world of influence, intrigue, dissimulation, feuds, and shifting alliances, all governed by and centered upon the uncertain regard of the emperor. The picture is all the more convincing because it is unexpected, in an ill-documented and highly respectable age, and from such a source.[123] The learned Fronto was sincere, he had no inclinations to be a courtier, but the role was thrust upon him. His intimacy with the palace was unsought but unavoidable: he was teacher of the imperial princes.

VIII

THE TEACHER OF EMPERORS

In the end, Fronto is remembered for better or worse as the teacher of Marcus Aurelius, and it is as *magister imperatorum* that he heads the proud pedigree of his great-grandson.[1] The course of instruction in Latin rhetoric which he offered to the young Caesar can be amply reconstructed from the correspondence: thorough familiarity with the ancient poets and orators, the composition of verse, incessant practice in the invention and use of similes and *sententiae*, translations between Latin and Greek, and finally the composition of various exercises in rhetoric.[2] All of this is familiar, and its effect on Marcus' style may be taken for granted, but it cannot be proven in any detail.[3] More important and more exciting is the general effect of Fronto's teachings on the education of an emperor.

We are exceptionally well informed about the tutors of Marcus Aurelius, more so than for any other emperor. This is due in part to the prominence accorded to his preceptors in the acknowledgments to them contained in the first book of Marcus' *Meditations*, and in part to the fascination with the scholar emperor which induced later writers to preserve the names of those who taught him.[4] The most surprisingly meticulous of these lists is to be found in the *Historia Augusta*, recording no fewer than eighteen of these men, from the humblest to the most aristocratic. There are four elementary teachers (the *litterator*, the *comoedus*, the *musicus* and *geometer*, the *magister pinguendi*); then three grammatici, one for Greek and two for Latin; then four *oratores*, three in Greek (including Herodes Atticus), and in Latin Cornelius Fronto.[5] Then, reflecting the prince's own interests, come some six philosophers, five of them Stoics, one a Peripatetic; and in law, one renowned jurisconsult.[6] This register, surely complete, bears comparison with two others. The *Meditations* (I.5-15) thanks nine or ten of these eighteen men in different but not unexpected proportions: all six of the philosophers are there, but only one of the four orators (Fronto), one of the three grammarians, and two of the elementary teachers, both of them renowned for their wisdom, and an eleventh is added, a man met later in life and appointed ab epistulis, who is naturally enough remembered in connection with his epistolary duties.[7] Finally, the *Historia Augusta* again reveals its special knowledge of the Antonine princes in its enumeration of eleven teachers of Lucius Verus. His *educator* is named; then three grammatici, one for Latin, three for Greek; and then the orators Apollonius, Caninius Celer, and Herodes Atticus for Greek, and Cornelius Fronto for Latin; and the philosophers Apollonius and Sextus.[8] It is significant that none of the primary teachers were shared with Marcus, while all but one of the higher masters were inherited from the elder prince: that should suggest another and special dimension to the instruction offered by the second group.

The honor and influence accorded to these individuals, most of them familiar from other sources, is remarkable. For the lower masters, up to and including the grammatici, there is often the grant of equestrian rank and perhaps a minor post in the procuratorial hierarchy, certainly influence at court.[9] But a sharp distinction must be drawn between these teachers of the lesser disciplines and their successors, most of whom were men of rank already and, strictly speaking, amateurs. Senators at least could not think of accepting a salary from their prince, and five of Marcus' teachers were not merely senators but men of consular rank or close to their consulships: Cornelius Fronto (cos. 143), Herodes Atticus (143), Iunius Rusticus (133), Claudius Maximus (c. 144), Claudius Severus (146).[10] Two more were equestrians high in the emperor's service when they came to Marcus: Caninius Celer was probably the Celer who was ab epistulis Graecis under Hadrian and Pius; and he was thus an associate of the jurist Volusius Maecianus, who was already "a libellis Antonini Aug. Pii sub divo Hadriano."[11] A simple but important conclusion must be drawn, that Antoninus Pius chose as teachers for his sons men who were not only masters of their chosen disciplines but also well-acquainted with the running of the state. Their influence may best be seen in the first book of the *Meditations*, wherein much of what Marcus has learned from them concerns not philosophy or rhetoric, but precisely the conduct of the prince in society.

Most honored of all his teachers was the redoubtable Iunius Rusticus, and here at least honor is an easy indicator of influence commanded, for Rusticus was Marcus' mentor in every affair, public or private. Marcus' biographer rightly singles him out as the greatest influence on the philosopher emperor, revered and followed first as a teacher, then as a friend; and Marcus privately recognized him as one of the three men he was thankful to have known in his life: Rusticus, not Fronto, was the true successor of Seneca.[12] What then did he teach the emperor, as distinct from the man and the philosopher? It is all but impossible to say. Marcus' account in the *Meditations* of his debt to Rusticus well demonstrates the limitations of that work for the reconstruction of external history. The weighty impression made on the inner man is captured in the initial sentence: Rusticus was the first to show him the need to reform and to take care for his character. Next, he taught the avoidance of ostentation, be it in rhetoric and other literary endeavors or in dress and comportment. An example follows, the writing of letters in simple style, like the one addressed by Rusticus from Sinuessa to the mother of Marcus. Then the lesson to forget anger quickly and to be reconciled with those who wish it, a precept with personal significance, for elsewhere Marcus thanks the gods that, though often angry with Rusticus, he never went to extremes, which he would soon have regretted.[13] Then the lesson to think carefully about all that he read or heard, and finally, a precious memory, an introduction to the *Discourses* of Epictetus with Rusticus' personal annotations. The most striking element in these acknowledgments is their random nature; topics are mixed, personal detail is juxtaposed to general observation. In this first book of Marcus' thoughts we are dealing not with a systematically drawn-up account of debts entered with a loving hand, but with a sketch designed to recall notable traits and significant moments in the lives of those who formed Marcus' character, more an aide-memoire than a record. Thus we are in one sense defeated by the very private nature of the *Meditations*, for we are no closer to any estimate of the influence exercised by the philosopher Rusticus on the emperor's policy or the day-to-day running of his government.[14]

The memorial to the orator Fronto is the briefest of all those assigned by Marcus to his teachers: "From Fronto: to observe how vile a thing is the malice and caprice and hypocrisy of absolutism; and generally speaking that those whom we entitle patricians are somehow rather wanting in natural affection."[15] The brevity comes as a shock when set against the extravagant affection of the correspondence, but there is no need for disquiet. Marcus' tributes to his mentors are in essence character sketches, and Fronto is deftly portrayed here by two dominant and related traits, candor and warmth of heart; even the most casual reader of his letters will agree that Marcus has remembered the two most obvious and attractive facets of his tutor's personality. And, more important, we can see from the letters that Fronto did devote special interest to the two subjects selected for remembrance by the emperor; witness his concern as a courtier for the tensions surrounding a prince, and his concern as a new man and a senator for the Roman lack of *philostorgia*. Marcus' remarks on Fronto thus recall the caution that without the context supplied by another source, his memories of his tutors must remain one-dimensional jottings. Fortunately, we possess Fronto's correspondence.

The standard perception of Fronto's relations with Marcus Aurelius might be summarized as follows: upon his appointment as tutor, Fronto quickly won his pupil's love and thoroughly instructed him in the art of Latin rhetoric; but in the course of the 140s the young prince was converted to philosophy, to Fronto's dismay and over his protests; and thereafter, although personal relations remained warm, Fronto never won back the earlier intimacy and authority.[16] The picture must be redrawn. Above all, there was certainly no sudden conversion to philosophy. From his earliest days Marcus was attracted to the pursuit, assuming at the age of twelve (and long before he met Fronto) the dress and conduct of a philosopher, to the detriment of leisure and other studies.[17] A sudden and total conversion is suggested by only one source, a letter to Fronto the relevance of which must be questioned, for it can be argued that the subject concerned is jurisprudence, not philosophy.[18] And significantly, when this letter is subtracted, we are left with a correspondence between Fronto and the Caesar Marcus which reveals almost no concern for the perils and attractions of philosophy: Fronto's skirmishes with the discipline are confined to letters and essays composed in his old age and after Marcus' accession as emperor.[19] It is easy to be blinded by the image of Marcus as the philosopher king, an image quickly fastened upon by subsequent generations but not so completely overwhelming for his contemporaries; for the corollary to the nonconversion is true as well, that there was no abandonment of literature and eloquence. His abiding interest as emperor in Greek sophistry is amply recorded by

Philostratus, and a valuable letter written soon after his accession demonstrates deep anxiety that his own powers of eloquence were in a decline.[20] The historian Dio recalled his weak health, linking it to the devotion of most of his time to study: even as emperor Marcus still attended lectures, Sextus for philosophy, Hermogenes for rhetoric.[21] Herodian, before his brief remarks on Marcus' well-deserved reputation as a philosopher, names him as surpassed by none in his love for the archaic writings of Greeks and Romans, as his speeches and writings testify.[22] And later chroniclers duly note that he excelled in both philosophy and eloquence.[23] It should be abundantly clear that neither did philosophy conquer nor were letters vanquished. The search for Fronto's influence on the emperor thus receives considerable justification.

Most of the orator's ideas on eloquence are set down or repeated in a recognizable dossier of five heavily mutilated letters or essays addressed to Marcus as emperor, which have been assigned the title *De Eloquentia*. In the first item (as we have it) Fronto appears to be resisting a suggestion by Marcus that he change his style in old age. Every poet, historian, and orator has an instantly recognizable style, he argues; even philosophers have personal rhetorical traits.[24] This introduction is significant, for we appear to have the philosopher emperor drawn into a discussion on matters of eloquence. This is followed by a defense of Fronto's guiding principle, the careful choice of words, for Marcus has expressed doubt over the value of such pedantic labor. Again Fronto appeals to those philosophers, famed as much for their eloquence as for their wisdom, who did not spurn the active pursuit of rhetoric. This first item in the group thus sets the theme for the remainder.

In the next, Fronto moves over to the attack. Words are not to be piled on indiscriminately but marshaled by rank and file, the difference being that between chaos and rational order. Then (he continues in a military vein) one can levy them at need, be they volunteers or no; thus one is never left at a loss for words, gaping foolishly. None of this is very new, but in the next section – two intervening pages are lost – Fronto advances with some temerity into the enemy's territory, relying on old memories of his own studies in philosophy. The subject is an important one, *officia*, of which there are two *genera* (never explained) and three *species* or *rationes*: *substantia*, *qualitas*, and *res*.[25] The third category, *res* or *negotium*, the purpose of one's life, is for the wise man *sapientia;* but Fronto argues that, although the first two categories have no direct bearing, they are nevertheless essential for the existence of the third. Thus, with regard to *substantia,* while a man does not live to eat he must eat to live (and hence, of course, to be wise). As for the second species, *qualitas,* each man's *officia* are suited to his individual character, or, to continue the metaphor, each man takes a different meal. "Consider then whether in this second category of obligations be contained the pursuit of eloquence." The line of attack now becomes clear: while eloquence (*qualitas*) does not lead to wisdom (*res*), like eating (*substantia*) it forms an essential precondition:

> For it falls to a Caesar to carry by persuasion necessary measures in the senate, to address the people in a harangue on many important matters, to correct the inequities of the law, to despatch rescripts throughout the world, to take foreign kings to task, to repress by edicts disorders among the allies, to praise their services, to crush the rebellious and cow the proud. All these must assuredly be done by speech and writing. Will you not then cultivate an art, which you see must be of great use to you so often and in matters of such moment? Or do you imagine that it makes no difference with what words you bring about what can only be brought about by words?[26]

The force of the argument is evident. Eloquence is the duty of the emperor, its mastery essential to his success: "Can anyone fear him whom he laughs at, or could anyone obey his order, whose words he despised?" Disregarding the rhetoric of the plea, we can see at once why Marcus never abandoned eloquence, and in the context of the senate alone it can be urged that Fronto's arguments enjoyed a real effect.[27]

The fundamental utility of eloquence for a Caesar may be taken as the major attraction, but Fronto buttresses it with other appeals to philosophy. First, the wise man is distinguished from the foolish mainly by "consilium et delectus rerum et opinio"; indeed, it is his duty to choose rightly, not wrongly to put one thing before another, that is, philosophy before eloquence.[28] Second, while eloquence is not to be coveted, neither ought it to be disdained (an appeal to moderation), for if a choice must be made eloquence is far preferable to speechlessness. Third, and cleverly, if Marcus is repelled by the thrill of saying something beautifully, the fault lies not in eloquence but in his own limitations as a philosopher, a view for which good support can be found in Plato.[29] Nevertheless, Fronto returns to pragmatism for his best argument. He remembers having heard that even philosophers must sometimes follow practices which diverge from their tenets: "Suppose that you, O Caesar, succeed in attaining to the wisdom of Cleanthes or Zeno, yet against your will you must put on the purple cloak, not the philosopher's mantle of coarse wool."[30] Further arguments are added, of less weight and therefore greater in rhetoric. Appeal is made to history: is the forum which echoed to the triumphs of Cato, of Gracchus, and of Cicero, to be rendered silent in the age of Marcus? Appeal is made to religion, to the gods who patronize eloquence and who will be angry at its abolition, Minerva, Mercury, Apollo, Liber, the Fauns, Calliope the mistress of Homer, Homer the master of Ennius, and even Sleep.[31] A specious argument is then advanced, contrasting the slovenly dialectics of Diodorus and Alexinus with the majestic eloquence of Plato and Xenophon and Antisthenes; and yet again the claim is reiterated in great detail, that the best of philosophers did not spurn the use of eloquence. The essential argument is summed up thus: "Dabit philosophia quod dicas, dabit eloquentia quo modo dicas."[32] As a reconciliation between philosophy and eloquence, the piece has little merit, attacking the dialectics for which Marcus himself had little love, while ignoring the charges against the equally empty but ostentatious trappings of rhetoric; but its main contention was surely valid in contemporary eyes, that a mastery of rhetoric was indispensable to an emperor.

The third letter in the series contains praise of a difficult thought brilliantly expressed by the emperor, presumably in a speech, thus following neatly upon the theme of the second letter, and coinciding with the favorable comments made elsewhere on Marcus' Cyzicene oration. Marcus is again worried about his eloquence, and once again Fronto is the not unwanted master. And for the fourth letter of the collection on eloquence, the Cyzicene letter (*Ant. Imp.* I.2) again provides similar context. Here the development of eloquence is traced back from orators to songbirds, then (with little real connection), Fronto considers the development of Marcus, whose genius was apparent from the earliest days of their studies: "From the very first there was no hiding your nobility of mind and the dignity of your thoughts: they wanted then but one thing, the illumination of words: that too we were providing by a varied course of study."[33] The illumination of words, *verborum lumina*, is a striking image, a memorable recasting of the simple dictum of the second letter, that philosophy tells what to say, eloquence provides the indispensable means of saying it. It is no surprise that the same idea appears stated in a similar fashion in the letter on the Cyzicene oration, quelling Marcus' doubts of his own ability: in his first long letter to the young prince, Fronto reminds him, the orator had remarked on his great abilities, assuring him that through his own application and Fronto's help he would win to the desired goal, "ut digna tantis sententiis verborum lumina parares."[34]

The letter on eloquence continues the story of Marcus' youthful development. "As young men will, wearied by the tedium of work," the prince seems to have deserted the study of eloquence for that of philosophy. Most unfortunately, at this point the text declines into indecipherability, but it is significant that when it recovers a page later, Fronto is found recalling at length the young Caesar's eager application to the study of rhetoric—that is, the abandonment of the study was merely a passing phase.[35] Next, after another obscure patch that was intended evidently to persuade Marcus that rhetoric was necessary whether he enjoyed it or not, we find the orator as *magister* again, advocating the judicious use of images; and again he lays stress on the practical benefits for statesmen: if Marcus conceives any startling new thought he must take great care in its expression, "for there is a danger that what is new to the hearers and unexpected may seem ridiculous unless it is embellished and made figurative." In closing, Fronto assures the emperor, in terms again remarkably similar to those of the Cyzicene letter, that his genius for eloquence shows no sign of flagging. The fifth and last item, *De Eloquentia*, is accordingly nothing less than a detailed critique of a recent speech of Marcus, which had imparted lofty *sententiae* in a language that occasionally fell short of its subject.

The file on eloquence thus contains some surprises, not a hopeless rearguard action against the victorious forces of philosophy, but a successful campaign to demonstrate to an anxious emperor that his faculty survived unimpaired, and to reconcile him to the important practical role of eloquence. Fronto is not appealing against Marcus' neglect of eloquence for philosophy, but vindicating a necessity which the emperor reluctantly admits.

The rambling treatise *De Orationibus* should be considered in this light. Knowing that Marcus will concede to him his old title of master—again a propitious beginning, indicative of the emperor's state of mind – Fronto arranges to set down some criticisms of Marcus' eloquence: "For I confess, what is the fact, that only one thing could happen to cause any considerable set-back in my love for you, and that is, if you were to neglect eloquence."[36] But better by far that he neglect eloquence altogether than that he cultivate a poor variety. This remark introduces a long and severe attack launched against the extravagant style affected by Seneca and his coterie. The only possible excuse for such a heated digression must be some error committed or contemplated by Marcus, and, if so, the passage should constitute further evidence of the emperor's continuing interest in the active pursuit of eloquence.[37] Next follows a lengthy and ecstatic review of a single image employed by Marcus, "oculos convenientes," which had won redoubled applause from his audience. For Fronto the words must be the triumphant reward of a careful search.[38] Following these remarks is a return to the Senecan theme: "Perhaps you will say, 'What is there in my speeches new-fangled, what artificial, what obscure, what patched with purple, what inflated or corrupt?' Nothing as yet; but I fear . . . "[39] The startling theme of the essay is thus explicitly confirmed: far from turning away from rhetoric, Marcus is indulging in it, but in a manner abhorrent to the advocate of the dry and compressed style. False rhetoric is as evil as false philosophy, Fronto solemnly avers, citing the exercises of a certain declaimer, Gallicanus.[40] But again, ever the pragmatist, he leads the discourse back to the practical evils of the Senecan style for an emperor. The first line of an imperial edict is dissected, examined, and harshly rejected, the primary indictment harking back to the general theme of the essay: it is too full of *ambitus* and *circumitiones*.[41] (If clarity is a virtue of the law, Fronto certainly has right on his side.) On a first reading, then, the salient point of the *De Orationibus* is the Frontonian vendetta against Seneca, but a closer consideration of the piece can discern a more important issue obscured by the rhetorical polemic, namely, a genuine concern for the proper governance of the empire.

This theme of eloquence and empire is carried forward in Fronto's relations during the same period with his other imperial pupil, and we may conjecture that it would have played a major role in the projected history of Lucius' Parthian Wars. There are some signs of this in the surviving *Principia*. For the early history of Rome, appeal is made to Cato – "in speech and action alike his reputation stands far the highest of all" – while accounts of the most recent events have been received from the warlike Lucius, "as one who had the rehabilitation of eloquence deeply at heart."[42] It was one of these dispatches to the senate which had previously elicited from Fronto a huge and fascinating epistle to Lucius on the theme.[43] The cause of his excitement in that instance was not Lucius' martial virtues and military deeds, but the triumph of eloquence displayed in their report. Now the emperor's master may die in peace, leaving behind "magnum monumentum ad aeternam gloriam," for while Lucius' military glory was won with the aid of thousands, his eloquence conquered under the leadership of Fronto alone. This concept is developed further (in a heavily lacunose text), but the recurrence of "verborum tuorum lumina" should prepare us for what follows: ". . . and so you may rule all with oratory . . ."[44] Several obscure passages succeed on eloquence and accession to power, but then we find a clear statement of the doctrine evident in the various letters to Marcus:

> Therefore, if you seek a veritable sovereign of the human race, it is your eloquence that sways men's minds. It inspires fear, wins love, is a spur to effort, puts shame to silence, exhorts to virtue, exposes vice, urges, soothes, teaches, consoles. In fine, I challenge boldly and on an old condition – give up eloquence and rule; give up making speeches in the senate and subdue Armenia. Other rulers before you have subdued Armenia; but by heaven, your single letter, your brother's single speech on you and your merits will be as regards fame more ennobling, and as regards posterity more talked of, than many a triumph of princes.[45]

Next follows a catalogue of past generals and princes, all of them struck dumb by the eloquence of Lucius. Moreover, because most of them were merely the mouthpieces of others, they were not fit to rule. Such a supposition demands a logical extension of the basic doctrine: "Now *imperium* is a word that connotes not only power but also speech, since the exercise of *imperium* practically exists in bidding and forbidding. If he did not praise good actions, if he did not blame evil doings, if he did not exhort to virtue, if he did not warn off from vice, a ruler would belie his name and be called *imperator* to no purpose."[46] In a subsequent section a further extension is added, with abundant illustrations from history, to the effect that in truth Lucius has acquired his military craft in the reading of his youth, culling *exempla* from histories and speeches as part of his rhetorical training. Thus it can be claimed that "you used eloquence as your mistress in the art of war."[47]

And after this (and an indecipherable page and a half) there seems to be a deliberate echo of the arguments used to Marcus earlier, in the assertion that neither the art of war nor philosophy (or rather "officii observantia quam philosophiam vocant") can claim to be complete without the aid of eloquence.[48] With this twin triumph of Lucius and Marcus, of war and philosophy, a triumph based on the indispensable aid of eloquence, only the conclusion remained to be added, and Fronto rises to the situation with feeling. Despite all of Lucius' triumphs, one citadel remains to be assaulted, Marcus' refusal to assume the title "Armeniacus," but Lucius has the supreme power of eloquence at his command. Marcus is vanquished, and Fronto apostrophizes him: "You have what you have asked for in all your prayers, a brave brother, a good man skilled in speaking." And he closes where he began, with his personal joy at the sight of his pupils united in brotherly love and triumphant through his teachings.[49]

In considering the significance of Fronto's teachings, emphasis should be laid not so much on the subject as on the pupils. By so doing we should only be following Marcus himself, who chose to remember the orator not for his doctrines of rhetoric but for his observations on the state. Fronto's importance here lies not in his theories of the art but in his insistence on its customary application to statecraft by the "vir bonus dicendi peritus." Information is found almost entirely in letters from the period after the accession of his pupils, but there should be no doubt that he had always advocated the utility of eloquence for princes. In one early letter to Marcus Caesar, he praises the care exercised, when Marcus addressed senate or assembly, in choosing the words and images suited to the eloquence of a Caesar. The young man was merely following the instructions of another letter wherein Fronto had advised him to adjust his oratory to his audience, not of course everywhere and anyhow but as much as possible, just as he attends to the popular wish in honoring or freeing a successful gladiator. And lest there be any doubt that a future emperor is being educated here: "You and your father, moreover, who are bound to wear purple and crimson, must on occasion clothe your words too in the same dress."[50] As to the result, a marked effect can be observed in Marcus' speeches to the senate, the only area in which we have sufficient material to form a judgment, and there it should be noted that the effect concerns not merely rhetorical opinions but imperial conduct. Fronto at least was well pleased with his handiwork: "As far as everything else is concerned, I have had my fill of life. I see you, Antoninus, as excellent an emperor as I hoped; as just, as blameless as I guaranteed; as dear and welcome to the Roman people as I desired; fond of me to the height of my wishes, and eloquent to the height of your own."[51]

Concern for the emperor shades into concern for Marcus the friend. An attractive packet of four letters survives, named for their subject, *De Feriis Alsiensibus*, which opens with a reluctant admission from Marcus that he will not tell Fronto about the imperial family's holidays at Alsium by the sea, lest his master trouble himself and scold his pupil. The problem is simply the emperor's overwork, and Fronto was not to be put off.[52] With heavy irony he assures how well he knows that Marcus has spent his holiday in the pursuit of relaxation, napping, reading, walking, boating, bathing, dining. He decides to play the fool for Marcus, claiming to be "a man greatly eloquent and a disciple of Annaeus Seneca" and rallying him for his refusal to indulge in pleasure: "It were easier to reconcile you to a polecat [*volpem*] than to pleasure [*voluptatem*]." Why bother going to Alsium; Marcus might as well work and starve at Lorium, as usual.[53] Marcus will insist that the affairs of the empire demand his constant attention, but Fronto forestalls him with examples of the idle pleasures indulged in by other men as busy as he.[54] At the very least, he begs the emperor to sleep, referring with a jest to the inconsistency of Marcus' "daily" business extending into the night, and concluding with the amusing fable "In Praise of Sleep." Despite the rhetoric in which it is wrapped, Fronto's concern is touching, and Marcus was moved by it; yet his reply ruefully reveals his obstinate addiction to work: on first receiving the exhortation, he had been compelled by the pressure of business to lay it aside, and he found time to read it only when his companions were eating and he was lying down. In mitigation he can plead only that Fronto knows better than anyone what an imperious thing is duty. But while declining the advice, he is obviously moved by the concern. In his turn he expresses anxiety over the pain in Fronto's hand, and his words are touched with real affection: "Farewell my best of masters, man of the warm heart." In the end it is this warmth of affection between master and pupil which lingers in the reader's mind, long after any embarrassment at the repeated and extravagant claims of love in the earlier books has faded away. One letter speaks for all, written by Marcus not in the enthusiasm of his youth, but in full maturity, after his accession to the imperial power: "I saw my little sons, when you saw them; I saw you too, when I read your letter. I beseech you, my master, love me as you do love me; love me too even as you love those little ones of ours: I have not yet said all that I want to say: love me as you have loved me. The extraordinary delightfulness [*mira iucunditas*] of your letter has led me to write this."[55]

APPENDIX A

The Dates of the Letters

FOR CONVENIENCE, the date for each item in the correspondence is listed below. The list is drawn in slightly modified form from my article "The Chronology of Fronto," *JRS* 64 (1974) 136-159; I am grateful for the permission to reprint it here. For the date 161, understand 7 March 161 throughout. Fronto's death is assumed to fall c. 167; *a* = after, *b* = before.

		Loeb	*Date*
M. Caes.	I, 1	I, 80	139/161
	2	80	"
	3	82	"
	4	90	"
	5	96	"
	6	154	Sept. 143/c. 160
	7	162	"
	8	168	"
	9	118	1 July/13 Aug. 143
	10	130	"
	II, 1	108	"
	2	112	"
	3	128	13/31 Aug. 143
	4	116	139/161
	5	136	1 July/13 Aug. 143
	6	140	July/Aug. 143
	7	116	1 July/13 Aug. 143
	8	140	13/31 Aug. 143
	9	144	"
	10	144	"
	11	146	"
	12	146	"
	13	150	139/161
	14	152	"

		Loeb	Date
M. Caes.	II, 15	152	139/161
	16	154	"
	III, 1	52	a. 139
	2	58	150s
	3	62	"
	4	66	"
	5	66	"
	6	68	"
	7	32	140s
	8	34	"
	9	18	139 or 140s
	10	50	139/161
	11	52	"
	12	12	140s
	13	14	"
	14	218	139/161
	15	100	"
	16	100	"
	17	104	early 140s
	18	106	"
	19	78	139/161
	20	170	140s
	21	172	"
	22	172	139/161
	IV, 1	70	150s
	2	74	"
	3	2	138/139
	4	174	139/161
	5	178	140s
	6	180	"
	7	184	139/161
	8	184	"
	9	186	"
	10	188	May/June 155?
	11	202	soon a. 30 Nov. 147
	12	202	"
	13	214	26 Apr. 146/147
	V, 1	188	139/161
	2	"	"
	3	"	139/c. 156
	4	190	139/c. 156
	5	"	139/161
	6-18	"	"
	19	"	139/c. 156

		Loeb	Date
M. Caes.	V, 20	192	139/c. 156
	21	"	1 Dec. 147/161
	22	194	139/161
	23	196	139/153
	24	"	139/161
	25	194	Apr. 145/161
	26	"	"
	27	198	139/c. 156
	28	"	"
	29	"	"
	30	200	"
	31	"	"
	32	"	"
	33	224	"
	34	"	a. 7 Mar. 149
	35	226	"
	36	"	139/161
	37	210	early 140s
	38	"	"
	39	212	c. 150
	40	"	"
	41	"	early 140s
	42	214	"
	43	208	"
	44	218	139/c. 156
	45	228	1 Jan. 148 or 149
	46	230	"
	47	"	c. Oct. 148
	48	232	"
	49	"	a. 7 Mar. 149
	50	234	"
	51	"	c. 158
	52	238	139/161
	53	240	154? (153/c. 156)
	54	"	"
	55	"	139/c. 156
	56	242	"
	57	244	7 Mar. 149/c. 156
	58	"	"
	59	246	139/c. 156
	60	"	Apr. 145/c. 156
	61	248	139/161
	62-64	"	"
	65	224	"

		Loeb	Date
M. Caes.	V, 66	226	139/161
	67	250	30 Nov. 147/161
	68	″	″
	69	″	139/161
	70	252	139/c. 156
	71	″	″
	72	″	″
	73	186	139/161
	74	52	early 140s
Ant. Imp.	I, 1	II, 30	?Oct. 161
	2	32	″
	3	118	late 161
	4	120	″
	5	122	″
	6	126	161/c. 167
	7-8	″	″
	9-10	128	″
	II, 1	94	summer 162/early 165
	2	96	″
	III, 1	158	161/c. 167
	2	168	″
	3	218	late 164/early 165
	4	220	″
	5	218	″
	6	″	161/c. 167
	7	″	″
	8	128	?summer 161/?early 165
	9	156	161/c. 167
	10	″	″
	11	218	161/c. 167
	IV, 1	I, 300	autumn 161/spring 162
	2	302	161/c. 167
Ver. Imp.	I, 1	304	″
	2	294	c. 30 Mar. 161
	3	296	″
	4	306	161/c. 167
	II, 1	II, 128	164
	2	116	c. spring, 163
	3	194	c. Jan./June 166
	4	236	c. summer 166
	4	″	″
	6	84	c. summer 162?
	7	150	163/166
	8	238	161/c. 167

			Loeb	Date
Ver. Imp.	II,	9	232	late 164/early 165
		10	234	"
Eloq.		1	46	161/c. 167
		2	52	?late Aug. 161
		3	70	161/c. 167
		4	72	"
		5	80	"
Orat.			100	"
Ant. Pium		1-2	I, 126	138/161
		3	254	146/c. 158
		4	260	"
		5	226	139/161
		6	228	"
		7	258	146/c. 158
		8	236	c. 158
		9	262	140s
Ad. Am.	I,	1	282	b. c. 167
		2	286	"
		3	278	157/158
		4	288	159/160
		5	290	?160 or 150s
		6	II, 190	164/166
		7	168	150s/160s
		8	190	140s/160s
		9	240	140s/150s
		10	242	b. c. 167
		11	86	?160s
		12	170	165/166
		13	174	b. c. 167
		14	98	c. 162/165
		15	88	"
		16	90	b. c. 167
		17	"	"
		18	—	"
		19	92	early 160s
		20	"	c. 163?
		21	192	b. c. 167
		22	242	"
		23	244	164/c. 167
		24-25	"	b. c. 167
		26	"	164/c. 167
		27	"	150s
	II,	1	I, 306	b. c. 167
		2	308	"

		Loeb	Date
Ad. Am.	II, 3	308	b. c. 167
	4	282	150s/160s
	5	258	146/c. 158
	6	II, 174	160s?
	7	176	163/c. 167
	8	188	?160s
	9	190	"
	10	I, 292	?c. 158
	11	"	c. 158
Princ. Hist.		II, 196	166
Laus Fumi		I, 38	c. 139
Laus Negl.		44	?
Bell. Parth.		II, 20	autumn 161/spring 162
Fer. Als.		2	161/c. 167
Nep. Am.		220	late 164/early 165
Arion		I, 54	early 140s?
Ep. Var.	4	264	b. c. 167
	5	268	"
	7	30	?139
	8	20	"

APPENDIX B

The Date of Fronto's Birth

I HAVE ASSUMED throughout that Fronto was born some time in the middle of the last decade of the first century after Christ.

There is no clear indication of the year in which he was born. The date of his consulship, almost certainly 143, provides some guidance. Some men reached the office of consul as early as age thirty-two (which would imply a birth date for Fronto of no later than 110), but such dispensation was granted only to men of patrician rank or outstanding talents. Forty-two was more likely for a new man in the consulship, the old republican minimum age; that would yield a date c. 100.[1] For lack of other evidence, it is thus commonly assumed that Fronto was born in the first decade of the second century.

There is, however, some slim evidence that he was slightly older, that is, his use of the treacherous phrase "nostra memoria." Several renowned philosophers living "within our memory" were as famed for their eloquence as for their wisdom: Euphrates, Dio, Timocrates, Athenodotus (*Eloq.* 1.4). The text is unfortunately much mutilated, so that it must remain unclear whether Fronto actually heard all of these great men, but his teacher Athenodotus at least is assured. Euphrates put an end to his own life in 119 (with Hadrian's "permission"), and Dio of Prusa is not heard from after 110. Athenodotus was but the subject of an anecdote for a young prince born in 121.[2] In addition to this, another memory also carries us back to Trajan's reign. In demonstrating to his pupil Marcus that one can dislike a thing without despising it, Fronto recalls the consular Crassus, who fled the light of day "nostra memoria."[3] This unhappy Crassus is probably none other than C. Calpurnius Crassus Frugi Licinianus, consul as long ago as 87, an inveterate intriguer of impeccable pedigree who was cautioned by Nerva, relegated to an island by Trajan (perhaps before 113), and there executed in the early days of Hadrian.[4] If so, the conspiratorial activities recalled by Fronto are confined to the period before this

Crassus' relegation. At what age the future orator began to take an interest in high politics remains a matter for speculation.[5]

Fortunately, there is a less ambiguous clue. Cassius Dio relates an anecdote from the period of Fronto's supremacy at the bar under Hadrian: "One night he was returning home from dinner very late, and ascertained from a man whose counsel he had promised to be that Turbo was already holding court. Accordingly, just as he was, in his dinner dress, he went into Turbo's courtroom and greeted him, not with the morning salutation, *salve*, but with the one appropriate to the evening, *vale*."[6] The emperor Hadrian had appointed the tireless Q. Marcius Turbo his praetorian prefect in 119, together with C. Septicius Clarus. Clarus fell from grace perhaps as early as 122, but probably later. The date of Turbo's departure or demise is quite unknown, but sooner or later he too was bitterly persecuted by his imperial patron; unfortunately, no successor is attested until the reign of Pius.[7] The length of Turbo's tenure is crucial. Under the principate only three exceptional men passed ten years in the praetorian prefecture: Sejanus, Claudius Livianus, and Gavius Maximus.[8] The long occupancy of Maximus was felt to be worthy of special notice by the biographer of Antoninus Pius, but in the life of the emperor Hadrian he gives no comparable hint about Marcius Turbo. The anecdote should therefore be assigned (at the least) to the 120s rather than to the 130s. It would have been an astounding feat if Fronto had won supremacy in the courts while in his twenties and perhaps still a student. The date of his birth should therefore be closer to A.D. 90 than to 100: let us say, very roughly, c. 95.

APPENDIX C

The Date of Fronto's Death

THROUGHOUT I have assumed that Fronto died in or very near the year 167. There has been considerable dispute over this, which is more or less the standard date, and powerful arguments have been advanced that he survived at least until the year 175.[1] As with much of his life, so with his death, certainty remains unattainable, but the standard assumption of an earlier demise appears to be correct.

The late dating is based upon the interpretation of a passage in the as yet undated treatise addressed by Fronto to the emperor Marcus, *De Orationibus*. The themes of this work are familiar from the correspondence, Fronto assuming his old magisterial role in order to criticize the emperor's lapses in rhetoric. Senecan circumlocution is the great enemy, and Fronto urges his pupil to remember his teachings that true eloquence is founded upon the pillar of the apt and carefully chosen word, and that the best vocabulary is to be discovered in the writings of the ancients. The crucial passage bears quotation at length:

> Hark back rather to words that are suitable and appropriate and juicy with their own sap . . . Cleave to the old mintage. Coins of lead and debased metal of every kind are oftener met with in our recent issues than in the archaic ones, in which is stamped the name of Perperna, fashioned with ancient art. What then? Am I not to prefer for myself a coin of Antoninus or Commodus or Pius? They are stained and contaminated and discoloured and spotted, aye more spotted than a nurse's apron.[2]

The problem here is the coin of Commodus, *nummus Commodi*: the first coins of the future emperor appeared in 175, in the context of his father's German victories.[3] A desperate remedy is to apply *nummus* not to coins but to medallions, perhaps an issue commemorating Commodus' promotion to Caesar in 166.[4] However, no such issue exists, and there can be no doubt from Fronto's words that he is referring to coinage in daily use. Therefore, the date of the epistle should be somewhere between 175 and 180.

An objection can be raised: who was Commodus? The future emperor Lucius Verus was known as Commodus from the time of his birth to the period of his accession, as Ceionius before his adoption, as Aelius or Aurelius or Aelius Aurelius after, but always as Commodus.[5] In 161, Marcus raised him to partnership and "ordered him to be called Verus, transferring to him his own name."[6] The move was significant, reflecting honor on both Augusti yet sharply defining their roles: Marcus advanced to their father's position as Antoninus, while Lucius assumed his as Verus. Fronto duly adopted the new etiquette in his salutations and even in the epistles themselves.[7] Nevertheless, a more intimate tone remains from earlier days. The old address "M. Aurelius" reappears once, the familiar "Marcus" three times, twice with "meus."[8] Before 161 the most common form is undoubtedly "M. Caesar." By comparison, after 161 Verus is still "Lucius tuus."[9] Before 161 he was surely known most simply as "L. Commodus." For thirty of his thirty-eight years "Verus" bore the name Commodus; it would be foolhardy to deny that he could have been called that after 161 by his old tutor in a private letter to his brother, especially if that letter was written soon after their accession.

The suspicion that "Commodus" is indeed Lucius Verus is strengthened by other indications that the crucial piece, *De Orationibus*, was written within a few years after 161. In one section of it (17), Fronto takes Marcus to task for an obscure circumlocution in one of his edicts, wherein he had meant simply to say that he wished to see the towns of Italy filled with a supply of young men. This has led to the plausible conjecture that the fitting occasion for such an edict was Marcus' augmentation of the alimentary system in commemoration of the betrothal of his daughter Lucilla to Verus in 162.[10] That same era is indicated by a phrase (11) from one of Marcus' speeches that Fronto praises highly: "oculos convenientes." The audience had applauded clamorously. It is a natural surmise that Marcus was making felicitous reference to the harmony or promise of harmony between himself and his new colleague Lucius, the twin eyes of the state.[11] A third passage, when supplied with the proper context, points decisively to the early 160s: "Perhaps you will say: 'What is there in my speeches newfangled, what artificial, what obscure, what patched with purple, what inflated or corrupt?' Nothing as yet [*nondum quicquam*]; but I fear . . .' "[12] It has been pointed out that if this work was indeed written in or after 176 Marcus Aurelius would have been at least fifty-five years of age, and somewhat elderly for his tutor to be anxious about impending decline in style.[13] Yet that argument is no less ludicrous when placed ten years earlier. The true significance of *nondum* must not be overlooked: it can only mean not yet *since your accession*. Eloquence for Fronto was the handmaid of empire, and nothing gave him more joy than the elevation to the purple of his best pupil. That was the proper test for his work, the time when Marcus' new imperial duties would require of him a flood of clear and elegant Latin, both spoken and written. Close reading of the letters *De Orationibus* and *De Eloquentia* reveals that in the period after his accession Marcus himself came to realize the problems in his own style and to fear for the consequences in his efforts to govern, and that he turned once again to his old tutor. It was not yet too late. The epistle *De Orationibus* must be assigned firmly to the early 160s.

With the only prop for a later date thus removed, the argument for assigning Fronto's death to a year very close to 167 may be restated briefly. The most powerful consideration is that no single item in the extant correspondence must be dated later than 166, and there is little chance that later epistles are lost in the lacunae of the manuscript, because the gaps are spread throughout.[14] By 166 Fronto was, as he constantly reiterates, an old man, over seventy if we accept the hypothesis that he was born c. 95 (see Appendix B). And his real ill-health must receive due emphasis. About one-quarter of the surviving letters deal in some way with his physical woes. The age was indeed one of hypochondria, but there should be no doubt that Fronto was for a number of years in very bad health, often crippled with disease.[15] After one terrifying attack, which occurred at least a decade before 166, his family had given him up for dead.[16]

The last certain items in his correspondence leave Fronto joyfully anticipating the triumphant return of Lucius Verus from the Orient in 166. With victory Lucius' troops brought back a devastating plague.[17] Many thousands were destroyed by the pestilence, according to the *Historia Augusta*, among them several of the nobility, for the most illustrious of whom Antoninus erected statues. It happens that Fronto too received a statue at his pupil's command, whether posthumously or not is unclear.[18] The coincidence suggests a connection. When the plague arrived Fronto was an old man, ill and stricken with grief at the loss of his wife and his grandson. And not only does his correspondence cease at this period, there is also no trace of the projected history of the Parthian War, in the preparation of which the elderly author had invested so much effort.[19] There can be little hope that the unhappy orator survived the year 167.

Notes

INTRODUCTION

1. R. Marache, *La critique littéraire de langue latine et le développement du goût archaisant au IIe siècle de notre ère* (1952). For general bibliography concerning Fronto, the reader is advised to consult that work and M. P. J. van den Hout's text of the correspondence (1954) lxxxiii-xciii. More recent material is considered in review articles by R. Marache, *Lustrum* 10 (1965) 213, and by P. V. Cova, *BSL* 1 (1971) 460; and in the standard bibliographical series, *L'année philologique* and *Collectio Bibliographica Operum ad Ius Romanum Pertinentium.*

I. AFRICA

1. Two letters (*Ad Am.* II.10-11) are addressed to "the triumvirs and decurions" of a state, the second referring to "our patria" and the neighboring and friendly community of Hippo: patently the unusual polity of Cirta. Note *CIL* VIII.10838, a boundary stone between the territory of the Cirtenses and Hipponenses. Also, after an allusion to his own career, Fronto mentions "the many other Cirtenses" in the senate; his tribe, the Quirina (*ILS* 2928) is that of Cirta; and he is referred to by an early third-century decurion, M. Caecilius Natalis (*ILAlg.* II.1.562, 674-678; cf. H. Dessau, *Hermes* 15 [1880] 471, and 40 [1905] 373), in the *Octavius* of Minucius Felix as "Cirtensis noster," at 9.6 (cf. J. H. van Haeringen, *Mnemosyne* 3 [1935] 29, on the value of "noster").

2. Cf. Pliny's close ties with Comum and his business there: *Epp.* 1.3, 8, 19; 3.6; 4.13, 30; 5.7, 14; 6.24; 7.11, 18; 9.7.

3. The best general account of Cirta remains that of S. Gsell, *Atlas archéologique de l'Algérie* (1911) fe. 17. C. Vars gave an exhaustive account of the antiquities existing in his day in *RSAC*, 28 (1893) 183 and 29 (1894) 281. L. Leschi offered a brief survey of Cirtan history in *RAf* 81 (1937) 25 = *RSAC* 64 (1937) 19.

4. Livy 30.12.5 ff., 44.12; Mela 1.6.30; *Bell. Afr.* 25.

5. On the Punic influence, see G. Camps, *Aux origines de la Berberie: Massinissa, ou les débuts de l'histoire* (*Libyca* 8, 1960) 258 ff.

6. Strabo 17.3.13. On the earlier Greeks, see Camps, 201 ff.

7. Sallust *Jug.* 26.

8. See the studies of H.-G. Pflaum on the nomenclature of Castellum Celtianum in *Carnuntina* (1956) 126, and of Cirta in *Limes-Studien* (1959) 96.

9. The efforts of J. Heurgon, *Libyca* 5 (1957) 7, and (much longer) of A. Berthier, *RSAC* 70 (1957/1959) 91, to show that the city was not part of Caesar's grant to the Sittiani are vitiated by Pliny *NH* 5.19: Caesar divided Juba's kingdom between Bocchus and Sittius (Appian *BC* 4.54); Bocchus' fief, according to Pliny, eventually became Mauretania Caesariensis; therefore, Cirta went to Sittius. For the *deductio* of 26 see *AE* 1955.202.

10. See Gsell 11-13 on the boundaries.

11. P. Veyne, *Latomus* 18 (1959) 568; U. Laffi, *Adtributio e contributio* (1966) 135 ff.

12. The best and most recent account of the Cirtan magistracies is that of P. Petitmengin, *MEFR* 79 (1967) 174.

13. Cf. Colonia Veneria Pompeiorum, the temple of Athena at Surrentum, and Nuceria on the river Sarnus: Heurgon 12.

14. J. Gascou, *La politique municipale de l'empire romain en Afrique Proconsulaire de Trajan à Septime-Sévère* (1972) 111 ff.

15. In 103/105: *ILAlg.* II.659. *ILAlg.* II.36, almost certainly Flavian, mentions Rusicade without the title of *colonia* under a *praefectus i.d.* Cf. Gascou, 111 ff.

16. For the limits see Gsell 11-13 and *ILAlg.* II, p. 40.

17. T. Mommsen, *Gesammelte Schriften* 5 (1908) 478.

18. Pflaum, articles cited in n. 8 above.

19. *M. Caes.* I.10.5.

20. *Ver. Imp.* II.1.6: "deosque patrios ita comprecatus sum: Hammo Iuppiter . . ."

21. Hence, perhaps, inquiry has been loath to admit his native blood; see, e.g., G. Picard, *La civilisation de l'Afrique romaine* (1959) 128, or Haines, xxiii, or *PW* IV.1313. This reluctance originated with Niebuhr, in the preface to his edition of 1816, xix-xx.

22. First, if the citizenship was the gift of a governor of Africa or legate of the third legion in Numidia, it was perhaps of Julio-Claudian vintage or even older; no Cornelius is yet recorded in the fasti of either office—which, it must be noted, are very incomplete—between 61/62 and c. 98/101; while before that period the nomen is found under Augustus and Tiberius—see W. Eck, *Senatoren von Vespasian bis Hadrian* (1970) 234, 246 f., and B. E. Thomasson, *Die Statthalter der römischen Provinzen Nordafrikas* (1960) II.41 ff., 147 ff. Second, the praenomen of Fronto's father was Titus, which is discovered in the name of only one obscure senatorial Cornelius (*PIR*² C 1410) in the first century; therefore, if the family's citizenship was received from proconsul or legate, it was probably not Fronto's father who received it.

23. For areas of cultivation see R. Cagnat, "L'annone d'Afrique," *Mém. Acad. Inscr.* 40 (1916) 247 ff., and H. Camps-Fabrer, *L'olivier et l'huile dans l'Afrique romaine* (1953) 25 ff. Note the boundary stones of a *fundus Sallustianus* directly adjacent to Cirta: *ILAlg.* II.1960.

24. For the structure and functions of the African aristocracies, see (e.g.) M. Jarrett, *AJP* 92 (1971) 513; J. Guey, *REL* 32 (1954) 115; J. Marion, *BAM* 4 (1960) 133; M. Torelli, *RAL* 28 (1973) 377.

25. *CIL* VIII.5528-5529. Note "M." and "Q." as praenomina in Fronto's immediate family.

26. *ILAlg.* II.10, 190.

27. *ILAlg.* I.2145.

28. *PIR*² I 284. On the family see J. Gascou et al., *AEHE* sec. 4, 1964/1965, 69. Note that this man's father-in-law was a P. Naevius, of a Cirtan family which appears in the next century with senatorial connections; see stemma ad *ILAlg.* II.640.

29. *Ad Am.* II.7.15 (the text seems corrupt). The father's name is certified as Titus by the filiation in *ILS* 2928. Only five T. Cornelii are to be found in Africa, three at Carthage (*CIL* VIII.11139, 11836, *AE* 1951.51), one at Ammaedara (*CIL* VIII.23269) – and one precisely in Cirta (*CIL* VIII.7314).

30. *Nep. Am.* 2.9; *Ver. Imp.* II.7.4; *M. Caes.* II.9, IV.8.1.

31. *CIL* XV.7438; *FO* xxviii; and *CIL* VIII.18081, on which see especially E. Birley, *JRS* 52 (1962) 225. The doubts of G. Alföldy, *Konsulat und Senatorenstand unter den Antoninen* (1977) 249 f., about the identity of the Numidian legate seem to depend on the inflexible application of "rules" which are no more than observed trends.

32. *Ad Am.* I.10.2. On *familia* cf. *Ad Am.* I.12.1, addressed to his son-in-law and praying that the gods will favor "familiam nostram."

33. M. Petronius Sura, *procurator aquarum* under Hadrian; M. Petronius Mamertinus, prefect of Egypt in 137 and of the guard in 139-143; M. Petronius Mamertinus, suffect 150; M. Petronii Surae Mamertinae, *ordinarii* 182 and 190. The family is treated by P. Lambrechts, *AC* 5 (1936) 187, and (with some dissent) by M. Corbier, *L'aerarium Saturni et l'aerarium militare* (1974) 285.

34. A. R. Birley, *BJ* 169 (1969) 259 f.

35. For extended speculation on the events connected with this letter, see *JRS* 64 (1974) 153 f.

36. The sense is effectively completed by P. Pescani, *Coniecturae atque Animadversiones Criticae in Frontonis Opera* (1961) 22.

37. The jurist and consular must be the distinguished jurisconsult and, as head of its leading family (if for no other reason), patron of Cirta, P. Pactumeius Clemens (cos. 138); see W. Kunkel, *Herkunft und soziale Stellung der römischen Juristen*² (1967) 155. Clemens' *ius respondendi* is certified by *Dig.* 40.7.21.1. The "greatest honor" won by three Cirtans remains a mystery: one of Cirta's many senators was praefectus urbi of Rome, Q. Lollius Urbicus; see *ILAlg.* II.3563.

38. "Illis moribus tantaque eloquentia – optimum et facundissimum – et morum et eloquentiae": the vocabulary has been carefully chosen and deployed.

39. As it happens, two of Fronto's nominees are noted elsewhere for their eloquence, Victorinus (Dio 72.11.2) and Postumius Festus (*ILS* 2929).

40. All consuls suffect, Victorinus in 155, Silanus in 152, Festus in 160 (*FO*). For the date of the letter, see *JRS* 64 (1974) 153 f.

41. Cf. C. Moussy, *Gratia et sa famille* (1966) 375 ff.

42. *ILS* 2928.

43. M. Jarrett, *ES* 9 (1972) 146.

44. The study by A. Pelletier, *Latomus* 23 (1964) 511, is incomplete, unoriginal, and often inaccurate. Better is the brief survey of G. Picard, *Karthago* 4 (1953) 126.

45. For the eques L. Iulius Crassus of Thugga, see *ILT* 1393, *ILAf* 520. For the Pactumeii, see n. 53 below. L. Albius Pullaienus Pollio (cos. 90), almost certainly African and perhaps from Thugga, was followed by Senecio Memmius Afer (cos. 99), certainly a Carthaginian; on the Pullaieni of Thugga see *PIR*² G 79, and note the consular of Bulla Regia, C. Memmius Fidus Iulius Albius (*ILAf* 453, etc.), with the stele of an Alb. Pullaienus Salvillus (*CIL* VIII.23396) and the inscription of Memmius Afer (VIII.24586). Then, under Trajan, Q. Caecilius Marcellus of Carthage and Q. Coredius Gallus Gargilius Antiquus, perhaps from Thugga: *PIR*² C 55 and G 78 (with *AE* 1973.551). There seems to be no good reason for making the Surdinius Gallus of Dio 60.29.2 an African.

46. There were two grants of the *latus clavus* (one declined) at Lepcis: *AE* 1957.238 and Statius *Silvae* 4.5.41-42. Others certainly African: Pliny *Epp.* 3.9.2-3 and *FIRA*² I.47. Possibly African are the Stertinii (coss. 92, 112) and the Servilii Pudentes (last consul in 166). The first senatorial Gargilius Antiquus, father of the Hadrianic consul, now appears to be Flavian: G. Alföldy, *Chiron* 8 (1978) 361.

47. Lusius Quietus (cos. 117), *PIR*² L 439; Sex. Cornelius Clemens (cos. by 170), C 1430.

48. For an introduction to the Punic problem, see F. Millar, *JRS* 58 (1968) 126.

49. Pliny *NH* 18.35 (with J. Carcopino, *MEFR* 26 [1906] 365); Petronius 117.8.

50. See, most recently, M. Bénabou, *La résistance africaine à la romanisation* (1976), with *Annales ESC* 33 (1978) 64 ff.; and the excellent survey by P. D. A. Garnsey, in P. D. A. Garnsey and C. R. Whittaker, ed., *Imperialism in the Ancient World* (1978) 223.

51. See (e.g.) M. Leglay, "Les Flaviens et l'Afrique," *MEFR* 80 (1968) 201; J. Gascou, *La politique municipale;* P. Salama, *Les voies romaines de l'Afrique du Nord* (1951).

52. M. Jarrett, *AJP* 12 (1971) 513; P. Lambrechts, *La composition du sénat romain de l'accession au trône d'Hadrien à la mort de Commode* (1941) 195 ff.

53. On the problems raised by the brothers Pactumeii, see T. D. Barnes, *CR* 21 (1971) 332. Q. Aurelius Pactumeius Fronto was consul in 80, his brother Clemens earlier. It is interesting, perhaps suggestive, to find another consular Cirtan named Fronto in a previous generation.

54. Cf. A. Stein, *Der römische Ritterstand* (1927) 195 ff., for the classic discussion.

55. He was not, however, an African by birth; on his career see H.-G. Pflaum, *Ant. Afr.* 2 (1968) 154, and R. P. Duncan-Jones, *ES* 5 (1968) 155. The second known flamen was a man of Cuicul.

56. Note also the unknown of *CIL* VIII.7069, patron of the Four Colonies.

For relatives of senators and knights at Cirta see *ILAlg.* II.794, 798; *AE* 1907.231; and above all *CIL* VIII.18864.

57. *PIR*[2] L 327; *Ad Am.* II.7.12.

58. Cf. A. Berthier, *Tiddis, Antique Castellum Tidditanorum* (1951).

59. *ILAlg.* II.645; *Dig.* 40.7.21.1 (Pomponius); *Ad Am.* II.11.2.

60. *ILAlg.* II.3610, with R. P. Duncan-Jones, *PBSR* 35 (1967) 154. For the career, see H.-G. Pflaum, *Ant. Afr.* 2 (1968) 173.

61. *ILAlg.* II.665, with M. Jarrett, *ES* 9 (1972) 170.

62. Gellius 19.10.1, 11 (cf. *M. Caes.* II.17.3 on the value of Ennius), with *ILAlg.* II.638. The man on the inscription is noted as "praetor kandidatus," rather than the more normal "candidatus"; the former spelling is not certainly found before the reign of Septimius Severus, hence G. Camodeca, in *AAN* 85 (1974) 261, denies identity with the friend of Fronto. However, several of the other instances are not securely dated, and, more important, the spelling "kandidatus" is precisely what one would expect from a fervent archaist.

63. *PIR*[2] I 340, with *M. Caes.* III.42. There are no other senatorial Marciani available; the term "noster" suggests real intimacy with Fronto; and the Cirtan connection should be conclusive.

64. He was the recipient of *Ad Am.* II.6-9. The most recent treatment of his career is that by G. Alföldy, *Konsulat und Senatorenstand*, 367 ff.

65. *ILAlg.* II.614, *ILS* 1118; cf. S. Gsell, *Atlas archéologique*, 237. C. Arrius Antoninus was *not* related to the imperial family through the grandfather of Antoninus Pius. That Arrius Antoninus, perhaps from Nemausus (R. Syme, *Tacitus* 605), was consul in 69, while the first African consul is certified as Vespasianic (i.e., Pactumeius).

66. *PIR*[2] A 754 (cf. 757), with S. Gsell and C. A. Joly, *Khamissa, Mdaouruch, Announa* III, *Announa* (1918) 81; the evidence on the family is conveniently gathered by F. Bertrandy at *Karthago* 17 (1973/1974) 195. Adventus was twice the commanding officer of the future procurator Ti. Claudius Candidus, who was probably a Cirtan by birth; see J. Fitz, *Latomus* 25 (1966), 833 f. And, most suggestive of Cirtan ties at Rome, Antistius Burrus (cos. 181), the son of Adventus and son-in-law of Marcus Aurelius, was accused under Commodus of conspiring for the throne with none other than Arrius Antoninus; *HA Pertinax* 3.7.

67. *PIR*[2] I 251, F 341. G. Alföldy, 179, conjectures that Castus was the son of the Castus who was consul in 165; M. Corbier, 398 ff. fixes the date of Festus. A good case has also been made that Saenius Donatus Saturninus, attested as a senator in 179 (*CIL* XIV.5356) was also Cirtan: R. Syme, *Historia* 27 (1978) 595.

68. *PW* Tullius 44.

69. *ILAlg.* I.447, 448.

70. See especially the remarks of R. Syme, *JRS* 58 (1968) 135 ff., on "Pliny country."

71. *JRS* 64 (1974) 153 ff.

72. *Ad Am.* I.3.1 ff.

73. Minucius Felix *Octavius* 9.6.

74. For his Greek friends, see Chapters III and V. Non-Cirtan Africans include only Iulius Senex and Iulius Aquilinus for certain; how Fronto met them is unknown.

75. *Silvae* 4.5 and passim. The man's origins are a real problem; see A. R. Birley, *BHAC* 1968/1969 63 and 1972/1974 63.

76. Apuleius *Apol.* 98.8; *HA Severus* 15.7. These and other references are gathered by F. Millar, *JRS* 58 (1968) 126, to which add the astonishing remarks of Ausonius on Septimius Severus (*Opus.* XIV.21.3-4, Peiper): "Punica origo illi, set qui virtute probaret / Non obstare locum, cum valet ingenium." The remark is particularly valuable if it can be supposed (with T. D. Barnes, *The Sources of the "Historia Augusta"* [1978] 103) that Ausonius' *Caesares* preserved the judgments of Severus' contemporary Marius Maximus.

77. Apuleius *Apol.* 24.6.

78. *Ep. Var.* 8.1.

79. Florus, *Vergilius Orator an Poeta* 1.4. On this work see H. Dahlmann, *MLatJb* 2 (1965) 9.

80. On the old controversy over *tumor Africus,* see the sane discussion of M. D. Brock in *Studies in Fronto and His Age* (1911) 161 ff. On its earliest figure, see P. Jal, ed., *Florus* 2 (1967) 107 ff.

81. Cf. M. Leglay, *Hommages L. Herrmann* (1960) 485; *AE* 1957, p. 56.

82. *ILAlg.* I.288, *ILAf.* 325, *CIL* VIII.2469.

83. Apuleius *Apol.* 4.1-2, etc. On the Greek language in Africa, see W. Thieling, *Der Hellenismus in Kleinafrika* (1911). Greek was not perhaps as pervasive as Thieling imagined; cf. T. Kotula, *Mélanges M. Renard* (1969) II.386 (probably too harsh).

84. A senator from Thamugadi put Attic *facundia* on a level with Roman *nitor* (*CIL* VIII.17910); a youth of Sitifis died at the age of twenty-two, "summarum artium liberalium litterarum studiis utriusq. linguae perfecte eruditus optima facundia praeditus" (VIII.8500); a knight of Cirtan Thibilis, an incomparable youth, was marvelously learned in both tongues (*AE* 1968.643): cf. *IL-Alg.* I.1363, 1364; *CIL* VI.1416. Above all, Apuleius plays on the distinguishing quality of Greek: he flatters his audience that they know it, his persecutor does not, even his wife can write letters in Greek (*Flor.* 18; *Apol.* 82 ff., 98.8).

85. *CIL* VIII.18864.

86. The corpus of African inscriptions records almost 300 metrical efforts. Everyone turned his hand to verse: the rhetor Florus (*VOAP* 1.3 ff.), the philosopher Apuleius (*Apol.* 6 ff.), the advocate Severus (Statius *Silvae* 4.5.57 ff.), the legate Tullius Maximus (*CIL* II.2660). Vergil especially was adulated, dissected, and imitated: Florus discussed whether he was a poet or a rhetor; Apuleius (*Apol.* 30) insinuated that his opponent had not read him. See, generally, J.-M. Lassère, *Bull. Assoc. G. Budé* 1965 220 ff. Fronto of course knew Vergil as a choice wordmaster (Gellius 2.26.11), perhaps imitating him: T. Schwierczina, *Frontoniana* (1883) 31, doubted by R. Marache, *La critique littéraire* (1952) 161 f.

87. G. W. Bowersock, *Greek Sophists in the Roman Empire* (1969) 17.

88. Augustine, *Conf.* 3.1 ff.; Tertullian, *Adv. Val.* 8; cf. T. D. Barnes, *Tertullian* (1971) 243 ff. What evidence there is for the schools is collected by F. Schemmel, *Phil. Woch.* 47 (1927) 1342.

89. P. Monceaux, *Les africains: étude sur la littérature latine d'Afrique* (1894) 186 ff., 243 ff. Note also Plutarch's Carthaginian friend Sextius Sulla (on whom see C. P. Jones, *Plutarch and Rome* [1971] 60); the poet and schoolmaster Florus, who bemoaned "fata Romam negant patriam"; Tuticius Proculus, the teacher of Marcus Aurelius; and the grammarian Fidus Optatus (R. Syme, *Historia* 27 [1978] 592).

90. *CIL* VIII.27573. For other equestrians in the imperial service whose offices required literary talent, see Jarrett, *ES* 9 (1972), nos. 18, 32, 34, 71, 85, 94, 102, 113, 119, 122, 138, 157. Two Africans were of course tutors of Marcus Aurelius: Fronto and Tuticius Proculus of Sicca Veneria; *HA Marcus* 2.3, 5, on which see A. R. Birley, *BHAC* 1966/1967 39.

91. *Apol.* 3.5 ff.; *Flor.* 18.15. We do find small-town African philosophers of no repute, an Epicurean, a Stoic, and a Platonist: *ILT* 1614, *AE* 1957.90, *ILAlg.* I.2115.

92. *Flor.* 20.4. It was also at Athens, not Carthage, that Apuleius met another young African, the knight of Oea and his future stepson, Sicinius Pontianus: *Apol.* 72.3.

93. *Sat.* 7.148-149.

94. See, e.g., *CIL* VIII.2393; *AE* 1917.73; *CIL* VIII.2734, 18227; *AE* 1911.99, *CIL* VIII.3506; *ILT* 1514. Apuleius' *Apology* is a defense before a proconsul, his troubles erupting in the midst of pleading in another case on his wife's behalf against a leading family of Lepcis (1.5; cf. J. Guey, *REL* 32 [1954] 116). His detractor Sicinius Aemilianus, uncle of a knight, had (among other past iniquities) personally contested the will of his own uncle before the prefect of Rome himself, and, refusing to accept the decision of that exalted judge and his consular *consilium*, he still obstinately maintained that the will was a forgery (2.10 f.). His associate, the knight's son Herennius Rufinus, was depicted by Apuleius as "omnium litium depector."

95. Lactantius *Div. Inst.* 5.1.21; cf. Minucius Felix *Octavius* 2.1-3.

96. See Jarrett, nos. 1, 7, 26, 34, 71, 81, 105, 113, 126, 131. Some rose very high: *ILS* 1451, 1347. Especially illustrative of the combination of rank, education, advocacy, and success in the emperors' service is *CIL* VIII.9249 + p. 974; cf. 20840.

97. M. Jarrett, *Historia* 12 (1963) 220.

98. Dio 78.11.1-3; cf. Herodian 4.12.1. The post of *advocatus fisci*, recorded by *HA Macrinus* and accepted by some scholars, is to be rejected: R. Syme, *Emperors and Biography* (1971) 81.

99. *Bell. Parth.* 1.

100. Cf. the question asked by a stranger of the provincial Tacitus: "Italicus es an provincialis?" (Pliny *Epp.* 9.23.3)—politeness or a real inability to distinguish? For the deeply ambivalent attitude of the provincial to his homeland, see the remarkable essays of a latter-day Cirtan, Albert Camus, in *Noces* (1938) and *L'été* (1954), particularly "Petit guide pour des villes sans

passé" in the latter collection, where he notes the fine quality of Cirtan ennui.

II. ITALY

1. Pliny *Epp.* 6.6.3, 5.8.8; *ILS* 2927.

2. *ILS* 2928: "tresvir capitalis."

3. Carthage was assumed by (e.g.) J. Heurgon, *RSAC* 70 (1957/1959) 142; but Alexandria is favored by most, by (e.g.) Niehbuhr and Haines in the prefaces to their editions, and by *PW*. In the latter case, it is argued that Fronto had many *familiares* in the Egyptian capital (*Ant. Pium* 9.2; cf. *Ep. Var.* 4-5); in the former, it might be urged that he addressed the Carthaginian Sulpicius Apollinaris as master (Gellius 19.13.2) and spoke *Pro Carthaginiensibus.*

4. *M. Caes.* I.8.3. On Dionysius see also *PIR*[2] D 106.

5. *M. Caes.* IV.12.2; *Eloq.* 5.4-5. The drift of the fable is easily surmised.

6. *Eloq.* 1-4; Marcus *Meditations* I.13.

7. *HA Severus* 1.5, with A. R. Birley, *Septimius Severus* (1971) 69. Note also *Dig.* 12.1.17: a youth at Rome "studiorum causa" in the time of Marcus. On the ages of students see, most recently, S. F. Bonner, *Education in Ancient Rome* (1977) 136 f. Also, an early third-century knight of Thubursicu Numidarum died while studying at Carthage at the age of eighteen years, four months, twenty-eight days: *ILAlg.* I.1363.

8. *M. Caes.* I.9.5; Horace *Sat.* I.8.

9. P. Grimal, *Les jardins romains*[2] (1969) 143 ff., 159 f.; cf. Platner-Ashby 269, and G. Lugli, *Fontes* 4 (1957) 112 ff.

10. H. Thylander, *Acta Archaeologica* 9 (1938) 101.

11. *CIL* XV.7438; these pipes should dispose of Ashby's doubts: first, 269, that Fronto is here referring to the well-known gardens of Maecenas; and second, 60 f., that the *auditorium* was actually within the gardens. Cf. G. M. Rushforth, *JRS* 9 (1919) 34.

12. *CIL* VI.31821, with Mommsen's discussion. A painted version of *Anth. Pal.* 12.118 was also found.

13. See G. Alföldy, *Fasti Hispanienses* (1969) 38 ff.

14. Magister Gregorius, *Narracio de Mirabilibus Urbis Romae* 19 (ed. R. B. C. Huygens, *Textus Minores* 47, 1970). See Juvenal *Sat.* I.12: "Frontonis platani convulsaque marmora clamant," with the comment of one scholiast, "in Horatiana domo, in qua poetae recitabant," and the explication of another, "Fronto orator Traiani temporis nobilissimus"; the confusion and its significance are well explained by Rushforth, 34.

15. *Epp.* 2.17.2.

16. *M. Caes.* IV.4.2.

17. For the ruins of the area, see *La Via Aurelia da Roma a Forum Aureli*, Quaderni dell'Istituto di Topografia Antica della Università di Roma 4 (1968), 13-73.

18. *Ad Am.* 1.6.1; *Ver. Imp.* 1.3.2; probably *M. Caes.* V.39-40; *Ver. Imp.* II.6.1.

19. *M. Caes.* IV.4.2, III.8.1-2, I.3.5.

20. *AE* 1945.38, with D. Mustilli, *Epigraphica* 2 (1940) 214; in general, see J. H. D'Arms, *Romans on the Bay of Naples* (1970) 210 and passim.

21. P. Mingazzini and F. Pfister, *Surrentum*, Forma Italiae I.2 (1946), 12, 70, 107 ff. ("palazzo").

22. By comparison, Pliny was probably much wealthier, but then we have more data for him; see the model discussion "The Finances of a Senator" by R. P. Duncan-Jones in his *The Economy of the Roman Empire* (1974) 17, superseding *PBSR* 33 (1965) 177.

23. Gellius 19.10.1-5; P. Mingazzini, 107 ff., H. Thylander, 120 ff.

24. *M. Caes.* II.1.1; *Nep. Am.* 9; *Ver. Imp.* II.7; *Ep. Var.* 4-5.

25. R. P. Duncan-Jones, 25; I. Schatzman, *Senatorial Wealth and Roman Politics*, Collection Latomus 142 (1975), 409.

26. *Ant. Pium* 3.3; cf. 4 and 7. Also *CIL* III.5174, 5181.

27. *Nep. Am.* 8, 9; *Ad Am.* I.12.2, from which we may infer that Fronto himself took no professional fees for his advocacy.

28. *Nep. Am.* 9. "Nostrae res haud copiosae," at *Ver. Imp.* II.7.5, is not to be taken too seriously, nor are the supposed claims of poverty in *Nep. Am.*, which (if anything) do not refer to present conditions; cf. Pliny's plaint, "sunt . . . nobis modicae facultates, dignitas sumptuosa" (*Epp.* 2.4.3): poverty is relative.

29. *M. Caes.* II.10.1, 11, 12; IV.6.2; V.20, 46. Note the particularly intriguing inscription *CIL* VI.13387, erected by an Aurelia Cratia Aug. lib.

30. *Ver. Imp.* II.9.1; *Nep. Am.* 4.

31. *M. Caes.* II.2.1, Marcus as Cratia's rival in love; II.10.1, Cratia and Marcus at Naples, "all my fortunes, all my joys are at Naples"; etc.

32. *M. Caes.* III.12.1.

33. *AE* 1945.38. Van den Hout prints the Greek *kratia* at II.12.1; the ms. has *krateia.*

34. Pape-Benseler 711 f. The Italian nomen Crattius appears to be derived from the Greek name. Of its occurrences in Italy, Greek origins are still manifest on *CIL* XI.4871 (Spoletium), VI.7087 (Rome), 13387, 13023, 16557, 16559; only VI.14983 and 23172 are indistinctive. No Crateia is found in Africa, Numidia, or Mauretania, but there was a Claudia Crateia at Cyrene: *QAL* 4 (1961) 40.

35. W. Schulze, *Zur Geschichte lateinischer Eigennamen* (1904) 156.

36. Cf. Ti. Crassius Firmus of Herculaneum: *CIL* X.8058.28, with 7450.

37. *AE* 1966.441. Klaudia Krateia's maternal pedigree as recorded there guarantees the highest social position in her native city; she was related to C. Antius A. Iulius Quadratus (cos. II 105), and perhaps through him to Fronto's Ephesian correspondent Ti. Claudius Iulianus (cos. 159?); and she was very closely related to one of the great representatives of the Second Sophistic, T. Flavius Damianus, subject of a laudatory biography by Philostratus, benefactor of his native city, and father or father-in-law of five consuls. Both families betray strong literary connections (see G. W. Bowersock, *Greek Sophists in the Roman Empire* 24-25, 78-79) and wide connections with the Roman elite.

On all these people and their connections, see now H. Halfmann, *Die Senatoren aus dem östlichen Teil des Imperium Romanum bis zum Ende des 2. Jahrhunderts n. Chr.*, Hypomnemata 58 (1979).

38. *M. Caes.* I.9.1, cf. 6; IV.13.1.

39. *HA Marcus* 3.8.

40. *Ad Am.* I.7, II.11.1.

41. *Ant. Imp.* I.2.3; *M. Caes.* V.59.

42. *Ad Am.* I.14.2.

43. *M. Caes.* V.25; *Ad Am.* I.12, 13, etc.

44. *Nep. Am.* 2.3.

45. For the ages of the grandchildren, see *JRS* 64 (1974) 155 f.

46. *Ad Am.* I.12.

47. *Ad Am.* II.11.1.

48. *Nep. Am.* 2.3; *Ad Am.* I.12.2.

49. See *ILS* 1129 (Pisaurum, the patria of the Aufidii); on the sarcophagus, see A. Giuliano, *PdP* 27 (1972) 271. The Macrinus episode is recorded in a lacunose section of Dio, 79.22; an eventual proconsulship of Asia is now confirmed by *AE* 1971.79. This Fronto was also pontifex, patron of Formiae, and husband of a Cassia Cornelia C.f. Prisca.

50. Listed on *ILS* 7218 (Pisaurum). Leo of Narbo, counselor of the Visigothic king Euric (466-484) was recognized by his friend Sidonius Apollinaris to be a descendant of Fronto, who would indeed have approved of him, for he was a poet and a lawyer; the data are gathered by K. F. Stroheker, *Der senatorische Adel im spätantiken Gallien* (1948) 187. Other descendants or collaterals could be conjectured, notably the Aufidia Cornelia Valentilla who, like Cornelius Fronto and Aufidius Victorinus, lived on the Esquiline (*CIL* XV.7398).

III. LITERARY SOCIETY AT ROME

1. *Elegantia* was the highest term of approval, and a hallmark of the Antonine age: R. Marache, *La critique littéraire* (1951) 146-147. The word appears in one form or another over thirty times in the extant manuscript of Fronto.

2. *Ekloge* 55, 306, 474-475, 482, 492-493 Rutherford.

3. Appius Apollonides was perhaps the surgeon Apollonides at Artemidorus 245.20 (Pack), Artemidorus being also a possible source for the partial cure of Fronto the arthritic recorded at 257.13: R. Pack, *TAPA* 86 (1955) 285. Note also the second-century doctor Apollonides, commemorated at Heraclea Salbace in elegaic distichs: L. and J. Robert, *La Carie* (1954) II.187, no. 88.

4. For the sources, see H.-G. Pflaum, *JS* 1961 29-31.

5. *HA Marcus* 3.3; Marcus *Meditations* I.14.1.

6. Galen XIV.613 K.

7. *JÖAI* 40 (1953) 14; Philostratus *VS* 588; cf. H.-G. Pflaum, *JS* 1961 29-31, and R. Syme, *Historia* 17 (1968) 102, for another possible connection.

8. Galen XIV.613, 629, 647. On Hadrian see *JÖAI* 40 (1953) 14, and Philostratus *VS* 588.

9. *IG* II/III[2] 4780; Galen XIV.651 ff. (on which see V. Nutton, *Chiron* 3 [1973] 429); Philostratus *VS* 559, 582. On the Quintilii, see J. H. Oliver, *Marcus Aurelius* (1970) 66 ff.

10. *Ad Am.* I.1.3, reading *sed* or *nam* with A. E. Housman, *PCPS* 1926 22, against manuscript *nec.* On Severus see the inscription in n. 7 above.

11. *Ad Am.* I.3.3.

12. *IRT* 533-535; *HA Pertinax* 1.5; cf. *Epitome de Caesaribus* 18.4.

13. Apuleius *Apol.* 24.1, 94.3-95.6 (with list of orators).

14. Lucian *Alex.* 57. This man might be the son of the proconsul of Africa (J. Morris, *PIR*[2] H, p. 55, and H.-G. Pflaum, *BHAC* 1971 114 ff.), but the evidence is inconclusive.

15. On Hedianus see *OGIS* 514 (the date is insecure). On C. Vibius Gallio Claudius Severus see *IRT* 533. Lollianus can be even further implicated in a web of kinship and culture. He was closely connected with the military Terentii Scaurianus (cos. 102 or 104) and Gentianus (cos. 116, before the age of thirty). Terentia, daughter of the former and sister of the latter, had inscribed on an Egyptian pyramid a touching memorial in verse to her brother (*ILS* 1046a: she was probably mother of Lollianus; cf. *PW* Terentius 97 and 48c, against *PIR*[2] H, p. 55). That verse offers an erudite reminiscence of Horace, in the same era that a commentary on Horace was published by the leading grammarian of Hadrian's reign, Q. Terentius Scaurus: the two were surely relatives (*PW* V A 671, E. Groag). Scaurus' son was *procurator aquarum,* his grandson tutor in grammar to Lucius Verus, from whose care the prince passed into that of the orator Fronto: *NdS* 1908.242; *HA Verus* 2.5.

16. See J. Guey, *REL* 29 (1951) 317n3, for a likely timetable of events.

17. *Apol.* 35.7 (*patientia*); 35.7, 55.12 (*humanitas*); 48.5, 2.5 (*sollertia*); 84.6 (*providentia*); 3.1, 102.5 (*iustitia*).

18. *Apol.* 36.5, 41.4 (Aristotle); 11.5, 25.10, 51.1, 64.4-5 (Plato); 38.1 (all).

19. *Apol.* 91.3; cf. 48.12, 60.3.

20. *Apol.* 81.2, 19.2.

21. On Pannonia see *CIL* XVI.99, 104. On the cursus of . . . Maximus see *ILS* 1062 + add., on which see J. Fitz, *AAntHung.* 11 (1963) 258; approved by R. Syme, *Danubian Papers* (1971) 235; doubted by A. Birley, *Marcus Aurelius* (1966) 125; cf. Syme, 190.

22. *HA Marcus* 3.2; Marcus *Meditations* I.15; cf. 16.10, 17.5.

23. *Apol.* 94.7, 95.7.

24. R. Helm, *Altertum* 1 (1955) 86.

25. Misconstrued by C. R. Haines as "thoughts"; Fronto's remarks here bear comparison with those of Pliny, *Epp.* I.10.5, on Euphrates.

26. *CIL* VIII.27572.

27. A. and E. Bernand, *Les inscriptions du Colosse* (1960), nos. 41, 42.

28. *ILS* 7776. The date of Julian's German command should be c. 152: E. Ritterling, *Fasti des römischen Deutschlands* (1932) 68. The nomen Aelius here is surely an error in the philosopher's name (prompted by the proximity of Aelia) for Acilius; cf. the African proconsul's father, M. Acilius Priscus Egrilius Plarianus (*PIR*[2] E 48).

29. Aristides *Or.* 48.9 K (Salvius), 50.23 (Evaretus). The philosophic in-

terests of the great jurist are also presumably reflected in the L. Salvius Epictetus who was an official of the *corpus pistorum* at Rome in 144: *ILS* 7269.

30. On his career see *AE* 1905.121; *ILS* 2907. His grandfather, like Severus', was a member of the group on *IGRR* III.173. Fronto's Iulianus might be the man who corresponded with Herodes Atticus: Philostratus *VS* 552; cf. G. W. Bowersock, *Greek Sophists in the Roman Empire* (1969) 78. Further, this man (or, just possibly, the jurist Salvius Iulianus) should be the Iulianus who was "consul under the emperor Marcus" and who patronized the philosopher-sophist Damophilus: *Suda*, s.v. Damophilus.

31. *Ad Am.* I.17, 19.

32. *Ad Am.* I.5.1.

33. "Prosus ego Statiani mei filium qualemcumque diligerem, tam Hercule quam Faustiniani mei patrem qualemcumque carum haberem," etc.

34. The list at H.-G. Pflaum, *Carrières* 684n1, is expanded by G. W. Bowersock, 50 ff. Add the sophist L. Iulius Vestinus, a Hadrianic ab epistulis (Pflaum 105), and T. Taius Sanctus (178 bis with *POxy.* 2760), a tutor of Commodus and ab epistulis Graecis of Marcus.

35. E.g., Iulius Secundus (*PIR*² I 559, with C. P. Jones, *HSCP* 72 [1967] 279), Titinius Capito (Pflaum 60), Suetonius Tranquillus (96), and note that Iulius Vestinus was a Gaul like Favorinus. These are admittedly combined Graecis and Latinis, but it would be difficult to account for any change after the offices were separated.

36. See *JRS* 64 (1974) 152.

37. *HA Pertinax* 12.7. Identity was assumed by E. Hauler, *WS* 53 (1935) 167 ff., and (even before Hauler had deciphered the word *magister*) by Haines, II.93n1.

38. Gellius 19.13; and n. 12 above for Avitus.

39. Dio 69.3.5, 71.22; *HA Hadrian* 15.5, 16.10; *BGU* 113; etc.

40. Aristides *Or.* 50.75 K; Philostratus *VS* 563.

41. The tribune Iunius Maximus might offer more hope. Two other letters are addressed to him, one apparently a consolation (I.23), the other a note of commendation, or at least one containing approval of a mutual friend (I.26). This friend, perhaps the "Ulpius noster" of the fragment surviving in the index, is a panegyrist of Maximus' honesty and dignity, and especially dear to Fronto for the usual reasons, as a partner in study and in the pursuit of the noble arts. The young Maximus might then also be a *contubernalis* of the orator. He is apparently the subject of *AE* 1972.576, which may refer to this visit to Rome; see G. Alföldy and H. Halfmann, *ZPE* 35 (1979) 195.

42. See H.-G. Pflaum, *CRAI* 1956 189 and also his *Les sodales Antoniniani* (1967) 41; but see G. Alföldy, *Konsulat und Senatorenstand* (1977) 361, rightly rejecting the attribution of *CIL* VI.1546 to Victorinus.

43. *Ad Am.* II.11.1, echoed at Dio 72.11.2: a commonplace, or did Dio know Fronto's letters?

44. *Ad Am.* I.14.2.

45. On the identity of Aquila, see *JRS* 64 (1974) 151.

46. *CIL* XII.701.

47. O. Hirschfeld, apud *CIL*; L. A. Constans, *Arles antique* (1921) 82; H.-G. Pflaum, *Hommages Bayet* (1964) 556.

48. Y. Burnand, *Mélanges Seston* (1974) 64; C. R. Haines, II.89n1.

49. Dio (Favorinus) *Or.* 37.25; Philostratus *VS* 489-492.

50. *AE* 1947.69 (Q. Trebellius Maximus, archon). Note also the Gallic sophist Iulius Vestinus (nn.34,35 above); and (e.g.) the early Narbonensian consuls (both ordinarii) under the Julio-Claudians, Valerius Asiaticus and Vestinus Atticus. The influence of Massilia is to be reckoned with.

51. Sources in n. 49 above.

52. Gellius 2.26.20 and passim; *Laus Negl.* 3.

53. I can find no parallels in this or Pliny's age.

54. "Ciceronianos" ought not to be "the books of Cicero," *pace* Haines. The terms used here by Fronto are technical, identical to those at Suetonius *Gram.* 24.3; cf. A. Grisart, *Helikon* 2 (1962) 379.

55. Gellius 13.22, 11.13.

56. Gellius 1.6, 2.27, and above.

57. *Ad Am.* II.3.

58. *JRS* 64 (1974) 153.

59. Note the awkward repetition of Fronto's obligation to *close* friends, and the jarring recurrence of *igitur.*

60. *Ant. Pium* 8.

61. *Ep. Var.* 4, 5.

62. Appian *Hist.* praef. 62.

63. For Appian's views on philosophers, see especially his *Mith.* 28.

64. *Ant. Pium* 9.1.

65. *M. Caes.* V.51; Marcus *Meditations* I.8; *HA Pius* 10.4; Lucian *Demonax* 31.

66. *M. Caes.* V.49-50.

67. *ILS* 1463 (Rome).

68. A. Stein, *Der römische Ritterstand* (1927) 188, 441; S. J. de Laet, *Portorium* (1949) 384-403.

69. *CIL* VIII.997; Apuleius *Flor.* 16.2, 23, 24; 18.37-43. Perhaps the man was known to Fronto, who spoke *Pro Carthaginiensibus.*

70. The praetor Sex. Iulius Maior Antoninus Pythodorus; *PIR*² I 398 with (probably) *Dig.* 5.3.25.16, and C. Habicht, *Die Inschriften des Asklepeions* (1969) 63, no. 27: descendant of kings and rhetors, son of a Roman consul, kinsman of the great Polemo, and presumably a friend of Aristides (*Or.* 47).

71. A connection with the Italian Q. Fuficius Cornutus (cos. 147) might be discounted on grounds of origin and grandeur (*PIR*² F 497), but note the relatively obscure Fuficius Candidus, procurator of Corsica in 125 (*AE* 1968.285).

72. Therefore, the standard accounting for the decline of Latin letters, that they withdrew from reality with the loss of political liberty (enunciated by E. Norden, *Antike Kunstprosa*⁵ [1958] 240; cf., e.g., *OCD*² [1970] 581), will have to be reformulated.

IV. THE MAN OF LETTERS

1. *Grammatici Latini* VI.496-497 Keil. Dating oscillates between the reign of Severus Alexander and the earlier years of Diocletian: H. Dahlmann, *PW* XXI (1951) 604.

2. *Inst.* I.2.20; cf. Pliny, *Epp.* 1.2.5, 1.19, 2.13.5, 4.27, 6.33.7, 10.4.1.

3. *Ad Am.* I.27.

4. *Ver. Imp.* II.7; *Ad Am.* I.5, II.7 sal., II.8.1. However, "mi fili" is not an unusual form of address used by an elder to a younger scholar; cf. Gellius 13.20.5; Apuleius *Apol.* 72.3, 97.1.

5. *Ant. Pium* 9.1; *Ad Am.* I.1.3, I.26, I.3.1-2.

6. Gellius 19.8.1.

7. *Ad Am.* I.15.1.

8. Gellius 19.10.

9. Gellius 19.8.

10. Gellius 13.29, 19.8, 2.26, 19.13.

11. R. Marache, *Pallas* 1 (1953) 84.

12. Gellius 1.2, 18.10.

13. Charisius 271 B.

14. *HA Pertinax* 12.8.

15. *Epp.* 3.7.4 (Loeb trans.).

16. Gellius 5.13.1.

17. E.g., Gellius 1.2, 18.5, 18.10, 19.5 (holidays); 2.2, 12.5, 16.3, 18.10 (visits); 4.1, 13.25, 20.1 (waiting); etc. *Sermones convivales*: 1.2, 2.22, 7.13, 9.9, 15.2, 17.8, 18.2, 19.9, 20.8.

18. E.g., Gellius 1.10; 4.1; 1.26; 5.21; 8.10, 14; 10.19; 13.20, 31; 15.9; 16.6; 18.4; 19.1; 20.10.

19. *M. Caes.* IV.3.1, III.3.1. A useful introduction to some of the social aspects of literature is provided by A.-M. Guillemin, *Le public et la vie littéraire à Rome* (1937).

20. Note the verse epitaph of a decurion of Aeclanum (grandfather of a senator): "Ne more pecoris otio transfungerer / Menandri paucas vorti scitas fabulas" (*CIL* IX.1164). In one splendid scene in Gellius, a doctor explaining a case to a philosopher and his disciple carelessly uses the word "vein" for "artery"; at this "loquendi imperitia" the learned men murmur and shake their heads, thus lending support to Galen's precept that in treating men of learning the doctor should strive to avoid solecisms and barbarisms lest his profession be brought into disrepute. Gellius 18.10.4-5; Galen XVII.2.148 K.

21. Gellius 2.26.20.

22. *Ant. Imp.* I.4.2.

23. Gellius 19.13.3; cf. Dio 57.17.1-3 (on Tiberius) with Suetonius *Gramm.* 22.2.

24. H. Peter, *Der Brief in der römischen Literatur* (1901) 216 ff.

25. Charisius 157, 177 B; *GLK* II.547, VII.33; *HA Hadrian* 15.5.

26. Macrobius *Sat.* III.16.6.

27. Gellius 13.18.2-3, 15.3-4.

28. *M. Caes.* I.19.1.

29. *M. Caes.* I.9.3.

30. *M. Caes.* II.3.1.

31. E.g., *Epp.* 1.1, 2, 20; 4.7, 26; 6.21; 7.4; 8.3; 9.11.

32. *Ad Am.* I.14, 15.

33. *M. Caes.* II.1.1. Cf. Apuleius *Apol.* 55.11, on his *De Aesculapii Maiestate*: "Ea disputatio celebratissima est, vulgo legitur, in omnibus manibus versatur."

34. *Ver. Imp.* II.9.1; cf. *Ant. Imp.* III.4, IV.2.3.

35. "The name of Poet was almost forgotten; that of Orator was usurped by the sophists. A cloud of critics, of compilers, of commentators, darkened the face of learning, and the decline of genius was soon followed by the corruption of taste" (Gibbon, chap. II). The last clause should be reversed.

36. *M. Caes.* I.9.4.

37. R. Marache, *La critique littéraire* (1951) 15-78, is the best account of the background of the movement. Note that Hadrian's archaistic tastes were considered perverse: *HA Hadrian* 16.6.

38. Pliny *Epp.* 1.13.1. Numerous items in Pliny, Martial, and Statius attest to widespread dabbling in poetry by the upper classes.

39. *Epp.* 1.16. See further R. Syme, *Tacitus* (1958) 86 ff., on literature under Trajan (88 ff. on poetry). Cf. the alarming versatility at *CIL* VIII.18864.

40. *Epp.* 7.4.4, 9.9-14. At 5.3.3-5 Pliny supplies a catalogue of those who have penned light verse before him. Advocates were particularly susceptible: Petronius *Sat.* 118.1-2; cf. *CIL* XII.4036.

41. *Epp.* 9.26, esp. 8.

42. *M. Caes.* III.17.3.

43. *M. Caes.* II.5.2, I.9.6.

44. *Nep. Am.* 2.7; *Ant. Imp.* IV.2.5.

45. *M. Caes.* IV.3.4: "insperata atque inopinata verba, quae non nisi cum studio atque cura atque vigilantia atque multa veterum carminum memoria indagantur."

46. R. Marache, 128-151, acutely analyzes Fronto's principles; see 155 ff. for Fronto and the poets.

47. *M. Caes.* I.9.5; Gellius 2.26.11.

48. I.7.2.

49. Gellius 19.8.3.

50. Gellius 1.22.9, 5.4.1, 16.10.9, 19.7 (where Ennius and Laevius are discussed); Apuleius *Flor.* 7.4; cf. 6.3.

51. By Alan Cameron in "Poetae novelli" *HSCP*, 84 (1980) in press; the work of E. Castorina, *I poetae novelli* (1949) (repeated substantially and often verbatim in his *Questioni neoteriche*, 1968) is erratic in concept and method. Similarly, the orator Fronto preached no doctrine of "elocutio novella": see Cameron, and L. Holford-Strevens, *CQ* 26 (1976) 140.

52. Gellius 6.7.1.

53. Gellius 6.7, 9.10, 20.8.

54. For the family see J. Fitz, *Epigraphica* 23 (1961) 84; however, the pedigree is quite insecure.

55. I will argue this identification in *HSCP* 85, in press. On Serenus' poetry, see A. Camerons and E. Zaffagno, *Argentea Aetas: In Memoriam E. V. Marmorale* (1973) 273.

56. See, e.g., *PIR*² A 650 (Florus), *CIL* IX.2860, 1663. There is a surprisingly large number of Latin verse inscriptions erected by senators and knights in the second and third centuries. Senators: *CIL* III.21, ?1395, ?7286; VI.132, 313, 319, ?1372, 9797, (31711); VIII.2581; X.1688; XIV.1; *IRT* 295; *AE* 1971.62. Knights: *CIL* III.45, 46, 47; VI.1609, 9241; VII.759, XII.103; *ILAlg.* I.2195. There is even a senatorial cursus honorum in iambic senarii: *ILS* 1195, prefigured a generation earlier by *CIL* II.2660. Tragedy in the age of the Antonines is represented by a miserable Vergilian cento, the *Medea*, by Hosidius Geta, who was almost certainly a senator (*PLM* IV.219; cf. *ILS* 7190); comedy was the preserve of the mimographer Marullus, who betrays some hints of social standing (see M. Bonario, *Dionisio* 35 [1961] 16).

57. *PLM* IV.169. For other professors in verse see *CIL* VI.33904/05, VIII.26671/72, XIII.1393.

58. *PIR*² I 604/605.

59. *GLK* VI.313 ff.

60. Fronto's historiography has received considerable attention. Most useful are the analyses of M. Leroy, *Musée Belge* 32 (1928) 241; S. Jannacone, *GIF* 14 (1961) 289; P. V. Cova, *Mélanges M. Renard* (1969) I.268, and (especially) *I Principia Historiae e le idee storiografiche di Frontone* (1970). M. D. Brock, *Studies in Fronto and His Age* (1911) 62 ff., confuses Fronto as historian with his letters as history; J. Revay, *AAntHung* 1 (1951) 161 (résumé in French at 190), attempts to reconstruct a *De Bello Parthico* from references in Lucian, although there is real doubt whether Fronto ever wrote this work.

61. P. V. Cova contends at length that the *Principia Historiae* is no more than a polite refusal to undertake a work on the war which Fronto never intended to write; the interpretation is not conclusive. Whatever his intentions, Fronto probably died before he could carry them out; see Appendix C.

62. Schanz-Hosius 58 ff.

63. *HA Hadrian* 11.3; *Ad Am.* I.13.

64. The long controversy surrounding these authors (one man or two?) has been summed up (and, I believe, settled) by T. D. Barnes, *The Sources of the "Historia Augusta,"* Collection Latomus 155 (1978), 90 ff.

65. Priscian, in *GLK* III.482; cf. II.250f.

66. Florus I.33.8: "It is a greater thing to keep than to conquer a province." Cf. W. den Boer, *Some Minor Roman Historians* (1972) 1; A. Garzetti, *Athenaeum* 42 (1964) 135.

67. R. B. Steele, *AJP* 38 (1917) 24 ff., esp. 40-41, adduces textual parallels, some of which are more convincing than others.

68. On Sallust see 33.8-13 Fl. On his family see *PIR*² L 247-249.

69. See S. Jannacone, 303 ff.

70. F. Bücheler, *Kl. Schr.* III.331 ff., against Hirschfeld and followed by all subsequent writers (see next note); his opinion is not conclusive.

71. O. Hirschfeld, *Kl. Schr.* 699 ff. Cf. H.-G. Pflaum, *Carrières* 651 ff., with references.

72. M. D. Brock, 78; M. Leroy, *Musée Belge* 34 (1932) 291.

73. See Chapter VIII for Fronto's teachings. For the folly of applying philosophy to life, see Tacitus *Dial.* 5, *Hist.* III.81, *ILS* 7778.

74. The fullest statement is found in the letters *De Eloquentia*; see also *M. Caes.* III.16; *Ad Am.* I.15.2.

75. Gellius 19.5.1.

76. Philostratus *VS* 566.

77. M. L. Clarke has argued ingeniously (*CP* 68 [1973] 19) that the poem compliments Herodes' presidency of the Panathenaia in 138/139. In support of this, the recipient of the poem, a Messalla, could be the patrician L. Vipstanus Poplicola Messalla, son of the consul of 115, and honored at Athens (*IG* II/III[2] 4208; cf. *ILS* 272, *CIL* XIV.4245).

78. R. Helm, *Altertum* 1 (1955) 86; T. D. Barnes, *Tertullian* (1971) 211 ("ecclesiarum sophista"); Cameron, "Poetae novelli." As for Fronto, the article of A. Ramirez de Verger, *Habis* 4 (1973) 115, is of no use; I have not seen H. Lannoy, "De invloed van de tweede sophistik op Fronto en Apuleius," diss., Louvain, 1948?.

79. See, e.g., *M. Caes.* IV.3.6, I.9.3.

80. Cf. the discussion of R. Marache, 120 ff.

81. E. Norden, *Antike Kunstprosa*[5] (1958) I.361 f.

82. M. D. Brock, 36; A. Cameron.

83. Gellius 2.26.20; *Ep. Var.* 7.2.

84. On Fronto and Greek literature, see R. Marache, 117 ff.

85. *Eloq.* 4.9; cf. *M. Caes.* III.9.2.

86. This rise is fully documented by H. Halfmann, *Die Senatoren aus dem östlichen Teil des Imperium Romanum bis zum Ende des 2. Jahrhunderts n. Chr.*, Hypomnemata 58 (1979).

87. Charted particularly in recent times by G. W. Bowersock (*Augustus and the Greek World*, 1965, and *Greek Sophists in the Roman Empire*, 1969), and by C. P. Jones (*Plutarch and Rome*, 1971, and *The Roman World of Dio Chrysostom*, 1978). See also R. Syme, *Tacitus* 504-519.

88. On the date and historicity of the characters, see the convincing discussion of W. Dittenberger, *Apophoreton. XLVII Versammlung deutscher Philologen und Schulmänner* (1903) 1; addenda by B. Baldwin, *Acta Classica* 19 (1976) 21.

89. Athenaeus I.1a-3b, II.50f-51a, etc.

90. *Inst.* 2.5.21; Gellius 13.29.3.

V. THE LAWYER

1. The vast material on Roman advocacy has been ignored by modern

historians. I know of no monographs later than those of J. Poiret (1887) and A. Pierantoni (1900).

2. *M. Caes.* V.42, 59; *Ver. Imp.* 2.7.3.

3. Dio 69.18.3-4: for the date see Appendix B.

4. For the prefect's jurisdiction see M. Durry, *Les cohortes prétoriennes* (1938) 171; A. Passerini, *Le coorti pretorie* (1939) 233.

5. *M. Caes.* V.49.

6. S. J. de Laet, *Portorium* (1949) 444 f., collects the relevant passages in the Digest, with penalties. I discount here the possibility of nonfiscal crimes committed in the course of collecting taxes.

7. On praetors and publicans see Tacitus *Ann.* 13.51; cf. *Dig.* 39.4.1 pr. De Laet suggests (446) the praetor "qui inter fiscum et privatos ius diceret," but he is attested only in the time of Nerva (Pliny *Pan.* 36; *Dig.* 1.2.2.32), and the fisc need not be involved in cases against *conductores.* On imperial intervention cf. Marcus as judge listening to his own *advocatus fisci* (*Dig.* 28.4.3).

8. *M. Caes.* I.6.2-7.

9. *M. Caes.* III.3.2.

10. By G. W. Bowersock, *Greek Sophists in the Roman Empire* (1969) 93-100; my account attempts no more than a summary of his results.

11. *M. Caes.* III.6.

12. Cf. *M. Caes.* III.3.2 with Philostratus *VS* 549.

13. *Ver. Imp.* II.9; cf. *Ant. Imp.* III.4, and G. W. Bowersock, 93-100. On the identity of Asclepiodotus, see n. 113 to Chapter VII.

14. Philostratus *VS* 559; cf. *IG* II/III^2 2342 (with stemma). The three archons were Ti. Claudius Demostratus, 4071.22; Aelius Praxagoras, 2067.2 (archon 154/155); M. Valerius Mamertinus, 1773 (archon 166/167).

15. Obscurities remain; I will argue elsewhere that Fronto's client in this speech was not the archon Demostratus but a senatorial kinsman.

16. *Octavius* 8.3-9.6.

17. *Octavius* 30.2-31.2.

18. Just how much of Fronto is embedded in the *Octavius* is very unsure, particularly with such a stylistic "mosaicist" as Minucius Felix; cf. further G. W. Clarke, *Kyriakon: Festschrift J. Quasten* (1970) 503. Certainly Frontonian is 9.6-7, possibly 9.5-7.

19. This was suggested by T. D. Barnes, *Tertullian* (1971) 161n2.

20. "The" speech occurs in the translations in Loeb, Budé, Ante-Nicene Christian Library 13, and (on the same lines) The Fathers of the Church 10.

21. P. Frassinetti, in the most imaginative attack on the problem (*GIF* 2 [1949] 238), dated the piece c. 162/164, because Pius' reign (138-161) was too lenient to Christians, and Minucius *Oct.* 7.4 demands a date before the end of the Parthian War (but see the sober introduction to the Budé edition of J. Beaujeu), etc.; the death of Justin Martyr is seen as an indirect result. But for M. Sordi, *Riv. Stor. Chiesa Italiana* 16 (1962) 3 ff., the speech was delivered c. 175/176, just in time to cause the massacre at Lyon and Athenagoras' *Legatio*. The latest embellishment is by M. C. Cristofori, *Riv. Stor. Chiesa Italiana* 32 (1978) 130.

22. Observed by R. Freudenberger, *ThZ* 23 (1967) 97.

23. *Legatio* 1-2; *HE* V.1.

24. *Legatio* 3.1; *HE* V.1.14.

25. R. Freudenberger, 103 f.

26. *Epp.* VIII.10.3 (Loeb trans.).

27. See (e.g.) P. Grimal, *Dictionnaire de la mythologie grecque et romaine*[4] (1969).

28. See, e.g., K. Baus, *Handbook of Church History* I (1965) 166; W. H. C. Frend, *Martyrdom and Persecution in the Early Church* (1965) 269.

29. Lactantius *Div. Inst.* V.1.21; cf. Jerome *Vir. Ill.* 58: "Romae insignis causidicus."

30. The only prominent Pelops known at this time was the teacher of Galen, who has accordingly been identified with Fronto's victim: *PW* Pelops 5; cf. Schanz-Hosius III (1922) 96. There is no reason why he should be.

31. *SEG* XIII.277 (Patras).

32. *Ant. Pium* 8.1.

33. Charisius 175.12-17 B. For punctuation see A. Mazzarino, *Maia* 1 (1948) 66.

34. The second person singular is used in the fragment on overseas wills, *M. Caes.* I.6.

35. There is no evidence as to the effect of the uprising on Ptolemais: C. H. Kraeling, *Ptolemais, City of the Libyan Decapolis* (1962) 17. For the extent of the devastation generally, throughout the province, see A. Fuks, *JRS* 51 (1961) 97, with evidence for Antonine reconstruction.

36. *Expositio* 35, p. 121 H.

37. Schanz-Hosius IV.2.202; *PW* VII.219 f.

38. *Ad Am.* I.15.1.

39. *Ad Am.* I.14.2.

40. Cf. Pliny and the Baetici: *Epp.* 3.4.2-7.

41. Tacitus *Ann.* 12.22.4; Dio 60.33.6; Tacitus *Ann.* 14.46; Pliny *Epp.* 4.9; Pliny *Epp.* 5.20, 6.5, 13, 7.6.10.

42. See (e.g.) Pliny *Epp.* 10.34, 58, 81; Dio *Or.* 48-41.

43. For senate trials in this period, see P. Garnsey, *Social Status and Legal Privilege in the Roman Empire* (1970) 59-63 (and 45-49).

44. P. A. Brunt, *Historia* 10 (1961), 189, collects the evidence for such trials from Augustus to Trajan.

45. *Ad Am.* I.15.3, with m^2.

46. Cf. Pliny *Epp.* 9.13.2, 21.

47. Chronic illness may be a factor here, prohibiting strenuous performance in court: note especially *M. Caes.* V.59, and *Ad Am.* II.11 declines a brief.

48. *Ad Am.* I.1.1. On *suffragium* in general, G. E. M. de Ste. Croix, *British Journal of Sociology* 5 (1954) 33, especially 43 f. (on this letter).

49. *Ad Am.* I.1.4.

50. "The broad wink of *gratia*" was discerned by J. M. Kelly, *Roman Litigation* (1966) 59-61; cf. P. Garnsey, 208 ff. At p. 60, Kelly improperly juxta-

posed to this letter *Ad Am.* I.4.1, a nonjudicial matter, to suggest quid pro quo.

51. *Ad Am.* II.7.

52. Lucian, *Toxaris* 24-26, tells a story with some similarities.

53. This was noted by A. Stein, *Der römische Ritterstand* (1927) 132; with *Ad Am.* II.7.15.

54. *Ad Am.* II.8.2.

55. *Ant. Imp.* II.2; *Ad Am.* I.14.

56. Egatheus will receive nothing; viz. T. Aurelius Egatheus Imp. Antonini Aug. lib. a codicillis (*ILS* 1529), who would presumably receive the inheritance whole if the codicils were disallowed.

57. *Ant. Imp.* II.1.1-2.

58. See nn. 71-73 below for the protests of modern students of Roman law.

59. *Ant. Imp.* II.2.2.

60. *Dig.* 35.2.26, first noticed by H. E. Dirksen, *Hinterlassene Schriften* (1871) I.248 ff. The details of that case are so reminiscent of those in the correspondence, yet so difficult to fit into any coherent reconstruction of the affair, that it may be best to view it as a hypothesis based by the jurist on an actual recent case.

61. Tacitus *Dial.* 3.4. Note Fronto's casual reference (*Ant. Pium* 8) to "duas amicorum causas" which he pleaded before the emperor.

62. A work on Roman advocacy would have to make social distinctions from the outset. For a tiny sample of motives, see Martial 1.76 and 5.18; Pliny *Epp.* 6.29.1-3; Dio *Or.* 24.3; and especially Tacitus *Dial.*

63. On Baetica see *Epp.* 7.33.4-10, etc.; Africa, 2.11, etc.; Firmum, 6.18.3; Comum, 1.3, etc.; Tifernum, 3.4, etc.

64. Another possibility might be pursued, the fragment (*Ad Am.* I.20.5) giving advice to his Ephesian friend Claudius Iulianus on the conduct of a trial: ". . . gravius eum tractavi quam Stratonabian aut Pyrallum."

65. Centumviral cases: *Epp.* 1.5, 18; 4.16, 17?, 24; 5.1, 9; 6.12, 33; 9.23.1. *Iudex*: 7.6.

66. F. Schulz was particularly harsh on the advocate: *Roman Legal Science* (1946) 43, 53, 71, 76, 108, 356. But (e.g.) Seneca *Apoc.* 12 seems insufficient for the claim of antagonism between advocate and jurist under Claudius; and most of Schulz' ammunition is drawn from the single source of Cicero. For one method of revising Schulz, see W. Kunkel, *Herkunft und soziale Stellung der römischen Juristen*[2] (1967) 325 ff., with *Dig.* 1.2.2.40, 43, 46, and especially 45.

67. Note particularly the evidence of Quintilian *Inst.* 12.3 (cf. 2.8.8); *Dig.* 1.2.2.43; Pliny *Epp.* 8.14.1-2; Martial 10.37.

68. Gellius 14.2.1-10.

69. *Epp.* 4.22, 6.22, 31; 6.11.

70. Dio 73.12.2: as an advocate he had successfully attacked Didius Iulianus in his youth (before 193, therefore while still in his twenties). On *cognitiones* see Dio 75.16.2-4, 76.17.1.

71. Especially by H. E. Dirksen, *Hinterlassene Schriften* I.243 ff., 276 ff.

72. Commentators include H. E. Dirksen, 276; G. Bortolucci, in *Studi Salvatore Riccobono* (1936) 433; and, best, G. Boyer, *Mélanges* I (1962) 271 = *Mélanges J. Magnol* (1948) 21.

73. B. Kübler, *Festschrift Paul Koschaker* (1939) II.353; H. E. Dirksen, 248.

74. Gellius 20.1; and it will be recalled that Gellius consulted Favorinus on the law.

75. *M. Caes.* IV.12.7.

76. *Ver. Imp.* I.3.2; *Ant. Pium* 8.1.

77. *Ep. Var.* 5.1.

78. *Ant. Imp.* I.5.1.

79. *M. Caes.* I.4.

80. *Fer. Als.* 3.8 ff.

81. *Fer. Als.* 3.8 ff.

82. *M. Caes.* II.15.1; V.74.1. *HA Marcus* 10.10 ff., 24.1 ff.; cf. (e.g.) *Dig.* 28.4.3.

83. *M. Caes.* IV.5.3.

84. *M. Caes.* V.43.1.

85. *M. Caes.* IV.13. For the interpretation proposed here, see my confused statement at *JRS* 64 (1974) 144.

86. See, e.g., Quintilian *Inst.* 12.11.5, or Tacitus *Dial.* 34.7, etc.

87. *Ver. Imp.* II.7.3-4.

88. *M. Caes.* V.59; *Ad Am.* II.11.

89. *Ad Am.* I.27.

90. *Ad Am.* I.10.1.

91. Cf. the sentiment expressed by Pliny in recommending a younger colleague: "Est indolis optimae brevi producturus alios, si interim provectus fuerit a nobis."

VI. THE SENATOR

1. *ILS* 2928.

2. I assume a date of birth c. 95; see Appendix B.

3. The minimum age for the praetorship is not necessarily the norm, and there is nothing in Fronto's previous career to promise any quick accession to high office. However, there is no need to assume any retardation; the *ius trium liberorum* may have worked to his advantage—he had or was to have six children.

4. *M. Caes.* I.3.4.

5. Cf. *JRS* 64 (1974) 141.

6. M. Corbier, *L'aerarium Saturni et l'aerarium militare* (1974), list at 570 ff.

7. *ILS* 2927, 8973. Of the two anomalies, one held the *aerarium militare* as his only praetorian post, having been adlected *inter praetorios* by Vespasian: *ILS* 1001. The other is an anonymous consul of the early third century who held another praetorian office not available in Fronto's day, an Italian juridicate: *ILS* 8842.

8. List at M. Corbier, 476 ff. Of the anomalies, two had been adlected *inter praetorios*: *AE* 1953.179, 1961.280. A third excused himself from a legionary legateship and was able to consider that office as a stage completed in his cursus: *ILS* 1071. The fourth went directly from praetor to prefect to ordinary consul, but he was a relative of the dynasty whose career shows other marks of special favour: *ILS* 1081.

9. F. Millar, *JRS* 54 (1964) 36; M. Corbier, 689 ff, 697. Pliny *Epp*. I.10.9-10 is essential for the duties.

10. Cf. M. Corbier, 528-538, confirming a standard observation.

11. Cf. the selective list of consuls in the late 30s and early 40s after Christ compiled by R. Syme, *JRS* 60 (1970) 29: "the results of late entry, slow progress or a setback."

12. This desire is useful for dating the letters: *JRS* 64 (1974) 140; cf. n. 21 below.

13. *Ant. Pium* 8 is generally taken as a request for *excusatio*, but there is no need: it may simply be an elaborate plea for extending the orator's stay in Rome beyond the latest date for departure allowed by the emperor (mid-April; cf. Dio 60.17.3). If *M. Caes*. V.51 is taken at face value, Fronto might appear to be in his province. Against this, it might be argued from silence that there is no other hint of such service in the letters and no sign of a separate book of official communications.

14. His career may be tabulated as follows (e.g.):

III vir cap.	c. 115/120
qu. prov. Siciliae	c. 120
aedil. pl.	c. 123
praetor	c. 125
praef. aer. mil.	c. 126-128
praef. aer. Sat.	c. 129-131
cos. suff.	143
procos. Asiae (se excusavit?)	c. 157/158

15. Seneca *Brev. Vit*. 20.4; cf. D. MacAlindon, *CR* 7 (1957) 108.

16. *M. Caes*. II.9, 10, 12.

17. Philostratus *VS* 555 f., *HA Pius* 7.3; cf. *Dig*. 40.5.12.1. *HA Pius* 7.3; cf. *FO*, anno 145.

18. *HA Marcus* 10.1, 25.6; Dio 71.28.2.

19. *M. Caes*. III.21.1; cf. *HA Pius* 7.1: "provinciae sub eo floruerunt," etc. Might the affair be connected with Fronto's *De Testamentis Transmarinis?*

20. *Ad Am*. I.20.3: ". . . roughly handled, I delivered in the senate . . . was asked to repeat it"; and I.20.5: "Our friend Valerianus has told you the great blows, which from all [quarters] . . . I treated him more firmly than Stratonabia or Pyrallus."

21. *Ant. Imp*. IV.2.3; *Pro Carthaginiensibus* (v.d. Hout 241 f.).

22. *M. Caes*. II.1.1.

23. Note the rosy picture of the empire to be derived from Aristides *Or*. 26K.

24. *Or.* 35K, reattributed by C. P. Jones to Aristides after decades of doubt: *JRS* 62 (1972) 134-152. The attribution, accepted here, has since been attacked in detail or in passing: S. A. Stertz, *CQ* 29 (1979) 172; J. H. Oliver, *GRBS* 19 (1978) 386 ff.; V. Nutton, in P. D. A. Garnsey and C. R. Whittaker, ed., *Imperialism in the Ancient World* (1978) 210 f. Defense of the attribution would require a long digression, and one concerned more with method than with fact.

25. *Rhetores Graeci* ed. Spengl, III.368 ff.

26. *Ant. Pium* 5.

27. *M. Caes.* I.10.4. Note the catalogue of Pius' virtues at *HA Pius* 2.1-2: the biographer may have been familiar with Fronto's speech, which circulated into the fourth century.

28. *HA Pius* 13.4; *Epitome de Caesaribus* 15.2-3. The latter source certainly derives from Marius Maximus: T. D. Barnes, *The Sources of the "Historia Augusta"* (1978) 98 ff.

29. *HA Marcus* 1.6 (citing Maximus as the source); cf. Eutropius 8.9. See W. Hüttl, *Antoninus Pius* I (1936) 173: "der neuer Numa" did restore a temple at Cures Sabini, the reputed birthplace of Numa; see also *PW* II.2509 f.

30. *Princ. Hist.* 2.10. Pius' name is lost here, but assured by the gloss of m^2: "Qualis et Antoninus Pius fuit." Ignorance of the attribution leads to serious error; see R. Zoepffel, *Chiron* 8 (1978) 391 ff.

31. Cf. *M. Caes.* III.8.2.

32. *Fer. Als.* 3.5.

33. *ILS* 341.

34. See the collection and discussion of the evidence by C. P. Jones, *JRS* 62 (1972) 142 ff.

35. *HA Pius* 5.4; *ILS* 340.

36. *Pan. Lat.* VIII(V).14.2.

37. *Or.* 35K. The Numan combination of peace and piety found itself exploited in a fragment of contemporary verse: "Germanos Maurosque domas sub Marte (?)Guitanos / Antonine tua diceris arte Pius" (*CIL* VI.1208).

38. *Ant. Imp.* IV.2.3; *Ant. Pium* 2.1.

39. Analogy can help, given the confines of the genre. Thus Pliny remarks upon various actions of Trajan, his benefactions to the people, administrative and legal reforms, public works, and (at great length) his relations with the senate. Aristides praises Pius' remissions of taxes, his humane administration of justice, his phil-Hellenism, his accessibility, and his restraint.

40. Pliny *Pan.* 83-84; Ausonius 2, 8, 10.

41. Probably not the consular *actio*; see *JRS* 64 (1974) 149.

42. *Ant. Pium* 2.2.

43. Ausonius 15.

44. *M. Caes.* I.10.4, II.3.3 (note the pun).

45. The fragments are preserved independently of the correspondence.

46. *HA Pius* 9.1-2; cf. Aurelius Victor 16.12, Pausanias 8.43.4.

47. A. Lézine, *Carthage-Utique* (1968) 1-75.

48. *CIL* VIII.12513.

48. *CIL* VIII.12513.

49. R. Cagnat, *RA* ser. 3, 10 (1887) 171, approved by P. Romanelli, *Storia della provincia romane dell'Africa* (1959) 362.

50. The Rhodian earthquake is fixed by Aristides, *Or.* 24.3 K, and the Opramoas inscription, *TAM* 905, c. 53, 59, 63; see W. Hüttl, II.38, for the computation.

51. B. Bischoff, *Der Fronto-Palimpsest der Mauriner*, SBAW, 1958 no. 2, 27 f. Van den Hout's text here must be ignored, but the paragraphs are retained for convenience.

52. The fragment runs: "regin <ae> Aegypt <i> amator Antoniu <s> ," a reading supported by the occurrence of "contub <ernalis/ernium?> " (followed perhaps by a feminine diminutive) five lines previously. The proposed restorations (which are highly conjectural) are mine, but B. Bischoff does suggest "reginae" in his critical apparatus.

53. It reads: "Orbi <s> securior videatur . . .," "aeru <mnae?> maximae illae," " <?tri> busque divisae," ". . . na aut aliena maria Carthaginem," "hac propin <quitate?> ," "seditionibus . . . mag . . .," "domant venan <tur> ." Or possibly the Punic Wars? (Italics indicate uncertain readings, here and in n. 54.)

54. Thus: ". . . do*mo* interrogan . . ." (that is, perhaps, trials in camera), followed by "novos incolum*i* libertate <n> os curarum" and ". . . nobis manibus bonis esse sine periculo licet nemo dives . . ." Then "nec sapien . . . <?ami> *c*itiam metri . . .," ". . . a crudi ce <rvices?> " (e.g.), and "patricium insidiator*is* nom <en> ," followed by "sentiamus nostr< enim a . . . *prosp* < sortem *te*mporum . . ."

55. *Ant. Pium* 2: "tam trita et assidua materia."

56. *M. Caes.* I.9.1, quoting Horace *Sat.* II.3.254-257.

57. Valerius Maximus 6.9.15.1; Lucian *Bis Accusatus* 16-17; Diogenes Laertius 4.16.

58. Fronto had a fondness for puns; see especially *M. Caes.* V.52.

59. *M. Caes.* I.9.2.

60. *Ad Am.* I.27.2 (similar to a sentiment in Apuleius, *Flor.* 16.31).

61. *Ad Am.* II.4.

62. The fragment reads: ". . . patricium insidiatoris nomen . . ."

63. *Ver. Imp.* II.7.7.

64. *Ad Am.* I.3.3.

65. Or, more harshly, the trait can be seen as evidence for the dilettantist search for the pure and simple life in an "age of anxiety"; cf. I. Lana, *Cultura e Scuola* 18 (1966) 90.

66. I.11 (also taught Marcus by Sextus of Chaeronea, I.9.3). Marcus took the lesson to heart; he was thankful that his wife had the quality, and he believed that an emperor should (I.17.8, 6.30.1). And in one letter (*Fer. Als.* 4.2), he addresses Fronto by the term.

67. R. Syme, "Novus Homo," in *Tacitus* (1958) 566 ff., surrounded by relevant chapters.

68. I have included among the senators the praetorian prefects Gavius Maximus and Cornelius Repentinus, each attested as *vir clarissimus.*

69. *Ad Am.* II.11.1.

70. *Ad Am.* I.4.2.

71. *Ant. Pium* 3.3.

72. *Ad Am.* II.7.15.

73. *Ver. Imp.* II.7.2. The enmity of a senator was particularly to be feared by a nonsenator: *Ad Am.* I.1.4; cf. Pliny *Epp.* 5.13.2.

74. *HA Marcus* 10.1-9.

75. *M. Caes.* V.37-38; the subject is M'. Acilius Glabrio, cos. 91, on whom see Dio 67.14.3 and Juvenal 4.94-101.

76. *HA Marcus* 10.7.

77. *Eloq.* 2.7.

78. *Eloq.* 2.7, van den Hout 136.31-32; cf. 25: "Quae res auctoritatem principum minuat."

79. *M. Caes.* IV.3.6.

80. *M. Caes.* III.1.

81. *M. Caes.* II.3.3.

82. *M. Caes.* III.18.2.

83. *Ant. Imp.* I.2.5.

84. *Ant. Imp.* 6, 9, 12. The *paraleipsis* no doubt went something like this: "As to the petition of the people of Cyzicus, conscript fathers, we pass over our hereditary ties with their city, for its present plight is sufficient to claim our urgent attention." Cf. *ILS* 7190.

85. 8.30 (Farquharson trans.).

86. This is well demonstrated by W. Williams, *JRS* 66 (1976) 78-82.

87. Dio 71.24.1-27.1. See further Chapter VIII and Appendix C.

VII. THE FRIEND OF CAESAR

1. *M. Caes.* I.3.4.

2. Note (e.g.) the tales about Marcus' wife: *HA Verus* 10.1; *HA Marcus* 19.1; *HA Avidius* 9.5; *HA Marcus* 24.6; Dio 71.22-23. Cf. R. Syme, *Emperors and Biography* (1971) 128, and for the identity of her alleged lovers, see H.-G. Pflaum, *BHAC* 1968/1969 223 ff. (add *AE* 1971.534). The career of Helvius Pertinax (*HA Pertinax* 2.4-6, confirmed in part by *AE* 1963.52, and Dio 71.22.1) is particularly rich in intrigues. Lucian, *Alex.* 30, 31, 48, 57, and cf. 39 (with A. Stein, *Strena Buliciana* [1924] 260), offers a picture of one man's overwhelming *gratia* at court. Fronto's friend Cornelius Repentinus (*Ad Am.* II.4) reportedly owed his praetorian prefecture to the influence of Pius' concubine Lysistrate: *HA Pius* 8.9 (see *ILS* 1836 for the woman).

3. *HA Hadrian* 16.6. Cf. the quaestor Salvius Iulianus (cos. 148), "cui divos Hadrianus soli salarium quaesturae duplicavit propter insignem doctrinam" (*ILS* 8973, on the meaning of which see D. Nörr, *Daube Noster* [1974] 242 ff.).

4. *M. Caes.* II.1.1.

5. *HA Hadrian* 15.10.

6. *HA Hadrian* 16.8-9.

7. *HA Hadrian* 16.10; Dio 69.3.4; and the treatise *De Exilio* (ed. A. Barigazzi, 375 ff.).

8. On Hadrian's treatment of Greek intellectuals see especially G. W. Bowersock, *Greek Sophists in the Roman Empire* (1969) 50-53. On his treatment of Latins, note the case of Suetonius (*HA Hadrian* 11.3), and the sharpness of the interchange with Florus (*HA Hadrian* 16.3-4).

9. *Fer. Als.* 3.5; *Ver. Imp.* II.1.12, *m*².

10. *Bell. Parth.* 2; *Princ. Hist.* 2.8-9. Fronto's opinions are of dubious value; see R. W. Davies, *Latomus* 27 (1968) 75.

11. *HA Hadrian* 15, with examples.

12. *Princ. Hist.* 2.8.

13. *HA Hadrian* 27.2 ("repugnantibus cunctis"); cf. *HA Pius* 5.1; Dio 69.23.3, 70.1.2-3. Hostility to Hadrian entered into senate mythology: Dio 76.7.5. It has certainly been observed in Aristides' panegyric of Pius: C. P. Jones, *JRS* 62 (1972) 151 f.

14. *Ant. Pium* 4.

15. *Nep. Am.* 2.8 ("saepe etiam cum periculo capitis").

16. See the exposition by R. Syme, *Historia* 17 (1968) 93-97. On Hadrian's first arrangements, see *ZPE* 21 (1976) 79; on the eventual settlement, see T. D. Barnes, *JRS* 57 (1967) 74 ff.

17. If the context is indeed the last years of Hadrian, the phrase "multa amice, multa fideliter" might recall the similar conjunction of the *familiaritas* with the lack of *fiducia* in Fronto's relationship with Hadrian.

18. Cf. Pliny as praetor visiting the philosopher Artemidorus at a time when philosophers were banned from the city and seven of his own friends had been slain or relegated: *Epp.* 3.11.

19. One of Fronto's primary occupations was acting in "amicorum causae": *Ant. Pium* 8.1; *M. Caes.* V.49, 59, etc. (see Chapter V). At this time Pedanius Fuscus (at least) probably stood trial: *Cat. Cod. Astr. Graec.* VIII.2.85 ff.

20. The best indication of the date lies in a letter written long after the event which recalled the speech delivered in the Senate by Marcus "when scarcely more than a boy," eliciting from Fronto "that first rather long letter from you" (*Ant. Imp.* I.2.5: A.D. 161). This first letter in fact survives, formal in tone and far removed from the intimacy which had arisen by the time of Fronto's consulship (*M. Caes.* IV.3). The speech concerned was probably Marcus' thanks for the Caesarship, or perhaps an address read in his capacity as *quaestor imperatoris* (5 Dec. 138/139). If Fronto's letter was indeed the first, it should have been dispatched soon after the commencement of their acquaintance. He therefore became Marcus' tutor either in the course of 139 or very late in 138, that is, after the death of Hadrian in the summer of 138, and when Marcus was of an age (seventeen or eighteen) to profit most from his rhetorical teachings. The timing is suggestive if Fronto's appointment was possible only under a new emperor.

21. Marcus *Meditations* I.16.6; *HA Pius* 11.3. Pius on Fronto: *M. Caes.* I.16.1.

22. *M. Caes.* II.1.1.

23. For the protocol, see J. Crook, *Consilium Principis* (1955) 23.

24. *M. Caes.* I.3.4.

25. *M. Caes.* III.14.3; Gellius 19.13 (cf. 4.1, 20.1).

26. *M. Caes.* V.63-64. Cf. II.16: "illa cottidie tua Lorium ventio, illa in serum expectatio" (but this might refer to some domestic crisis in the imperial family).

27. *M. Caes.* V.45-46. The restored reading mentioning Cratia is most probable.

28. *M. Caes.* V.57-58, 69-70.

29. *Ant. Pium* 6: "Cum bene perspectas habeam sincerissimas in me adfectiones tuas, tum et ex meo animo non difficile credo, mi Fronto carissime, vel praecipue hunc diem, quo me suscipere hanc stationem placuit, a te potissimum vere religioseque celebrari."

30. *Epp.* 10.35-36, 100-101; 52-53, 102-103; 88-89.

31. J. Crook, with the comments of R. Syme, *AJP* 67 (1956) 264.

32. *Ant. Pium* 9.

33. *Ant. Pium* 9: "ne inprobe peterem." Elsewhere in the correspondence the only other sign of Fronto's influence with Pius may appear in his attribution of his brother's success to the emperor's *bonitas*; and it is interesting that in the same passage he affirms that none of his own honors were sought *inprobis rationibus*: *Nep. Am.* 2.9.

34. On *suffragium* in general, see the survey of G. E. M. de Ste. Croix, *British Journal of Sociology* 5 (1954) 33. Epigraphy confirms that even imperial procuratorships could be secured by senatorial influence: *CIL* VI.1418 and *ILS* 1191 (both by consulars), *CIL* VI.2132 (by a vestal virgin).

35. Cf. the essay of R. Syme, "Pliny's Less Successful Friends," *Historia* 9 (1960) 362.

36. *ILS* 1011, 1545, 3832, 6698; *CIL* VI.1545; and especially *ILS* 1071: a man praetor, legate of the tenth legion Fretensis "a cuius cura se excusavit," curator viarum, prefect of the Saturnian treasury, consul.

37. Praef. 62.

38. Pius was particularly hard on sinecures, hence his general suspicions and Fronto's careful denial of sordid motives: cf. *HA Pius* 7.7. The interplay of interests in this case is remarkable, the reluctant emperor defending a principle, his friend urging a single exception, the client seeking imperial honor, and the host of rivals whose motives are less pure.

39. *Ant. Pium* 7 (= *Ad Am.* II.5).

40. *Ant. Pium* 4.1; *HA Pius* 8.7; cf. (e.g.) *ILS* 1325.

41. Text: van den Hout 160.20 f., restored by P. Pescani, *Coniecturae* 17. (Haines I.260 is obsolete.)

42. *Ant. Pium* 3.4.

43. E. Birley, apud H.-G. Pflaum, *Carrières*, pp. 227 f., observing that Maximus followed Niger as procurator of Mauretania Tingitana, suggested

that he was later promoted to prefect over Niger's head. However, Censorius Niger's very occupancy of the Mauretanian post is in doubt: the mutilated stone *CIL* XVI.176 (cf. *AE* 1969/1970.743) retains only the cognomen Niger. Thus Censorius' only surely attested office remains the governorship of Noricum, known from *CIL* III.5174, 5181.

44. On the phenomenon of *amicitiam renuntiare* in general, see R. S. Rogers, *TAPA* 90 (1959) 224.

45. *Ant. Pium* 4.2.

46. *HA Marcus* 6.7-8; Dio 71.35.4.

47. *M. Caes.* V.49; cf. 50.

48. *M. Caes.* IV.7, V.35, I.6.1, etc.

49. Haines I.239 translates "a pueritia me curavit" as "has attended to all my wants since I was a boy," surely wrong: Aridelus would be rather old for promotion, and one would have to account for his transfer from Fronto's service to the emperor's. Surely he has served Fronto from his own boyhood, a standard element in the letter of commendation; cf. *Ver. Imp.* II.7.2 ("a prima aetate sua me curavit Gavius Clarus") or *CIL* VI.2120 ("cognitus mihi ex longo tempore primae iubentutis").

50. The ms. reads: "procuravit vobis industrie"; van den Hout offers "procurabit," following an emendation of Mai. Textually there is little to choose, but the context surely demands the perfect tense: your *libertus* has cared for you well in the past, now he wishes to be an actual procurator. Commendation naturally praises past performance, and Fronto enjoys a word-play; cf. the uses of *forma* in this same letter.

51. *M. Caes.* V.52.

52. H.-G. Pflaum, *Les procurateurs équestres* (1950) 210; cf. P. R. C. Weaver, *Familia Caesaris* (1972) 268 f. The notion of rules is cogently criticized by F. Millar, *JRS* 53 (1963) 194.

53. The crucial phrase reads "e a o r m a suo loco ac i u o tempore." "Ex forma" is a marginal emendation, easily an inspired guess of a late Roman scribe in whose era *forma* could mean not just regulation but grade or rank: P. R. C. Weaver, 269n2. (But a word-play on *forma* is admittedly attractive; see n. 50, above.) Certainly "perpetua forma" at *CIL* VIII.10570.iii.16, iv.17 (reign of Commodus) appears to mean "hallowed custom," which is merely the forerunner, not the equivalent, of "regulation." As for "iusto tempore," "tuo tempore" seems just as likely a correction, and perhaps more attractive in the context.

54. *HA Marcus* 5.4.

55. *M. Caes.* II.5.1.

56. The key passage reads: "quei et regum filiis linguis faveant atque adnutent et subservient."

57. *M. Caes.* IV.1.

58. *Eloquentia: M. Caes.* I.5.6, III.16.1, 17.1; *Ant. Imp.* I.2.1, etc. *Ingenium: M. Caes.* I.9.3 (*eximium*), III.8.3, 12.1, 17.1; *Ant. Imp.* I.2.3, etc.

59. *M. Caes.* IV.2.

60. *M. Caes.* IV.2.2.

61. *M. Caes.* III.2.1.
62. *M. Caes.* III.3.
63. *M. Caes.* III.3.
64. *M. Caes.* III.4.
65. *M. Caes.* III.5.
66. *M. Caes.* III.6.
67. *Ver. Imp.* II.9.1.
68. *M. Caes.* I.6.8, producing I.8.
69. For instance, Fronto, the courtier exegete of the Orpheus legend, is thanked, appropriately enough, for demonstrating to Marcus the jealousy, caprice, and hypocrisy endemic to empire (I.11). Diognetus taught him to endure *parrhesia;* Rusticus, to be reconciled with those who offend him; Apollonius, to receive favors from his friends graciously and thoughtfully (I.6, 7.3, 8.2). Cf. especially I.9.1, 12, 13, 14.2; and in general see P. A. Brunt, *JRS* 64 (1974), especially 2n10, and 10 ff. Note also Marcus' many benefactions to his friends, and particularly his acquiescence to the opinions of his *consilium* (*HA Marcus* 22.3-4).
70. *PIR*[2] I 814; cf. 730.
71. Marcus *Meditations* I.17.5; *HA Marcus* 3.3-5.
72. *HA Marcus* 3.3-5. The *HA* omits two items of significance: the second consulship was as ordinarius for 162, the first such appointment of Marcus' reign; and it was accompanied or soon followed by the prefecture of the city (*Dig.* 49.1.1.3; *Acta Iustini*).
73. *Meditations* I.17.7.
74. *Meditations* I.7.1-2 (Farquharson trans., modified).
75. *Ant. Imp.* I.2.3.
76. Note particularly the remark of Dionysius of Miletus, himself of procuratorial rank, to the ab epistulis Avidius Heliodorus, that Caesar could give him money and honor, but he could not make an orator of him: Dio 69.3.5; Philostratus *VS* 524.
77. Philostratus *VS* 559-561.
78. *HA Marcus* 2.1, 6, 4.10, 15.1, 22.5; Dio 71.29.3-4. Cf. (e.g.) Suetonius *Augustus* 45.1.
79. *M. Caes.* IV.12.5.
80. *Fer. Als.* 4.
81. *Meditations* I.3, 17.7; cf. I.7.2, VIII.25, IX.21.
82. *M. Caes.* II.12.2.
83. Note the extraordinarily saccharine conversation reported by Marcus at *M. Caes.* IV.6.2.
84. *M. Caes.* V.20, 25, II.10, 14.
85. *HA Didius Iulianus* 1.3-4; *HA Marcus* 6.9; cf. *HA Pius* 11.8 (Homullus).
86. *M. Caes.* II.12.2.
87. A long list of offices won by imperial ladies for their favorites can be compiled, starting with Livia (Suetonius *Otho* 1.1, etc.)
88. T. D. Barnes, *JRS* 57 (1967) 65, is essential for Lucius' position.

89. *HA Verus* 3.3-5.

90. *HA Verus* 2.5.

91. See the prolegomena to van den Hout's edition, 1vi ff.

92. *M. Caes.* V.53; cf. 54.

93. Lucius has recently turned up on Pius' *consilium: BICS* 19 (1972) 103.

94. *Ver. Imp.* I.2-3.

95. The rest of the letter is fragmentary.

96. If he was identical with the Charilampes known to Galen (XIV.624 K); see J. Ilberg, *Neue Jahrbücher* 15 (1905) 288.

97. Cf. particularly Epictetus 3.7.29-31; Pliny *Pan.* 88. That Pius was able to dispense with the screen of *aulici ministri,* who thereby lost both power and profit, is a clear sign of their position under Hadrian: *HA Pius* 6.4; cf. 7.1.

98. *HA Verus* 9.3; *HA Marcus* 15.2. The exception was Eclectus, the assassin of Commodus.

99. *Ver. Imp.* I.2-3.

100. Cf. the close parallel at *M. Caes.* I.3; *Laus Fumi* 1.7.

101. This passage again recalls Marcus' characterization of their master, *Meditations* I.11.

102. *Ver. Imp.* II.2.1. Text: van den Hout 124, with P. Pescani, *Coniecturae* 19, for an adjustment.

103. *Imagines* 2, 10, and passim, with the apologia of *Pro Imaginibus*; cf. Marcus *Meditations* VIII.37. See the commentary by P. Gabrieli, *RAL* ser. 6, 10 (1934) 29.

104. The agent was his cousin, M. Annius Libo (cos. 161): *HA Verus* 9.2.

105. *HA Verus* 8.11: surely an authentically contemporary jest.

106. *Princ. Hist.* 2.18. The theme (cf. Juvenal 10.78 ff.) is developed further.

107. *Ver. Imp.* I.1.

108. *HA Verus* 6.7; cf. 4.5.9, 5.1-9, 8.9.

109. *Ver. Imp.* II.6.

110. *Ver. Imp.* I.4.

111. "Mea parum refert, quis me de caris tibi amicis diligat, nisi quod prior ratio est eius, qui minus est nostri fastidiosus."

112. Haines, for once less than sensitive in his translation, here makes "cum frigeret" into "when he had a cold" (I.307).

113. *Ver. Imp.* II.9.1. Who was Asclepiodotus? Five individuals may be relevant: M. Aurelius Aug. lib. Asclepiodotus (*CIL* VI.25044; cf. M. Aur. Asclepiodotus Augg. lib., VI.13028); Asclepiodotus, the favorite of Lucius, attacked with Herodes Atticus in the *Pro Demostrato*; Asclepiodotus, poet and procurator in Egypt (A. and E. Bernand, *Les inscriptions . . . du colosse* 153 f., no. 62); Asclepiodotus a libellis in 177 (*AE* 1971.534); Asclepiodotus a rationibus and a memoria in 185/189, and co-heir with the notorious Cleander of T. Aius Sanctus (*AE* 1961.280). *If* these individuals may be combined into a plausible and consistent person, we can see the rise to power of an imperial freedman with pronounced literary interests, a man whom Fronto might dislike on both counts.

114. *Ver. Imp.* II.8. Appian's procuratorship is a clear illustration: *Ant. Pium* 9.

115. *Ver. Imp.* I.1.

116. *Ver. Imp.* II.7. Clarus is noted on *SEG* XVII.584-585 as the son of L. Gavius Aelianus, qu. propr. of Lycia-Pamphylia (cf. *AE* 1897.72 and *JRS* 54 [1964] 103), and grandson of the knight L. Gavius Fronto, a soldier high in the favor of Trajan. A relative was the knight and priest M. Gavius Gallicus, honored throughout Asia and an advocate who had appeared before governors and even emperors (*IGRR* III.778 [Attaleia], with *SEG* XVII.585 [above], erected by a P. Gavius Gallicus, friend and client of Gavius Fronto).

117. *Ver. Imp.* II.3.1.

118. *Ver. Imp.* II.3.3.

119. *Ver. Imp.* II.1.

120. *Princ. Hist.* 2.1. Sallust is also invoked to show that great deeds demand great historians, witness also Cato and Xenophon; cf. Sallust *Cat.* 8.2-4.

121. *Ver. Imp.* II.9-10, 4-5.

122. Another example of such activity may appear in a letter to the senator Claudius Iulianus (*Ad Am.* I.20.2): "A dominis nostris imperatoribus non propter aliud adamari me opto quam ut te quoque participem mei corporis et animi diligant, et propter bonitatem tam certus tu fueris quam ego sum ita fore."

123. The picture is in fact very close to that which may be derived from better documented and more uncertain ages; cf. (e.g.), F. Millar, "Epictetus and the Imperial Court," *JRS* 55 (1965) 41; M. T. Griffin, *Seneca, a Philosopher in Politics* (1976) 67-128.

VIII. THE TEACHER OF EMPERORS

1. *ILS* 1129.

2. For a quick survey, see C. R. Haines I.xxxv-xxxvii.

3. It is particularly dangerous to press the correspondence into providing background for the *Meditations, contra* M. P. J. van den Hout, *Mn.* ser. 4, 3 (1950) 330. Much of the evidence he cites is fortuitous; much could just as easily be derived from Marcus' other teachers; some is absurd, e.g., the suggestion about XII.27. More substantial are the comments of W. Williams, *JRS* 66 (1976) 78, on Marcus' style as observed in his constitutions.

4. See, e.g., Dio 71.1.2; Eutropius 8.12.1.

5. *HA Marcus* 2.2 (with 4.9); 2.3 (with A. R. Birley, *BHAC* 1966/1967 39); 2.4 (with Birley, *BHAC* 1966/1967 41).

6. *HA Marcus* 2.7, 3.2-3, 7.

7. *Meditations* I.12; "my tutor" may be the man mourned at *HA Pius* 10.5.

8. *HA Verus* 2.9, 2.5-6, with T. D. Barnes, *JRS* 57 (1967) 67.

9. See, e.g., *ILS* 1740 (with the acute comments of H.-G. Pflaum, *Carrières* 163); *HA Verus* 9.3 (cf. *HA Marcus* 15.2); *HA Marcus* 2.2; *AE* 1954.64 (with Pflaum, *Carrières*, pp. 991 f.); *HA Marcus* 2.5; Aristides *Or.*

47.23 K. Each gives an example of honor or influence enjoyed by the early teachers of the imperial princes.

10. And from his names alone, the otherwise unknown Cinna Catulus (*HA Marcus* 3.2) looks like a senator.

11. On Celer see Philostratus *VS* 524; Aristides *Or.* 50-57 K (with G. W. Bowersock, *Greek Sophists in the Roman Empire* [1969] 53). On Maecianus see *CIL* XIV.5347. Gratitude to the higher teachers is of course recorded as well: *HA Marcus* 2.5, 3.5 (perhaps an insertion); *HA Alexander* 29.2 (suspicious, but perhaps an extravagant development of a legitimate note in the life of Marcus).

12. *Meditations* I.17.5. Note also Rusticus' unusual position in book I, out of order, immediately after the primary teacher Diognetus, who introduced Marcus to philosophy.

13. *Meditations* I.17.7.

14. A possible glimpse of Rusticus the statesman appears in the *Acta Iustini* (the primitive and most authentic text is in Knopf-Krüger-Ruhbach, *Ausgewählte Märtyrerakten*[4] [1965] 125): see T. D. Barnes, *JTS* 19 (1968) 516 f.

15. I.11 (Farquharson trans.).

16. See (e.g.) A. R. Birley, *Marcus Aurelius* (1966), chap. 4 and 5 (although not, of course, so crudely as stated here).

17. On Marcus the philosopher see *HA Marcus* 1.1, 2.1, 6, 3.1, 4.10, 8.3, 16.5, 23.5, etc.

18. The argument will be found at *JRS* 64 (1974) 144, on *M. Caes.* IV.13; and above in Chapter V.

19. *M. Caes.* III.16 is the only evidence of Fronto's defending rhetoric against the Caesar's doubts. *M. Caes.* IV.3.1 is neutral, and *Ep. Var.* 7 (e.g.) appears to show Fronto and Plato coexisting in harmony; cf. S. Frasce, *Argentea Aetas* (1973) 261.

20. See *HA Marcus* 3.8 for his assiduous attendance at the lecture hall; the biographer's claim is illustrated by *M. Caes.* II.7 (Polemo), II.8 (encomiographi); Philostratus *VS* 539 (Herodes), 577 f. (Hermogenes), 582 f. (Aristides), 588 f. (Hadrian of Tyre). Marcus personally chose Theodotus to be professor of rhetoric at Athens: Philostratus *VS* 566 f. (dated c. 174, according to I. Avotins, *HSCP* 79 [1975] 313).

21. Dio 71.1.2.

22. 1.2.3.

23. Aurelius Victor 16.1; *Epitome de Caesaribus* 16.7.

24. *Eloq.* 1.1-3.

25. *Eloq.* 2.5 ff.

26. *Eloq.* 2.7, on which see particularly F. Millar, *The Emperor in the Roman World* (1977) 203 ff.

27. See Chapter VI and A. Beltrami, *Le tendenze litterarie negli scritti di Frontone* (1907) 10 ff.

28. *Eloq.* 2.9.

29. *Eloq.* 2.11-12.

30. *Eloq.* 2.14; cf. *margine* "Cleanthes aqua de puteo extrahenda victum quaerebat; tibi saepe numero curandum in theatro crocum longe adque alte exprimatur."

31. *Eloq.* 2.15.

32. *Eloq.* 2.19, *margine.*

33. *Eloq.* 4.4.

34. *Ant. Imp.* I.2.5.

35. *Eloq.* 4.6-7, a useful catalogue of the course of instruction given by Fronto to Marcus. Were the text sound at this point, we might have proof that Marcus' exclusive addiction to philosophy never existed.

36. *Orat.* 2.

37. Cf. *Orat.* 10, *margine*: "Clipeo te Achillis in orationibus oportet, non parmulam ventilare neque hastulis histrionis ludere" (with the emphasis on *te*).

38. *Orat.* 11-12.

39. *Orat.* 13; see also Appendix C.

40. *Orat.* 14-15 (or "a Gallic declaimer").

41. *Orat.* 17.

42. *Princ. Hist.* 2.2, 20.

43. *Ver. Imp.* II.1, with the additions and emendations of B. Bischoff. It must be emphasized that the following remarks are based on his reordering: cf. the text at Portalupi, 272 ff.

44. B. Bischoff, 20.

45. *Ver. Imp.* II.1.7.

46. *Ver. Imp.* II.1.10.

47. *Ver. Imp.* II.1.21-23. Cf. various collections of stratagems, notably that of Polyaenus, which was compiled precisely for the use of Marcus and Lucius in their Parthian Wars (I, praef. 1).

48. B. Bischoff, 23; *Ver. Imp.* II.1.19, where a military metaphor is developed.

49. *Ver. Imp.* II.5-6.

50. *M. Caes.* I.9.3, III.1, I.9.2.

51. *Ant. Imp.* I.2.2. Cf. *Ver. Imp.* II.1.16, where Fronto considers Marcus and Lucius to be his *sectantes* (in the technical sense, members of his *secta*).

52. *Fer. Als.* For oppressively erudite analysis, see J.-M. André, *REL* 49 (1971) 228.

53. Cf. *M. Caes.* I.2.2, II.15.1, III.14.1, 2, IV.7.1; *Eloq.* 4.7, 5.1; *Bell. Parth.* 9.

54. *Fer. Als.* 3.4-6.

55. *Ant. Imp.* I.4.1-2.

APPENDIX B. THE DATE OF FRONTO'S BIRTH

1. R. Syme, *Tacitus* 652; J. Morris, *LF* 87 (1964) 316.

2. Euphrates: Dio 69.8.3. Dio: last heard of in Pliny, *Epp.* 10, perhaps surviving even into Hadrian's reign; cf. C. P. Jones, *The Roman World of Dio Chrysostom* (1978) 55. Athenodotus: Marcus *Meditations* I.13.

3. Combine *Eloq.* 4.8 with the comment thereon by m^2.

4. *PIR*[2] C 259. If Dio 68.16.2 is pressed to imply Trajan's presence in Rome, 113 is the latest possible date for Crassus' exploits.

5. The phrase "memoria nostra" need not, of course, imply personal involvement; cf. *Princ. Hist.* 2.4, on Trajan's Parthian War.

6. Dio 69.18.3 (Loeb trans.).

7. Appointment of Turbo and Clarus: *HA Hadrian* 9.4-5; fall of Clarus: 11.3 and 15.3; fall of Turbo: 15.7. These events and their wide repercussions in the political and literary history of Hadrian's first decade have engendered considerable debate, but comment here will be held to the minimum. The date of 122 for Clarus' fall is certainly delusive, resting on a clear insertion by the biographer into a continuous narrative of the events of 122; see R. Syme, *Emperors and Biography* (1971) 114 f. The date of Turbo's disgrace is quite unknown, and it is not even clear that he was in office when the attack came. But the date of Hadrian's appointment of the two men to the prefecture is generally held, on good grounds, to be 119, and there is no call to impugn the biographer's accuracy here; see the exemplary discussions of Turbo's career by H.-G. Pflaum, *Carrières* 94, and R. Syme, *JRS* 52 (1962) 87. That much seemed certain, whatever the ramifications. Now, however, an important military diploma, dated to 10 Aug. 123, has appeared to upset things (published by I.I. Russu, *Dacia şi Pannonia Inferior* [1973]). It is addressed by Hadrian to troops who served either in certain units presently in Dacia Porolissensis under a commander whose name is too mutilated for confident restoration, or in another unit presently in Pannonia Inferior, no commander named (for a parallel to this sequence, see *CIL* XVI.61), "quinis et vicenis pluribusve stipendis emeritis, dimissis honesta missione per Marcium Turbonem, quorum nomina subscripta sunt." From this, H.-G. Pflaum has deduced (*AEHE* 1975/1976, 373 f.) that Turbo was still in his attested special command on the Danubian front in August 123, and hence that he and Clarus had not yet been appointed to the praetorian prefecture; and this in turn has led to an important reconsideration of the much-disputed career of Suetonius, who fell with Clarus, by J. Gascou (*Latomus* 27 [1978] 436). The deduction about Turbo is highly improbable in itself; and, unfortunately for it, the diploma suggests the reverse, that Turbo was *not* in the province at that time. Compare another and closely contemporary diploma of Hadrian, dated 17 July 122 and addressed to the veterans of a long list of units "qui sunt in Britannia sub A. Platorio Nepote, quinque et vigenti stipendis emeritis, dismissis honesta missione per Pompeium Falconem, quorum nomina subscripta sunt" (*CIL* XVI.69; see 43 for the same sequence). Platorius Nepos is the present commander of the troops, Pompeius Falco the former commander, from whom the veterans received their discharge; Nepos had of course succeeded Falco as legate of Britain (A. R. Birley, *ES* 4 [1967], 69 f.). By the same formula, Marcius Turbo is now attested as a *former* governor in Dacia and Pannonia; but that was already known.

8. A. Passerini, *Le coorti pretorie* (1939) 275 ff.

APPENDIX C. THE DATE OF FRONTO'S DEATH

1. By T. Mommsen, A. Stein, and (most recently) G. W. Bowersock, *Greek Sophists in the Roman Empire* (1969) 124-126, with bibliography.

2. *Orat.* 17-18. C. R. Haines misleadingly inserts *ista* before *polluta,* thus destroying the meaning; it is current coins that are befouled by use, not ancient ones.

3. See *BMC Cat.* IV, Marcus Aurelius 625, 633 ff.

4. A. R. Birley, *Chiron* 2 (1972) 469 f. But where is Commodus' twin Annius Verus (died 169)?

5. *PIR*² C 606.

6. *HA Verus* 4.1.

7. *Ant. Imp.* I.2.2 and 4, II.1.1; *Ver. Imp.* II.1.5 and 6.

8. *Ant. Imp.* IV.2.1; *Eloq.* 4.10; *Fer. Als.* 3.14; *Nep. Am.* 4.

9. *Ver. Imp.* II.2.1; cf. *Princ. Hist.* passim.

10. A. R. Birley. Unfortunately, another of his arguments is based on a faulty text of Galen, at XIV.651 K; see V. Nutton, *Chiron* 3 (1973) 429.

11. C. R. Haines, II.109n1. Note also Apuleius *Apol.* 9.12 for a contemporary reference to two brothers as *oculi.*

12. *Eloq.* 13.

13. C. R. Haines, II.111n1; A. R. Birley.

14. The evidence is set out at *JRS* 64 (1974) 136; see also A. R. Birley, 473, on the lacunae. I believe that attempts to date *Ad Am.* I.1 and I.10 later are mistaken; see my discussion.

15. C. R. Haines, II.333 affords a somber list of ailments and attacks; cf. the unsympathetic views of J. E. G. Whitehorne, *Latomus* 36 (1977) 413.

16. *M. Caes.* V.55: gasping for breath, pulse stopped.

17. On the plague see J. F. Gilliam, *AJP* 82 (1961) 227, with A. Degrassi, *MAL* ser. 8, 11 (1963) 153.

18. *HA Marcus* 13.5, 2.5. On Marcus' statues, see A. E. Gordon, *Quintus Veranius* (1952) 325.

19. Cf. A. R. Birley, 473.

Index of Passages Discussed

General Index